Rich Men Have No Friends

The Capitalists

By Phineas McNabb

Copyright © 2024 by Phineas McNabb

All rights reserved. This book, or parts thereof, may not be reproduced in any form without permission.

This book is dedicated to the three most important people in my life, my wife who supports me unconditionally without fail and has had my back for thirty years, my children who continue to teach me that it really is about your fellow man and to be thankful for today and not worry about yesterday or tomorrow. Yesterday is already in the past and tomorrow is not promised.

Rich Men Have No Friends

By Phineas McNabb

Phineas McNabb

1

My name is Theodore Hightower. I am the richest man in the world. Forbes estimates my net worth to be over 400 billion dollars. I am an investor. My house is huge, my cars all go fast, and my yacht is the biggest one in the world by exactly 11 inches. How do I know that? I had someone on my team provide the measurements of the largest yacht in the world and then I had my yacht built to be exactly 11 inches higher, wider, and longer than that yacht. The name of my yacht is *wife#_*. Why the name? I have been married five times and grew tired of renaming the yacht for each new wife.

I am a graduate of the University of North Carolina at Chapel Hill with a dual degree in Computer Science and Economics. I have master's degrees from the University of Michigan and Harvard in both Business and Information Systems. My PhD is in Computational Science and Engineering from MIT. I graduated high school at the age of 15, college (bachelors and masters) by 18, and finished my Ph.D. at 23. While in college, I was solely responsible for over 30 patents that made me rich by the time I received my Ph.D. While I made a lot of money, one hundred million dollars to be exact, none of the patents currently belong to me.

Given my extensive education, I became an investor and turned one hundred million into four hundred billion dollars. To this day, I have a small team of 20 people who work for me and most of them have been with me for over twenty years. Many of them are millionaires in their own rights. I don't pay salaries to any of my staff. If I make money, they make money. If I lose money, they get nothing. I don't regularly engage my team and hardly interact with them. I have an assistant, Shelley, and all communications go through her. She has been with me for the past ten years and is invaluable to me. I treat her like crap, she knows it, but I pay her handsomely to manage the team.

Rich Men Have No Friends

Shelley is smart but I hired her for her street smarts. She grew up the child of military parents. When I met her, she was the owner of a small coffee shop. It was my favorite place to get coffee and I admired her no quit attitude. I trust her because she comes from a background that does not look favorably on being disloyal, and frowns altogether on being a snitch as they say in the streets. She will do anything for me, and I appreciate that unbeknownst to her.

I turned fifty-eight this year. I have been my own boss for a very long time. I am a deal maker. I invest heavily in companies, take over their boards, then I pounce. My only goal is to get the stock price as high as possible and then dump it quickly. It is what we in the investment world call the "pump and dump". I have no interest in the company, its mission, and I really don't care about the employees who work there. They are just numbers to me. Companies get nervous when they know I have an interest in them. Whatever it takes to make me money. That's all I care about.

You see I am a capitalist to my core. Money is all I think about. I prefer money to sex. That may explain why I have had so many wives, none of whom I really cared about that much. They were something to do, another conquest in the hunt. What type of women do I marry? Preferably young, drop dead beautiful, with nice curves, and not much else. I am smart, I don't need someone nagging me or trying to get into my business. Every wife I have had to include my current wife was required to sign a prenup that guarantees them twenty million at signing, five million if they stay with me at least two years, and ten million ten years from the official date of divorce as long as they don't discuss the prenuptial agreement and say nothing bad about me that could be published.

I have three children, Jonathan, Christopher, and Amy. Jonathan is twenty years old and in college at Penn. I had him with my first wife. Christopher is 17 and lives with my second wife. I hardly see Jonathan or Christopher. We talk occasionally but they don't call much because they don't have my direct number and are screened by Shelley before they can talk to me. They don't care for me, and I don't blame them. I really have not been involved in their lives. Gave them everything they needed and more and will continue to do that until the day they die. But I was not very good at being a decent father until Amy came along. I

Phineas McNabb

cheated on their moms with what would be the next wife and they resented me for that. And then there is Amy, who is the love of my life.

Amy was the sweetest daughter a man could ever want. She would have been five years old today. Two weeks ago, my fourth wife, Isabel had a big party at her house in Malibu.

Amy was with her. I could not make the party as I was traveling to China on business. I don't have a lot of close friends and I loathe pretending to like people that frankly get on my nerves and don't add a lot of value to me. If you can't make me money, then I don't need to be speaking to you. That's what Shelley does. Anyway, there was a party, a lot of people showed up, celebrities, athletes, movers, and shakers from Hollywood. Isabel knew most of them through her career as an actress.

Yep, I saw her on the big screen and decided that I wanted to be married to a movie star. She was a two-time Oscar winner, and the highest paid actress in Hollywood. Over twenty million followers on social media, loved by every producer worth their salt in making movies. She is the first person they call, regardless of the role. We have been married a little over four years now, though we see each other very little. She is in love with me, but I have never really been in love with her. I spend most if not all my time in Houston where my company is located.

When we first met, it was love at first sight for Isabel. I flew to Hollywood, convinced a producer to get me in the room with Isabel by investing six million dollars in a movie he was making, and I handled it from there. (I ended up making 10 million off that investment by the way) I have always kept myself in good shape, and I am easy on the eyes. I am six feet tall, dark curly hair, well-kept beard, and I have green eyes. Oh yeah, and I am rich. When I met Isabel, she was 29 years old and full of life. Everyone in Hollywood loves her, she never meets a stranger, and loves the finer things in life.

I agreed to marry her only because she had her own money (net worth of $20 million) and it was good for both our careers given our connections in the business world and celebrity world combined. I never really loved her. She was just a deal to me, and once the deal was completed, it was time to move onto something else. I respect her as the mother to our daughter, and I love her for that. Unfortunately, that does not make for a strong marriage.

At the party that weekend, the pool was opened for everyone. When Amy was born and started to walk, we installed an electronic gate around the pool that is always up unless there is an adult using the pool and Amy must be with that adult or is closely guarded by the housekeeper or nanny. The night of the party, everyone went inside and said their goodbyes to Isabel. While she was saying her goodbyes, the electronic gate was not monitored, and it was turned down as the party was ending and everyone had made their way to the front of the house to leave.

Amy was playing in the living room and disappeared from Isabel's sight. She walked out the patio doors, and while outside she noticed one of her favorite toys was floating near the edge of the water. It was determined that she reached for the toy and fell in the water. By the time Isabel and the housekeeper realized what had happened, it was too late. They pulled Amy from the water. They tried to resuscitate but it did not do any good. By the time the paramedics arrived, Amy was gone. She was the one bright star in my hard charging, take no prisoners life and she was gone. We buried her over a week ago and when we put her in the ground, a part of me went with her. For the first time in my life, I have this void that I can't fill, and money is useless to fix the emptiness I am feeling right now.

Isabel is mad at me and wants a divorce. May have something to do with the fact that I blamed her for being more concerned with being famous and not doing her job as a mother. We had a real falling out the day of the funeral. She called me a heartless bastard, and I told her she was probably right. She asked for a divorce, and I said okay. Much like in the business world, it was time to divest the marriage. The only asset we had together was gone so there was no need to continue the relationship. And that was how I put it to her right before she called me an arrogant son of a bitch and the biggest asshole she has ever met in her life. I walked out the door and never looked back.

What Isabel did not know was that I would have stayed married to her if Amy was happy. Amy was the bond between us. She made me appreciate Isabel as her mom, not so much as my wife. That mutual respect that we displayed towards each other was a direct result of Amy being the sweetest daughter and probably the best thing either of us had ever done. Amy had significantly minimized all the Oscars, business deals, and the quest to accumulate money neither of us really needed. Amy was gone now, so the deal or marriage was off. Period.

Phineas McNabb

2

It is Monday morning, and I have asked Shelley to meet me in the office first thing. I own the building that our headquarters is located in. It is a fifty-story building, and our offices are on the 49th and 50th floor. My office along with Shelley's is on the top floor and the team is located one floor beneath. The building sits on San Felipe Street here in Houston, Texas. It has a glass exterior, with an atrium that rivals the Sistine chapel. As you walk in, the artwork decorates the walls and the roof. It is beyond description. I selected three of the top artists in the world and allowed them to do whatever they wanted if the art meshed in a way that it provided scenes that were beautiful, made you think, and represented everything that is capitalism.

There are nicely done pictures of money floating through the sky, the bull from wall street, a ticker tape, brokers with bull heads screaming out orders, and other signs of opulence that are beyond description. The walls are made of white marble that I imported from Greece and the front desk is also made of white marble. There are two couches in the foyer that sit on either side of a rectangular white marble coffee table, and they sit on a rug that I had imported from Italy.

All my tenants are movers and shakers. I charge a hefty price to be in my building and they all want to be in the building of the richest man in the world. I have not met any of them, but Shelley knows most of them. Before anyone can rent in our building, I must sign off and Shelley is charged with working with the property manager to vet them. One company per floor, and they must have assets of at least one hundred million dollars that they are investing on any given day. My thoughts were if they have that kind of money, they can afford the rent and won't spend time trying to meet the rich guy on the top floor. Being in the building alone should get them the best clients. They each pay me two hundred and fifty thousand dollars per year to be a tenant, with the entire year due the first day of January. I make twelve million dollars a year in leases for this one building.

There is a guard at the front desk. His name is Harold. There are elevators to the left of his desk and there is one right behind his desk. The elevator behind his desk only has three numbers on it, one, forty-nine, and fifty. It has two passengers, Shelley, and Me. It uses three-step authentication, all of which work simultaneously. Card, fingerprint, and a four-digit code in that order. If any of those is not properly executed, the elevator takes you back to the first floor and stays open until you exit. It has made me angry on more than one occasion when I have had too much to drink and forget the right order to do it in. The good news is there are two buttons on the elevator, both for emergencies. One for the authorities in case of fire or I get stuck. And the other button goes directly to Shelley who can override the system from wherever she is and get me to the top or fiftieth floor.

My office, along with Shelley's takes up half the 50th floor and I live in the other half. There is ten thousand square feet of space in total. I have a two-bedroom living space with all the amenities of a man of my wealth. There is a private gym, a screening room for watching movies, a chef's kitchen, a living room, and a playroom built for Amy that leads off one of the bedrooms. There are only two bedrooms because there was one for me and one for Amy.

There are views of the city from every single room. At night, you can see the beauty and the splendor of Houston, but no one can see in. When it is time to go to bed, the windows have technology that blocks out the lights of the city and creates a darkness that brings complete calm.

The office space has two offices, and no reception area. Shelley resides in one of the offices and I am in the other. Her office is very nice with a glass desk, a great view of the city, and one chair for me to sit in when I visit her and discuss business. Other than that, no one comes on the floor, so she does not need any furniture to accommodate anyone. She also maintains an office on the forty-ninth floor to interact with the team.

My office has a glass desk as well, three computers, two phones. There are two televisions on an internal wall, both 65-inch flat screens. I use them to watch the weather, the news and to occasionally check on the team below. There are no filing cabinets on this floor as everything is filed away electronically. I do not use e-mail. I communicate with Shelley, and she talks to the rest of the world as well as the team on the floor below. I do a lot of research in my office, and I don't really use the phones much. The reason I have two phones is one was dedicated to Amy so she could always reach me, and the other is for Shelley to reach me when she is out of the office or downstairs and needs to speak with me. With Amy gone now, there will need to be some renovations to the living space and the phone in the office needs to go.

Phineas McNabb

I arrive at the office around 6:30 am. I could not sleep so I decided to walk down and sit at my desk until Shelley comes around 8:00 am. The Wall Street Journal and the Houston Chronicle have been delivered and are already sitting on my desk. Not sure how they get there but Shelley takes care of making sure they are here and that I am not disturbed when they are delivered. I have always wondered if she lets Harold in the space to get me my papers since no one can get to this floor without her override.

The phone for Amy has a beeping light so I check it. "Daddy, this is Amy, are you coming to my party? Mommy says you can't make it, but I really would like you to be there. Anyway, I love you. And I miss you. And make sure Mr. Wimples is taking care of you and Shelley. Tell him and Shelley I said hi." That would be the last message I ever received from my dear Amy. She was calling her dad to be at her fifth birthday party, and I was not able to make it. Jerk!

Mr. Wimples is a teddy bear I had specially made for Amy. He is about 15 inches tall, wears a polo shirt, shorts, and small Nike tennis shoes. She fell in love with him. She felt sorry for me being up here all alone when Shelley was not around and made him my best friend and business partner. This little girl even convinced me to have a small desk built for him to sit at in my office. Mr. Wimples sits in the corner of my office, always at the ready in case I need him.

"Well, Mr. Wimples, I have some bad news for you. Amy is gone. I had been intending to tell you last week, but you know, business comes first, and I did not get into town until late last night and did not want to bother you.

Now, you are going to have to be strong for me and help me get through this. She had a beautiful funeral, and I am quite sure that she would have wanted you to know that she really loved you. She told me that many times. Don't worry, you are safe here with me. I won't abandon you. Amy would not want that. As my only business partner and best friend, I need you to help me figure out how I get through this. They don't teach you in business school how to deal with this. So frankly, Mr. Wimples, I am at a complete loss. Will you help me?"

Mr. Wimples just stared at me, not saying anything. I knew he could not say anything, but in my mind, I felt like he was sincerely listening and was at a complete loss for words given what I had just told him. It almost looked like his normal smile was not there anymore. At that point, Shelley walked through the door.

"Good morning, boss. I have your coffee just like you like it. Black, no cream, no sugar. Boss, I just want you to know that……."

"Save it Shelley, did the Hartwell deal get done yet?"

"Ummmmmm, yes, but boss………"

"Shelley, is the deal done or not?"

"It's done, boss."

"Are you able to give me your full attention, or you going to continue to be distracted by something that I don't care to talk about. Amy is gone, and that's that, got it!!!!!"

"Got it boss."

"Okay then. I am headed to the airport for the Baker deal. Have you crunched the numbers? Everything in order? Is all the paperwork filed?"

"Yes, boss." Shelley was confused and I knew why. We had not talked about Amy at all and yet she and Amy were the best of buds whenever Amy visited the office. Amy spent time in Shelley's office, sat in my chair and they would have lunch and tea parties together. I am not good at that stuff and Amy understood. On more than one occasion, I would be running late, and Shelley would stay over and keep Amy company. Amy also convinced Shelley that while I was an asshole, I had a heart. I am sure that she did not quit on me because of that.

"Okay, I am headed to the airport. You are in charge as usual, and tell the team please stop sending me cards. I am shredding them. I have not read any of them and don't need them at this point. The next person that sends me a card, a flower, or leaves something at the guard desk for me is fired. Understand?"

"Got it boss. Won't happen again. See you when you get back."

"Shelley?"

"Yes boss?"

"She really loved you. I just want you to know that."

"I know boss. I loved her too."

"One more thing. Mr. Wimples will be traveling with me on this trip. I promised Amy I would take him with me on my next trip and looks like he finally gets to go."

"Okay, boss. You all have a safe trip."

"See you Friday."

"See you Friday, boss."

Phineas McNabb

I grabbed my briefcase, Mr. Wimples, and proceeded to the condo to pack. I put Mr. Wimples in a backpack that I used when I would venture out for a short walk downtown and we proceeded to head to the elevator. I called down for my limo but made a change in plans. Harold arranged all my transportation. He was an elderly black man who I hired when we first moved in the building. He always speaks to me and is a genuinely nice fellow. He is married, and he and his wife live in Cypress. Harold is a veteran, and I only knew that because he liked to wear baseball hats that have symbols on them that indicate he had served in the military. Like Shelley, he could be trusted. I did not know much else about him. Shelley knew that he was to never be fired or replaced. When he was on vacation, the desk was empty.

"Harold."

"Yes, Mr. Hightower."

"Cancel the limo and have my Bentley brought around please. Have them bring the convertible."

"Mr. Hightower, I am really sorry to hear about........."

"Harold, my Bentley?"

"Yes sir, Mr. Hightower, right away. See you when you get downstairs."

The Bentley was my favorite car. It had all the amenities of a six-figure car. It was black with green and black interior. The green was for the color of money and the black was because I was always in the black. There was no red obviously.

On occasion, I would sneak off and drive it to San Antonio. There was a nice hotel downtown, the Valencia. I have a room that I like that has a nice balcony. And when I wanted to get away, that is where I would go. Sometimes I would take Amy with me. She liked to look over the balcony at the people and gaze at the big buildings that you could see from just the right angle. I was a very private person, who maintained a very low profile. Harold knew that if I took the Bentley out, I must be going to San Antonio.

"Harold, it looks like a nice day for a drive today."

"It does indeed, Mr. Hightower. Headed to your normal destination."

"Not today, Harold. I am headed to the airport. Just wanted to put the top down for Mr. Wimples."

"Oh, I did not know that you had a VIP with you today. I am sure he will enjoy the ride."

Rich Men Have No Friends

"That he will, Harold. That he will. See you, Harold."

"See you, Mr. Hightower."

I put my things in the trunk and buckled Mr. Wimples in the passenger seat. The shock of what I had told him this morning was still weighing on him. He did not handle grief well, so he chose to be quiet the entire time. I turned on the engine and put the radio on a nice jazz channel. Houston in April is not that bad. The weather is mild, and there is an occasional thunderstorm or rain shower. Hard to predict where it is going to hit but overall, the weather is good. My flight was leaving from Hobby Airport, so I put the convertible top down and headed downtown to catch the freeway.

As we were going to the airport, it hit me. I had been fine or so I thought until it hit me. Amy was gone. My childhood had been rough, a struggling mom, a bunch of deadbeat stepfathers and a dad that was never around. I had basically raised myself. Mom had died a long time ago and the last stepdad disappeared after that. I have a sister who lives in Florida, but we have not spoken much since I went off to college. You could say that I had been a loner and took no crap guy most of my life. People were of no use to me, either they were a value add to my investments or they were just objects that could be discarded at any time. And I did not care either way.

Amy had a way of making me smile and brought stability to my money making, women chasing, hard charging, take no prisoners life. And she was gone. And since I had never really prayed or even picked up a Bible in a very long time, I was at a loss as to why my Amy was gone. All I knew was that a part of my soul, if I had one at all, was gone. I had been humbled in the worst way possible. I was a parent whose child had died while they were still alive. No parent wants that, and I was at a loss.

Phineas McNabb

3

"Call Shelley." I had the latest technology in the Bentley and one of the benefits was a system that allowed me to give the car verbal orders, which it carried out without fail. I needed to speak with Shelley as there had been a change in plans.

"Yes Boss."

"Shelley, I need you to cancel the trip. The Baker deal will have to wait. Postpone the meeting until further notice. I don't have a date yet. Tell them you will get back to them soon."

"Boss, this is a five-billion-dollar deal. We jumped through a lot of hoops to get the two countries to agree and had to go through a lot of red tape. There will be a lot of pissed politicians, shareholders, and employees in complete limbo. And I know how you feel about the employees. Not your problem but this is a big deal to say the least. Are you sure?" Shelley was confused and it showed on her face.

"Shelley, are you done?"

"Yes, boss."

"Shelley, Mr. Wimples and I are taking a trip, and I am not sure when I will be back. I need some time to think. The loss of Amy is more than I thought it would be. I am going to do the deal, just not today and not this week. Can you handle that for me, please?"

"Sure, boss." In the ten years I had known Shelley, I had never said please to her unless it involved Amy. And that was because Amy would always say "Please" when I requested something of Shelley which would then make me say "Please" very reluctantly.

"Boss, where exactly are you going and how will I be able to reach you?"

"Shelley, you won't be able to reach me. If I need you, I will call you. If Isabel calls, tell her I am out of town on business and can't be reached. Bad reception in the area or something. Shelley, I am taking a sabbatical of sorts. Keep the team going and not a word to anyone about what we discussed today."

"Boss, you have not told me anything except you won't be available."

"Perfect, tell them that. Thanks for covering for me." Shelley was not amused as I had not told her anything. I sure hope she does not quit on me now that Amy is gone.

4

"Good morning, Stella."

"Good morning, Pastor. How are you today?"

"I am good. Weather looks pretty good today."

"It is looking good today, Pastor. I stopped by to drop off the mail and pick up that package you need me to send. What a great thing you are doing, Pastor. Sending clothes and shoes to those who are less fortunate is such a kind gesture on your part."

"Would not have it any other way, Stella. Those folks live in countries where the littlest act of kindness goes a long way. And besides, we throw away so much in this country that can be still used by someone."

"Pastor, you are a good man. If not for you, what would Greensburgh Church have become. I know the folks around here really appreciate you for all you are doing for the community and all that you are doing to touch others."

"I am not doing as much as I would like to, Stella, but every little bit helps."

"That it does, Pastor, that it does. Well, I must go. Duty calls, rain, snow, or sunshine…."

"I know, Stella, the mail must be delivered. Have a great day today and remember to act like it is your last day. And if you do, you will have a great day by default."

"Pastor, I was here for the service on Sunday, received the message loud and clear."

"I know you did, Stella, a little positive reinforcement can't hurt though." They both laughed and Stella went her way.

Pastor Cletus "C.J." Johnson is the senior pastor of the Greensburgh Church in Greensburgh, Texas. He has a congregation of about three hundred members. He is African American, six foot two inches, athletic build, bald headed and wears an earring in each ear. He wears black t-shirts all the time, even when he preaches. He has been the pastor of the church for some five years now. Prior to that, he was the leader of one of the largest mega churches in the country, The Greater Gospel Church in Houston, Texas. He had a membership of over ten thousand and was a successful book writer having made the New York Times Bestseller

Phineas McNabb

lists ten consecutive times. His net worth is believed to be a millionaire with a net worth of some twenty million dollars. In his mid-fifties, he was educated at Morehouse college getting dual degrees in theology and economics while being the starting point guard for the basketball team. He then went to Harvard to get his dual MBA/Law Degree.

His father had been a preacher in Houston, walked with Dr. King during the Civil Rights movement and was a well-known figure in the black community. His dad and mom had been his rocks all his life until they both passed away in a tragic auto accident some twenty plus years ago.

His dad pushed him hard providing tough love and discipline coupled with the teachings of the bible. His mom had provided him with unconditional love and support and was his biggest cheerleader.

His father had wanted him to become a preacher, but he had his sights set on Wall Street. He dreamed of being an investment banker. The promise he always made his dad was that he was going to go make a bunch of money which his father would not be fond of, and then give back to the community. And he promised him that he would come back one day if that was the Lord's calling and take over his dad's church.

After graduating from Harvard, he became an investment banker working for the top investment bank in the world, French-Helliman. French-Helliman managed assets of over fifty billion dollars and he began as an investment analyst and quickly moved up and made partner, the first African American at French-Helliman to accomplish such a feat. At the point he made partner, he took over one of their funds that at the time was valued at a little over one hundred million dollars. He quickly grew that to one billion dollars inside of a five-year period. His bonuses and salary eclipsed ten million dollars annually in any given year.

Instant success changed Louis. His visits home were less frequent and his calls home to his mom were hit or miss. He was living the life, fast cars, penthouse apartment, house in Hawaii and acceptance into an old boy's club that rarely accepted people who looked like him. But there is always an exception when you make the kind of money he was making for French-Helliman. They did not treat him like a black man, but instead they treated him like a green man, because money was green, and he brought plenty of it to the firm.

He was asked to serve on boards of two fortune five hundred companies and had memberships to two of the most exclusive golf clubs in the United States. And in New York City, he was a rock star. He became a very famous man and much like the rappers and athletes he associated with, the ladies loved him, and the young kids admired him. But not for his intelligence or hard work. They admired him for the money, the glamour and the women that were always on his arm. Never the same one, always someone different at every event he went to. And as for church, he stopped going when he made partner. His dad would have more than one conversation with him about his lifestyle and money, but he would not listen. As much as his dad said the grass is not always greener on the other side, he was not listening because not only was his grass green, but it was so tall he could not cut it. He was a multi-millionaire, and no longer thought of himself as a black man, an African American man, a southerner from Houston, or a preacher's kid. He thought of himself as a rich man. He was a one percenter and that was all that mattered. All at the ripe old age of twenty-nine years old.

Phineas McNabb

5

One New Year's Eve almost twenty-six years ago now, Louis or C.J. was preparing to go to a party with some of his friends from the athlete and entertainment world. His girlfriend for the moment was getting ready in the next room. He had not been home for Thanksgiving or Christmas. He sent his dad and mom matching Cadillacs and his dad had told the dealership to take them back. He wanted nothing to do with them. That offended Louis and he had not talked to them since. He was getting ahead of himself.

The call came around nine that night. He recognized the number as it was an old friend from college who lived in Houston and attended his parents church at his urging. The strange thing about Louis is that he encouraged anyone who would listen that if they were in Houston to go to his dad's church. Yet he had not been in years. The foundation was there, but it had slowly started to slip.

"Louis?"

"What's going on, frat?" Thomas was a fraternity brother of his who kept an eye on his mom and dad and kept him informed when he failed to check in or call his mom.

"Louis, I have something to tell you."

"What is it, Thomas? I am late for a party. Man, you should be here. You name the star, and they are going to be in the house tonight. I mean every Oscar winning, Grammy nominated, MVP of whatever league and the models, my goodness! You should really be here. You want me to have a private jet to come get you. I can have you here a little after midnight and we can party till the morning. I mean I have a date, but I can dump her for you, man. You are my boy!"

"Louis, there's been an accident. Your mom and dad were in an auto accident. And........." Thomas wailed up at that point and had to catch himself. Louis had fallen back on his bed and what was three seconds seemed like an eternity.

"Thomas, how are they? What happened? Where are they? What hospital are they in? Thomas, talk to me......."

"Louis, your mom is in ICU at Baton Rouge Memorial and your dad, man I am so sorry. Pastor Johnson did not make it. He passed away before they could get him to the hospital."

Rich Men Have No Friends

What Louis did not know is that his parents were worried about the life he was living. His mother had demanded that his father drive them to New York to have a talk with Louis. His father being a man of God, he turned her concern into a positive opportunity. They had never been to New York so he convinced his wife rather than worry about Louis, they would surprise him. In all his years on this earth, yes, he had been a little more absent than they wanted, but he had always been the most respectful man and son. When he did come home, he was lowkey, less flashy, and knew not to talk about money and the life he was living to his dad or mom.

He cut the grass, washed the dishes, and did whatever they needed him to do. He was not a fraud, but a son who really loved his parents. Without them there every day in his life, he was caught up and could not see the forest for the trees. Or better yet, the jungle for the snakes.

"Thomas, I understand mom is in ICU but how is she doing?"

"Louis, she has been in ICU for the past three days."

"What, how come you are just calling me about this?"

"Louis, no one knew how to contact you. It was Deacon Jones who remembered that you and I went to college and so he found me with the hopes I could locate you. Louis, they were on the way to see you. They wanted it to be a surprise. You know your mom does not like to fly and your dad thought it would be a nice trip. They would take their time and get there after the holidays. I am telling you what Deacon Jones told me, Louis. He said your mom was worried about you, but your dad had convinced her you were fine. You were just a young man trying to find his way, but you were fine. Anyway, they were passing through Baton-Rouge and a bad fog appeared out of nowhere. Apparently, there was a stalled tractor trailer on the road and before your dad could react, well.........."

"No, man. No. You are lying. No way, man. No way." Louis started to sob uncontrollably and dropped the phone out of his hands.

"Louis, Louis, are you there man? Louis?" Louis was gone. At that point, his heart dropped, his body went limp, and he cried himself to sleep. His phone lay beside him with Thomas calling for him in the background. He would not respond.

The next day Louis caught a plane to Baton Rouge. He arrived at eleven that morning. The weather there was balmy and cold. There was overcast and drizzling. He met Thomas at the airport, and he drove him to the hospital.

"Thomas, how's mom?"

"Louis, we need to get to the hospital. It is not looking good, man. How about you let me concentrate on driving given the weather and let's get moving."

The drive from the airport to the hospital was about twenty minutes but it felt like hours. Everything had slowed to a pause. Louis noticed the stores off the exits, the cars that were stalled in traffic because of the weather. He noticed that a tree limb had fallen possibly from lightning the night before. He saw every inch of the road. He noticed the homeless couple on the side of the road with a sign that read "homeless, with two young children, please help". He noticed the big white stucco-looking building with all the windows that appeared to have some green tint to them. He noticed the elderly gentleman getting out of his car with the help of someone who could be his son. He noticed everything. His life, while fast to this point, had slowed to a screeching halt.

"Louis, your mom is not able to speak and has not opened her eyes the entire time. She is hurt pretty bad. She has slipped in and out of a coma twice now. I just want you to know when you get up there."

Thomas pulled the car up to the front door and let Louis out. Hospitals tend to have a lot more cars near the front entrance and Louis needs to get his mom now. Thomas will park and head up afterwards. Louis makes a mad dash to the elevator. Thomas said fourth floor and to your right.

Louis exited the elevator, and what he saw next was not what he expected. In the visitors' area were people of all walks of life. All races, all nationalities. There were very important people from Houston who had flown or driven in to be there for his mom. Deacon Jones spotted him and ran right up to him.

After giving him a hug that felt like an eternity, he greeted Louis. "Louis, how was your flight?"

Louis just looked at him, and said "Fine, Deacon Jones. Where is mom?"

"Right this way, Louis."

The corridor in the hospital was about 20 yards long and his mom was in the last room on the right. Word had gotten to the hospital administrator that Louis and his dad were prominent people in the clergy and investment world, so his mom was to get the best treatment possible. He passed several rooms, and the theme was consistent. Family members gathered around a sick or hurt family member. Tubes, EKGs, blood pressure monitors, nurses everywhere all going about their jobs dressed in scrubs and clog mules.

His mom was in room 15B. There was a bathroom to the left as he entered, her bed sat in the center of the room and there was a dresser and TV in front. Off to the left side of her bed was a recliner and a couch that could be pulled out to make a short bed for a family member who was sometimes allowed to stay given the condition of the patient. His mom was in her early sixties and had beautiful grey hair. She showed little signs of her age. There was an IV running out of her arms and a tube leading to her mouth to help her breathe. She had a collapsed lung, broken collar bone, and her back had been injured. She had also taken a very hard hit to the head which caused her to go in and out of the comas. The concussion was what worried the doctors the most. She had been non-responsive and had not uttered a word since being rescued from the accident and moved to the hospital.

Louis walked into the room, where Deacon Jones's wife was sitting by the bed holding his mom's hand. He walked up to the bed, looked at his mom, and tears began to slowly come down both cheeks. He spoke.

"Hey, mom. It's me, Louis. I'm here mom. I'm here."

"She's been asking about you, Louis. I am sure she is glad you are here."

"Mrs. Jones, how are you? Asking about me? I thought they said she has not spoken since the accident."

"Louis, your mom has been asking about you every day for the past two months. When you did not come home for Thanksgiving or Christmas, she started to worry. So, I am one hundred percent positive that she is happy you are here today, young man."

"Yes ma'am, Mrs. Jones. You are right." Just then, his mother's eyes started to move as if she was trying to open them. He could see her mouth trying to move as well.

"Get the doctor, mom is moving! Get the doctor!" The doctor came in and he slowly pulled the tube out of her mouth. She opened her eyes and began to say something, but no one could hear her. Louis leaned in and put his ear as close to her mouth as he could. "Mom, are you trying to say something?"

Phineas McNabb

"Hey, baby."

"Hey, mom. How are you?"

"Louis?"

"Yes, mom."

"Keep your promise. Okay?"

"Yes, mom, I will."

"I love you, Louis."

"I love you too mom."

That was the last words Louis would ever say to his mom. The beeping line on the heart monitor trailed off and a solid beep followed very quickly. His mom had lived long enough to see her son one more time. In an instant, Louis had just become an orphan. Both his parents were gone.

The next two weeks went by very quickly with planning a double funeral, working through the probate and wills, and trying to assimilate to the passing of the two people Louis loved more than anything in this world.

Louis had been racking his brain trying to remember what promise he had made that his mom wanted him to keep. He had been so out of touch he had forgotten what the promise was. But he had been a lot of things, but he did not lie to his dad and mom, and he always kept his promises. What promise had he made?

The Monday after the funeral, he was sitting in his father's office at the church. His father had a very nice, but modest office. Nice Oak Desk with two chairs in front. Behind the desk was a book cabinet that took up the entire wall. Every book you could imagine. History books, religious books, books about business, books written by authors who his father deemed to be spiritually motivated when they wrote. On his desk was a computer that was hardly used and a phone that was used quite often to check in on members and for his charitable work in the community and across the world.

On the wall were plaques from other churches, cities he had impacted through his charitable work and honorary degrees from colleges and universities in the local area and nationwide. But in the middle of all this was a blown-up picture from Forbes magazine. On the cover was a picture of Louis. And the title of the picture was the "King of Wall Street, the Rockstar of French-Helliman, Louis Cletus Johnson." Forbes had written a piece about him, and his father had been given the magazine by one of the members of the church. He had reproduced the front cover, had it enlarged and hung it on the wall.

Louis did not know it, but his dad was very aware of who he was, how much money he was making, and the concern his mother had for him was real. His dad had always preached to him as a kid that it would be harder for a rich man to get into heaven than it would be for a camel to go through the eye of a needle. Despite that, his picture hung proudly on his wall. That was his son, and that was never going to change.

"So, Pastor, when will you be ready for your first sermon?" Deacon Jones had entered the office and had been watching Louis admire his father's accomplishments, both big and small. He was a tall heavy-set man who was always very serious about life. He ran a non-profit organization in town and was the most trusted adviser of Louis's dad. Deacon Jones and his dad had been friends since the sixth grade. Went to college together, roomed together, married two girls who were the best of friends, and ultimately settled down in Houston in houses right across the street from each other. Louis had not noticed him enter the office as his back was to the door and he was oblivious to what was going on around him.

"Funny, Deacon Jones. Deacon, did my father know who I was? He never talked about this magazine article when I came home. We never discussed my career at all. Whenever he asked, I told him I worked for a bank, and I was doing okay. Never went beyond that. And mom never inquired at all. Not once in all these years."

"Louis, your dad knew exactly who you are. He knew everything about you. He was proud of you but concerned that life was moving too fast, and the money would get the best of you, and you would lose sight of what really mattered in this world."

"Deacon, I am really not up for a sermon right now."

"Louis, you asked the question, I just answered."

"You are right, Deacon, my apologies."

"So, when will you be ready to preach your first sermon?"

"Deacon, what are you talking about?"

"The promise, Louis. You don't remember the promise, do you?"

"What promise, Deacon?"

"Think back, young man. Think back to when you went off to college and told your parents what you were going to do and what you promised them when they agreed to let you chase your dreams."

"I am sorry, Deacon Jones. I really don't remember."

"Your father said this might happen. Money has a strange way of affecting all of us. Don't get me wrong. Nothing wrong with having it or making as much of it as you can. But what you do with it is what determines how it ultimately affects you. You told your father that if he let you go chase your dreams, you would come back and take over the church when he retired. Well, unfortunately, Louis, he retired sooner than any of us could predict, and the ball has been passed back to you. Time to suit up, son. You are now a point guard for God."

"But Deacon, I have never preached a day in my life. I have not read the bible in years and my lifestyle has been on public display for years. You think the church wants a woman chasing, alcohol drinking, party as hard as I could millionaire preacher who hardly has showed up for anything at this church in the past few years."

"No, the church is not ready for that. And we may lose some members because of it. But that was your dad's wish, and the board wants to honor that wish. Frankly, there are more than a few skeptics but that is what he wanted, and we want to honor his wish. He believed that it would be good for the church and more importantly, it would be good for you."

"Can I think about it, Deacon Jones?"

"You just did."

"Huh?"

"Louis, you did not say no, so I am taking that as a yes. I will let the church know that you need three weeks, and we will go from there. And Louis, you will be fine, you will see."

So just like that, the Rockstar of Wall Street would pack up and move back to Houston to fulfill a promise he had made to his father.

Rich Men Have No Friends

6

"Well, Mr. Wimples, what do you say we make a pit stop and stretch our legs? I could use a cold drink right now. How about you? Good, I thought you would say that." Mr. Wimples stared straight ahead looking at the glove compartment of the Bentley. For whatever reason, Mr. Wimples was in the right place at the right time. Without him, Theodore would be lost. He had checked out mentally from work for now. What he could not afford to do was check out totally. That would not be good.

He and Mr. Wimples were just on the other side of Beaumont, Texas headed east on I-10 when he saw up ahead a small convenience store. They took the exit and followed the feeder to the store. To the right and left of the highway were farms. What they grew he was not sure, but he could tell they were farms from the neat rows of greenery that seemed to stretch forever all ways.

As he exited the Bentley, he noticed that his car was the only one in the parking lot. "Be right back, Mr. Wimples. You need anything? No. How about a nice Coke? I tell you what, I will bring us a Baby Ruth and a Diet Coke. We will share. Sounds good to me."

The convenience store was a brick building that had been there since the early sixties. Standard red brick building with a black shingled roof. Inside the store were three to four small aisles. Snacks on one aisle, candy, and sweets on the other aisle. Drinks on the third aisle, and miscellaneous things on the last aisle, oil for the car, gas can, tissue, and stuff you buy when you are traveling but forgot at home. It was a good model. If you leave it at home, must buy it in the store. Charge twice as much for it. These little stores were profit machines. "Maybe I should investigate buying a chain of them." Mental note to remind Shelley to investigate this when I return to work.

Theodore walked up to the counter, and the gentleman behind the corner was an older man who appeared to be in his late seventies. He had a beard and had on a plaid shirt and overalls. He had a baseball cap on that looked every bit as old as him. The hat indicated that he was a Vietnam Veteran and a proud Army Veteran. "Thank you for your service, sir. How much for the drink and candy?"

"One hundred dollars, mister." Theodore was not amused.

"You are kidding, right?"

Phineas McNabb

"Of course, sonny. Four dollars and two cents. Sound better."

"For a candy bar and a soda?'

"Let me ask you something, sonny. When is the last time you bought anything for yourself?"

"What does that mean?"

"Well, you pull up in your fancy millionaire's car, wearing a watch that cost more than my house, and you are surprised by how much a soda and a candy bar cost. That means you have not shopped for anything in a long time. No offense, sonny."

"None taken, you made your point."

"Where you headed today? Lake Charles, New Orleans, Biloxi, or Baton Rouge. Like the dice, do you?"

"Not headed to any of those places. Not today anyway. How do you know that I play craps? I do like to shoot the dice on occasion, but not often. Silly way to lose money. But it is a good stress reliever. Plus, the ladies like to gamble as well as some of my business partners."

"So, you are a businessman."

"You could say that."

"Well, I don't know where you are headed but I hope you find what you are looking for."

"Thanks."

"Safe travels, Mr., I did not get your name."

"Ted, Ted is my name." No one had ever called Theodore Ted before, but he was trying to fall off the grid and the easiest way to do that was to maintain a very low profile.

As Theodore exited the store, he noticed that a black pickup truck had pulled up beside his car.

An elderly man who looked to be in his seventies stopped at the store. He had on blue jean overalls the kind of pants that hooked liked suspenders over your shoulders, a black baseball hat, some black work boots, and a white T-Shirt underneath the overalls. He was about the same height as Theodore, had long hair and a long beard. His truck was very plain, appeared to be several years old with a set of new tires. It was black with silver trim and a rope held up the rear guard.

It had dings all over from many miles on the road. Nothing fancy about it, matter of fact it did not appear to be of this time at all. Windows had to be rolled up by hand, and there was a radio that looked like something from an antique store. Where did this truck come from and what time machine had it passed through?

"Nice car. What did it cost you?"

"More than I care to talk about. How about your truck, where did you get this beauty? Must cost you a lot. What is it, from the sixties or early seventies?"

"It is a 1978 Ford to be exact. I have driven it for a very long time. Gets me from point A to point B. I have never seen the need to trade her in. We go everywhere together. I guess you could say the truck reminds me that there is more to life than shiny objects. It has a way of keeping a person grounded."

"Never thought about it that way. Your name, sir."

"My name is Abraham Esau Jacob. Your name?"

"Ted Hightower. Good to meet you, Abraham. Never met someone with three first names before."

"My father gave me those names."

"Let me ask you something, Abraham."

"Sure, what is it?"

"I will trade my car for your truck. And I will throw in my watch, this bracelet, and the clothes I have on. You appear to be the same size as me. How about it?'

"You serious? Hey, is this car stolen? Are you running from something? You one of those drug dealers?"

"No, I am not any of those things. I am just kind of turned off by the car at this moment. You would not understand if I explained it to you."

"I tell you what, Ted. I will take you up on your offer. If I understand you right, you are going to give me your car, your watch, and that fancy bracelet you have on as well as your clothes for my clothes and in return you just want this old truck."

"That's right."

"Are you sure?"

"Positive."

"You got yourself a deal. One small problem. What if the police pull me over thinking I stole this car?"

"I will sign it over to you right now. Follow me."

Ted and Abraham went back in the store, and he asked the gentleman behind the counter for a piece of paper. He wrote a statement "I Ted Hightower give free and clear my 2019 Bentley to Abraham Esau Jacob and that includes my watch, bracelet, and the clothes I have on. If anyone has any questions, they can call this number and a woman by the name of Shelley can vouch for this exchange." The gentleman in the store witnessed the exchange by signing the piece of paper as well. Ted took a picture and messaged it to Shelley.

They made the exchange, Ted grabbed his suitcase, and Mr. Wimples and they loaded up the truck. He was not sure why he had done that but something about this man in the truck had affected him in a strange way. It had something to do with the comment about the shiny object.

"Where you headed, Ted?"

"Not sure, just want to take a little time off and clear my head."

"You ever been to Greensburgh, Texas?"

"Never heard of it."

"I think it would be the perfect place for a guy in overalls driving an old truck who wants to get away and fall off the grid for a while."

"How did you know that I ...."

"Ted, I have been in your shoes before. Not sure what happened to you, but whatever it is, it has you hurting badly. Up the road is a restaurant in Beaumont called Pappadeaux's, a seafood place. It will be on your left, can't miss the sign. Exactly 10 miles from there you will find an exit on your right. There is a big red barn at the exit. Take the exit, turn right, go about twenty miles and you will be in Greensburgh. You will be completely off the grid. Cell service is spotty, and the internet works on occasion. But it is a great little town full of nice people. Not as big as it used to be, but still a nice place to visit."

"What happened to it? I mean, what do you mean not as big as it used to be."

"Big business, Ted. Big business. You will see it when you get there. Drive safely and thanks for the car. And Ted, you are embarking on a journey that will help you deal with the pain you are feeling right now. That hurt you feel will turn to joy again; you will see. Drive safe. Who knows, we may see each other again soon."

"See you, Abraham." Theodore, now Ted, got in the pickup, tried to start it a couple of times, it finally backfired loudly, and he and Mr. Wimples were on their way. Couldn't hurt to stop in Greensburgh for one night.

Back in Houston, Shelley was receiving the message with a photocopy of the agreement about the car. Was Theodore losing his

Rich Men Have No Friends

mind? Was he okay? She would not worry yet. He was a survivor and the fact he contacted her was a good sign. Oh well, back to work.

Phineas McNabb

7

Louis Cletus Johnson had left Wall Street as he had promised his mom and dad. Sold off all his material things, gave ninety percent of his money to a foundation that did good things to change the world, and settled into his role as Pastor of the Greater Gospel Church in Houston, Texas. He put the ten percent that was left or roughly seven million dollars into a trust account that paid him a decent return annually to offset the salary he was getting from the church. While he had agreed to pastor the church, he was not able to let go of the money he was used to having. He would not spend the money, but allowed it to accumulate in an account, just in case he changed his mind about the whole preaching thing. And it gave him a false sense of satisfaction knowing that he was still a baller, although no one else knew.

He was 29 years old, in the prime of his life, and had given up a life that was beyond unbelievable. He had learned that money can provide you with a sense of heaven on earth, until it can't. Money would not bring back his parents, even if he were the richest man in the world like Theodore. When he took over Greater Gospel, the membership was right at about 350 members. The church was in the historic section of Houston, a predominantly African American part of town that dated back to the 1950's.

After the first year, Louis had done a fairly good job of taking over his dad's church. Membership stayed constant and the congregation had long forgiven him for his previous life and lifestyle. They had also admired the fact that he had given over 90% of his wealth to charity. They did not know what his net worth was at the time he did that, so the assumption was that he had sacrificed everything to be a soldier for the Lord. Only he knew how much money he had and what his true net worth was, and it was starting to grow again.

By the second year, he became bored with the now consistent routine that was required of him as the Pastor of the church. Same meetings every week, Easter and Christmas celebrations coupled with the church anniversary and retreat. He did a very effective job, but he was not happy. Not happy in the sense that he loved preaching at the church but there had to be more to life than this. After all, he had once been the darling of Wall Street, living a life that was like being in Heaven on Earth as he would tell his friends in New York quite often. And if it was up to him, he would get that life back. Even if he had to do it as the Senior Pastor of The Greater Gospel Church of Third Ward, a black community in the heart of Houston, Texas. It would take him almost twenty years to do it, but he would get the lifestyle he so badly wanted while not breaking the promise he had made to his dad. But at what price?

Phineas McNabb

8

Abraham pulled the Bentley into the garage. Abraham was a guardian angel charged with seeking out those whose faith had been challenged or who in some cases lacked any faith at all. The black pickup truck was his way of reminding people that life could be as simple as they made it.

If someone he encountered understood the message he was delivering, they would normally trade their vehicle with him on the spot. Or he would convince them to take the truck if they had nothing to offer but needed reliable transportation. He had an unlimited supply of black pickup trucks.

"Hey, Pete. Got another one for you."

"Abraham, where did you get this car?"

"Another lost soul on the side of the road. He traded it for the pickup, did not have to do any convincing at all."

"Wow, he must be in a lot of pain."

"Lost his daughter in an accident. Divorcing his wife. Two sons that he hardly speaks to and not the easiest person to work with. The only constants in his life right now are his assistant Shelley and a Teddy Bear named Mr. Wimples."

"Wow, he seems like he is bad off. I thought you said he was the richest man in the world before you left?"

"He is the richest man in the world, Pete. But all the money in the world can't solve what he is dealing with right now. Smart fella, and somewhere inside of him is a kind heart. He just needs some help. I sent him to C.J. in Greensburgh."

"That's probably the best place for him. I still have C.J.'s Escalade in the back just gathering dust. What should I do with the Bentley, Abraham?"

"Park it in the rear, Pete. And put all this stuff in the trunk for me. If everything goes right, he won't be needing that car anymore." Abraham handed him the watch, the bracelet and changed back into his normal outfit, overalls, t-shirt and an old black baseball hat and black work boots.

"I will take care of it, Abraham."

"You have my truck ready. Need to get back on the road. Never know when I am going to be needed."

Rich Men Have No Friends

"It's ready now, keys are in the ignition."

Abraham walked to the rear of the garage, opened the door to a black 1978 Ford Truck and started the engine. He pulled out of the garage and headed back out onto the road.

"See you in a few days, Pete."

"See you, Abraham."

Phineas McNabb

9

"Well, Mr. Wimples, what do you think of our new ride? No air conditioning, no electric windows, and an am radio of all things. Not sure what I was thinking there but something told me to give that fella my Bentley. He looked like he could use the money. Now hold on a second, I have not gone and gotten soft on you. It had nothing to do with helping him. It had more to do with blending in and not being noticed. With this old truck and these clothes, no one will be the wiser. We will stop at a Wal-Mart and pick up some things and dump those clothes in my suitcase. For this trip, you and I are just two old buds on a road trip taking a break from life. Know what I mean?"

Mr. Wimples continued to look straight ahead at the glove compartment. He did not move at all. Theodore or Ted as he was calling himself now looked over at him and they continued their journey.

"Well, there's the Pappadeaux's, Mr. Wimples Now I need you to pay close attention as we must go exactly 10 miles until we see the Red Barn. That's our exit."

As they were getting close to their exit, the phone rang. It was Shelley. "Hey, Shelley, what you need?"

"Boss, you okay. I received your message and wanted to be sure you were okay. Did you really give your Bentley away?"

"I did give the Bentley away. Mr. Wimples and I are trying to blend in and it's hard to that in a Bentley."

"Boss, are you sure you are okay? I can send someone to get you. You have been through a lot these past few weeks."

"Shelley, I am fine. I just need some space right now. Did you postpone the deal?"

"I did and the folks are none too happy about the delay. They agreed to wait one week exactly. They understood that this is a tough time for you and for that's the reason they agreed to the delay, but not more than one week."

"Very good. Look, Mr. Wimples, there's the Red Barn. Shelley, we need to go. Our exit is approaching. I'll keep in touch. Don't call me, I'll call you." Ted hung up the phone and proceeded to take the exit.

"Red Barn. What in the world?" Shelley hung up her phone and was as lost this time as she was when she received the text message about

Rich Men Have No Friends

the car. The good news is that she spoke to Theodore, and he appeared to be okay, for now.

Greensburgh, Texas is a small town just on the other side of Beaumont. The population of the city is about two thousand people, down considerably from the twenty thousand that used to be there in the early seventies and up until the plants all closed. It was home to three of the largest plants in Texas employing over five thousand people at its peak.

Those plants had closed in the late nineties, early part of the two thousands and the city just kind of drifted away. The schools closed, and now the few remaining kids are bused over to the next county.

In its heyday, there was a bustling downtown, with shops, and restaurants all locally owned by the citizens. Many of them had been in the families for generations. Greensburgh was a town where you could realize the American Dream regardless of your race or educational background. It had some challenges during the sixties, but the town grew closer once the plants opened and opportunities were given to everyone to have a job, raise a family and own a home. It was always sort of funny how that worked out. Give people a chance, a fair chance, and concerns with inequality, and dislike towards one another for whatever reason tend to go away or at least subside.

There were three churches in town, the Greensburgh Baptist church for the blacks, the Greensburgh Baptist Church for the whites, and the Greensburgh Church for the Hispanics. The town was very diverse as the plants had created so much opportunity that folks moved in from Houston to get the good paying jobs being offered. Starting pay was fifteen dollars an hour, with full medical benefits, educational reimbursement, and once you had three years with the plants, they would even assist you with buying a home. To ensure that the banks would approve the mortgage, the company that owned the plants would guarantee twenty percent of the loan just like the Veteran's program that some of the plant workers were able to take advantage of.

Times were good in Greensburgh until all the jobs were sent overseas. No one really knew the full details, except there was this gentleman who was making a name for himself in the investment world who had purchased the company, drove up the stock price, and gutted all the assets. Within six months of purchasing the company, all the plants were notified that the jobs were going overseas. All the employees were given six months to sell their homes and find new jobs. The only problem was the plants were the largest employers in the town.

Many of the citizens got out early, but the majority ended up abandoning their mortgages, and moving back to Houston or relocating out of the state. Those who hung around were either retired or ended up not fairing so well leading to an uptick in suicides, drug addiction and falling below the poverty line. That eventually worked itself out but not without a lot of lost souls and broken dreams. Greensburgh had gone from a thriving town to a ghost town overnight. Almost all the shops on the main drag had closed or been boarded up.

Now it is just a shell of itself. The downtown was making a comeback with a few places of business that somehow closed but had recently come back. No one knows where the money came from but over a few years the town was able to reopen a Diner, a Motel, a Gas Station, a Bar, a Grocery Store, a Hardware Store, and one of the Churches was saved. They even opened a Post Office. With everyone leaving, the churches lost so much membership they could not afford to keep the Pastors on board. You see, they also worked at the plants as well while holding down their duties as clergy.

Greensburgh had been able to rebuild one church because of a man by the name of Cletus Johnson. He had relocated from Houston. Apparently, he had been the pastor of one of those megachurches with over ten thousand members and they say he burned out and wanted to go back to his roots. They said that he was a rich fella a long time ago. Anyway, he moved into town, was able to secure financing to expand the church, and to the town's credit, everyone goes to the same church now and it has been renamed the Greensburgh Church, for all those who want to come.

As Theodore and Mr. Wimples got within ten miles of Greensburgh, they noticed that there were boarded up homes on the side of the road. There were bulldozers tearing down homes in what appeared to be neighborhoods from times past. There was an old high school that was no longer being used.

Further up the road, they saw a farmer plowing his land and some kids playing in the front of an old home adjacent to the farm. Where had Abraham sent me?

When Theodore and Mr. Wimples finally were close to town, there was a Green Sign that read, "Greensburgh, Texas. Welcome to God's

Rich Men Have No Friends

little town." He passed the post office and before he knew it, he was in the middle of town. He figured he was there because he had passed one of two stop lights one for when you come in and one for when you exit on the other side. "Mr. Wimples, this seems like a bad idea. Maybe we should get back on the highway and head to Lake Charles. What do you think? That's my kind of town and we can get rid of this old truck and pick us up another convertible. What do you say, sound like a plan?"

Just at that moment, the truck backfired loud, the engine made a slow purring sound that lowered in volume as the purring died down, and then it backfired again before it finally cut off. They were directly in front of the Gas Station aptly named "The Gas Station." Everyone ran out, looked to see what the commotion was and went back inside their respective businesses. A young man that was about twenty-five or twenty-six years old came out. He had on a gray jump suit and an old towel draped over his shoulder. He had a gray baseball hat on and some old military style black boots. On his hat and left breast pocket were the letters TGS.

"I see you met Abraham. Pop the hood for me, sir." Not knowing what he was talking about, Theodore just looked at him. He opened the door, pulled this latch beside Ted's left foot and there was a thump and then the hood moved slightly. He went around to the front, opened the hood and then he said "Yep, there it is." Mr. Wimples and Ted were a little dumbfounded. Ted was not used to this as had not driven a car that had broken down since undergrad.

"So, what seems to be the problem, Ken?" Ken was on his sewn-on name tag.

"Well, sir, you have a few problems that need addressing. I am going to need to order the parts, could take a few days to get them in, no later than Wednesday I can have you back on the road. Should not be more than a couple of hundred dollars. I only take cash." Ted had officially gone to the Twilight Zone.

"Not a problem, any chance you can jump it and get me back on the road. I was headed to Lake Charles to trade it in anyway."

"Abraham would not take too kindly to that, Sir. He gave you his prized truck and expects you to take care of it."

"He did not give me anything! I gave him my car in exchange for his. And now I am stuck in this one stoplight town!"

"Two."

Phineas McNabb

"What, Ken?"

"Two stoplights, sir. We have two stoplights."

"Whatever. How can I get in contact with this Abraham guy to get my car back?"

"You can't, sir. Abraham is a hard man to find but he seems to show up at just the right time. Can't believe he gave you his prized truck for your car. He doesn't just give his truck away. You must be down on your luck. Nice of him to help you like that." What in the world was going on? This guy was acting like Abraham got the worse part of the deal and Ted stuck him with a lemon of a car. The nerve of this guy. Where was Ted and when was this nightmare going to end?

"Well, that's just great. No transportation, a guy is riding around in my car that works mind you and I am stuck in the one, I mean two stop light town. This Abraham guy really got me good. Is he a scam artist who preys on travelers?"

"Sir, I am going to need you to take that back, and I mean right now. Let me ask you a question, who initiated the trade, you, or Abraham?"

"Well, Ken, if you must know, I initiated the trade. I was tired and did not want to drive my car in this part of the country. I thought it might stand out. So, I initiated the trade. And the name is Ted, stop calling me sir."

"Okay, Ted. If you initiated the trade and you wanted this fine piece of machinery made by none other than the greatest car maker ever, then I think you owe Mr. Abraham an apology."

"He's not even here. What are you talking about?"

"No apology, no fixing the truck. I will just wait for Abraham to come and get it back. So, what do you say? How about that apology?"

"My apologies, Abraham. I did not mean to insult your truck. I did not mean to offend you. Happy now, Ken?"

At that very moment, a voice that only Theodore could hear spoke back in a silent whisper "None taken."

"What did you say to me?"

"What are you talking about, Ted?"

"Never mind, Ken. You can have it ready for me on Wednesday, not a day over!"

"Wednesday it is, Ted. And welcome to Greensburgh. Ruby over at the hotel can help you with your room. You might want to hurry though, because the diner closes at six and Myrtle likes to get home in time for Jeopardy.

"Well, Mr. Wimples, a fine mess you have gotten me into today. Come on, let's go check in the hotel."

Ted and Mr. Wimples walked across the street to you guessed it right, "The Motel". That was the name plain and simple. No fancy signs, no bulbs just a sign that looked recently painted that said, "The Motel".

The thing with Ken and the voice from Abraham concerned Theodore but he chalked that up to a long day and fatigue. Anyway, he was tired, and he needed a shower and something to eat at you guessed it right, "The Diner."

Phineas McNabb

10

Louis has been preaching at his dad's church now for some twenty plus years. He has grown the membership to over ten thousand members and the church has moved from its original home. He was able to acquire some land just on the outskirts of the beltway near Cypress, almost twenty acres.

The Greater Gospel Church was now a sprawling campus with a main building that could house up to fifteen thousand worshipers, a gymnasium, a private Christian school for grades 6-12, enclosed Olympic sized pool, a bowling alley, two restaurants, a coffee shop, and office space for Louis and his now full-time staff of some twenty people.

About a mile up the road he had built a two million dollar ten thousand square foot home that sat on an additional five acres with two guest houses, a pool, a stable for his horses, and a five-car garage. The house had a staff of four people, a housekeeper, a butler, a groundskeeper, and someone to maintain his horses. He had one of his horses finish third in the Kentucky Derby one year. The horses' name was The Chosen One.

Louis had taken all he learned on Wall Street and applied those same theories and principles to the church. He had taken what was once a community-based church serving one of the oldest communities in Houston and grown it into a big business.

And who should appear on Forbes Magazine some twenty plus years later, "Louis Cletus Johnson, the King of the Megachurches and Best-Selling Author." Louis had written books on how to grow churches, being fiscally responsible as a church member, how to save your marriage and other self-help books tied to his faith. The only problem was there was a conflict.

Louis had some twenty years ago given away ninety percent of his wealth to charity and kept ten percent or seven million dollars for himself unbeknownst to anyone at the church. He had been investing that money as well as the money from his book proceeds and had turned that into a substantial amount of money, somewhere north of forty million dollars. It would have been seventy million dollars, but thirty million had gone towards the purchase of the land, building the new church and his new home for him and his wife, Sarah. They had two children, Adrian his son and Adriana his daughter who were now grown and had lives of their own. He had done everything right and believed that his mother and father were proud of him as they looked down from heaven.

There was one problem, no one at the church knew that he had personally financed the church and his life of opulence. Rumors started to spread that he was going back to the lifestyle he had once left, and the members of the church were concerned that their hard-earned money given through tithing was taking care of his lifestyle.

Louis did not help things any by wearing five-thousand-dollar custom made suits, one thousand-dollar shoes, watches that cost more than the average salary of his congregation and cars that screamed I am rich.

He had a Rolls, a Bentley, a Range Rover, a Maserati, and his wife drove a Jaguar. Everything about him said rich and the church members thought they were paying for it. He was trying to fulfill the promises to his parents while holding on to a life that he had left behind, or so he thought.

It all came to a head one Sunday when he informed the church that the air conditioning unit for the church would need repairing. The cost to repair the unit and to maintenance all the units on the campus was almost fifty thousand dollars. A unit would also need to be replaced for another fifty thousand dollars. The total cost was one hundred thousand dollars. The overhead for the church was almost two hundred thousand dollars a month, or over two million dollars a year. Church members were starting to get a little restless and concerned.

The following Monday, a young lady came to visit him. She was a single black woman with three children, all under the age of ten. She was neatly dressed, appeared to be in her mid-thirties and looked like she worked in an office of some sort. Her clothes were nice, but modest and she had very little jewelry. She had requested to see Louis and for some strange reason, his calendar, which was normally packed, was wide open that afternoon. He had long gotten past knowing all the members of his church since his church membership was almost the size of a small Texas town. His job was to pack them in, preach the gospel and continue to build the membership. He was striving to be the biggest megachurch in the United States. And nothing was going to stop him from that goal. His moving to the new campus was based on an old saying "If you build it, they will come" except he had misinterpreted the true meaning of what the saying intended.

She came in and sat down in a chair in front of his desk. His desk was the same one that his father had used at the old church downtown. "Pastor, Johnson, you don't know me, but my name is Cynthia Leakes. I have been a member of this church my entire life. My mother was a member when your father was the preacher, but she found a new church when we moved to the new campus. Pastor, I am concerned about the direction the church is taking."

"What is your concern, sister Leakes? Are those your children sitting by my assistant?"

"Yes, those are my children. They were all baptized in this church. You would probably not remember because you were traveling for each of their baptisms on church business. Your fill ins did a great job."

"Well, they are well-mannered sitting back there. Now, what is your concern?"

"Pastor, I am a lawyer, and I work for a very large bank here in town. I work in the mergers and acquisitions department. I worked hard to get to where I am. I did it as a single mom, with no assistance from my children's dads and I make a pretty good living. The problem is that I have a concern with the ten percent you are requesting of me. I have no problem with giving you ten percent of my earnings but what I do have a problem with is keeping up your lifestyle. I know who you are, I know who you used to be, and I know you are a best-selling author, but book sales alone can't sustain such a high lifestyle. It's not my business to tell you how to live your life, but it is my business to know where my money is going."

"Well, sister Leaks, one, kudos to you for being a single mom who is balancing a career with raising three wonderful children. Second, the church pays me no salary and my books have done well. But you are right, the book sales alone can't sustain my lifestyle."

"I knew it!"

"Hold on, don't get ahead of me. I have been blessed over the years to put a few nickels away here and a few quarters there. That has allowed me to sustain my lifestyle, as you call it, as well as do other things in the name of the Lord."

"Well, Pastor. If that is true, then why don't you take a few of those nickels and a couple of those quarters and pay for the air conditioning unit to be replaced and repaired. Yesterday, during service, we were asked to not only tithe our ten percent, but also to give to the homeless fund, the single parents fund, and now the air conditioning fund. That's a lot to absorb and all independent of themselves deserve some attention. But again, not if the money is not going to those things but instead to a church campus we don't really need and supporting a lifestyle that is a bit much even for a successful pastor as yourself."

"I see, Sister Leakes. You feel strongly about this. Let me ask you a question. What do you see as the main cause of your frustration getting beyond just the money aspect of it?"

"Well, Pastor. You are not the same person anymore. You allowed the money to get you again. I mean we all thought it was commendable when you gave up a substantial amount of your net worth many years ago to come back and take over the church for your dad. And you gave up the lifestyle, the clothes, the women, and whatever else you were involved in.

And I understand how difficult that was, particularly given the circumstances of losing both your parents at the same time. But when you came home, you promised your parents you would carry the torch for your dad."

"And I did that, Sister. I not only did that, but I grew the church leaps and bounds."

"But how did you grow it, and what was your reason for growing it?"

"I don't understand your point."

"My point is, did you do it for your parents or did you do it for yourself? I mean we have celebrities, athletes and all sorts of national and local political officials that take up the front rows of the church on any given Sunday. You know their names, their kids, and have officiated the marriages and funerals for most, if not all of them. I have three children, was here long before they ever set foot in this church, and you don't even know who my children are."

"So is that it, I didn't baptize your children. For that, I apologize. But you do understand that we have over ten thousand members, don't you?"

"No, Pastor, what I understand is you took what was once a community church that kept the community together and you moved it out in the suburbs to be closer to your house since you chose not to live in the community you were serving. I also understand that you could not let go of your rock star status and wanted to be in the limelight again.

You could not resist the spotlight and now it's back on you again. And my question to you is are you happy?"

"Of course, I am happy, I mean look at all the success we have had over these past twenty years."

"Pastor, where did you grow up?"

"Sister Leakes, I grew up in Third Ward, a block from the old church. We lived in a nice, but modest three-bedroom two story house on Peach Street. I went to school a few blocks from my house and right around the corner from the church. As a matter of fact, those are the best memories of my life and I fall back on them when I miss my mom and dad. Those were good times. Third Ward shaped me into the man I am today."

"Think about what you just said, Pastor. And now think about your current situation. Do you know your neighbors? Is this beautiful campus in the neighborhood it should be or just in the neighborhood? How many of your congregants who come to this church live within a block of this beautiful complex? Other than building one of the preeminent megachurches in the country, how does this church benefit Third Ward that is being slowly gentrified almost every day. And how does this church help to build communities when it left the community that built it many years ago?"

"I never thought of it that way, sister Leakes. You make a lot of good points."

"Pastor, I know you are a good man and I know you want to do the right thing. But at this point, you have made Greater Gospel Church a business. You kept investing in the church, but did you really invest in the people it is supposed to serve? Much like businesses that get so big they can't fail; you have done the same thing to Greater Gospel. The catch here is that much like a big business, I am just a number to you but instead of being employee number two hundred or two thousand, I am member number two hundred or two thousand. I have friends that have telemarketers calling them to come to the church. Let me ask you something, did telemarketers help build this church or was it your dad living right and getting out in the community?"

"Sister Leakes, I so badly want to refute you, argue with you, or convince you that you are wrong but to your credit, you are right. My intentions and my expectations were not aligned with the very thing that made this church one of the most respected churches in Houston. And for that, I am sorry."

"You see, Pastor, when we lose sight of who we are, don't know our neighbors, and all that matters is money, well, growth becomes greed, and membership becomes a commodity. You are a former investor, so I know you get it."

"Sister Leakes, you have given me a lot to think about."

"And Pastor, thanks for seeing me today and listening to me. I did tithe yesterday, and I gave what I could to fix the air conditioner. I don't want to be sweating in this church. Might scare me the next time you are talking about the alternative to Heaven." They both laughed.

"Thank you, sister. And you can come by and see me anytime. We could sure use you around here to help with our mission. Over ten thousand members and the same people are always volunteering to help usher, sing in the choir, or teach a class. Not sure what causes that, but that's a story for another day. You have a safe trip home."

"I will Pastor, now to fight the traffic and make this thirty-mile commute back into town."

"Where do you live?"

"Third Ward, Pastor. One block from the old church. Three houses down from your parents' old place. Paid a lot for the place, but I wanted my children to have the same experience you and I did. Not quite working as planned with gentrification and all but we can't give up. Too much to lose."

"Keep the faith, Sister Leakes. Keep the faith." Sister Leakes gathered up her children and left. Louis sat back down in his chair, stared out the window and was for that moment at a loss for words. She was right. In his efforts to do the right thing, he had become misguided in his true mission as the Preacher of the Greater Gospel Church of Third Ward. It was never about growth, but the binding of a community. The rock was gone, so the foundation had been torn apart. At that point, he asked his assistant to come to his office. "Yes, Pastor?"

"Have Deacon Jones to come see me if he is around today."

"Will do, Pastor."

Phineas McNabb

11

Abraham pulled into the parking garage of the pretty white building and parked his truck in the visitor's spot. He had changed into something a little more formal. He had on a blue button-down short sleeve shirt, some jeans, his old baseball hat, and his favorite boots. He got out of the truck and headed towards the door.

"Good morning, Harold, old friend. How are you doing??"

"I am good, Abraham. Missed you. I have not seen you in a while. Still driving that black pickup truck?'

"Yes sir, would not have it any other way."

"So, Abraham, what brings you to the big city. This ain't your part of the country."

"Well, I wanted to know why you called me about this Ted fellow. He's not that bad. Do you know he gave me his car, his jewelry, and the clothes off his back? And he offered up, I did not have to convince him at all."

"I called you because when I went to deliver the paper the other morning, I found this." Harold reached in his pocket and handed Abraham a piece of yellow lined paper that had been pulled from a notepad.

Rich Men Have No Friends

The writing on the note said the following:

Shelley, by the time you find this note, I will have embarked on a trip with no final destination, and I will not be returning to the office or the company. It is best that I ride off into the sunset with Mr. Wimples. I want you to know that you have been nothing but loyal to me these past years and for that, I am very grateful. But the loss of my Amy is more than I can handle. She was my light in this world of darkness.

I have no real friends although I would like to think of you as my friend. I learned ten years ago, when Pierre slept with my wife. He was my right hand, sat right beside me on the forty ninth floor. He and I had been friends dating back to grad school. When he slept with my wife, I declared that I would no longer trust or be close to anyone again in my life. But then I met you. I can always count on you.

As for fun, the only thing I like to do is make money and make Amy smile. As long as I could look forward to making Amy smile, making the money seemed worthwhile so that I could provide for her when I was no longer here on this earth. I have not been the best dad as you know with the boys, but I felt like I was making it right with Amy. And now she's gone. All I had in this world is gone.

My last will and testament is current and you can call Jess Witherspoon to get the details if ever the need arises. Jess also has the necessary paperwork that gives you full authority to run the company in my absence. Given that I hardly interact with the staff, and you have been my go between all these years, it should not cause any problems at all. Other than that, keep running the company and as I told you before I left, don't call me, I will call you. Oh yeah, one last thing, renovate the fiftieth floor however you see fit. I won't be needing that space anymore. Goodbye, Shelley, and take care.

Phineas McNabb

"Abraham, that is why I called you. I did not quite know how to interpret this note."

"Harold, this note was not for you to interpret. Nor am I going to interpret it. And the reason is that if we try to interpret it and we are wrong, we could alter the future in a way that was not intended. You know, self-fulfilling prophecy."

"You are right, Abraham. So, what do I do with the note? Shelley will fire me on the spot if she knows I took this note. In all my years of working here, I deliver the paper to Mr. Hightower's desk, and I have never touched anything or read anything on his desk."

"Harold, you are fine, don't worry. It was meant for you to see this note just like it was meant for me to run into you when I did years ago. How you and Marjorie doing?"

"We're hanging in there. Taking it one day at a time, that's all we can do. She is my light, you know. We would not have made it if not for you, Abraham."

"Good to hear. How's that truck doing?"

"Running good as always. Stop backfiring years ago. Runs like a sewing machine now."

"Good. Harold, here is what you are going to do. Put that note in an envelope. And when you see Shelley, tell her that Mr. Hightower left this for her. Don't tell her how you got the note. It will all work out fine, okay."

"Will do, Abraham, and Abraham?"

"Yes, Harold."

"Thanks. I don't know what would have happened to me if I had not met you. What did you do with my Hummer?"

"I still have it; you want it back."

"Nope, I am good with my truck. Life's much simpler now and I want it to stay that way."

"Good, now I must go. There are people waiting for me. See you, Harold."

"See you, Abraham."

Abraham would leave and go back to his truck. Harold had met Abraham much like both Louis and Theodore had met him. Harold's wife had many years ago recovered from surgery for breast cancer and was in remission. She and Harold grew apart during the worst time of her sickness although they still lived together and appeared to be happily married. He had told her that he was going on a business trip for work where he was the top salesman for a large pharmaceutical company. Instead, he took his girlfriend to Vegas for a few days of fun and relaxation. He was not able to handle his wife's sickness so he was checking out with the hopes that it would help him deal with her death one day.

He never stopped loving her. He just did not know how to deal with the sickness. He was the highest paid salesman at his company, they lived a good life, and he paid for the best medicine his money could buy. t frustrated him that he could not rush the process of her getting well so they could go back to happier times of traveling and doing the things they used to do skiing, rock climbing and visiting exotic places.

When she found out about his cheating, he felt so guilty, he took some time off, packed up his Hummer and headed cross country. On his way, he pulled off at an exit to use the bathroom. He met this guy named Abraham, and Abraham convinced him that while he went about it wrong (trips to Vegas and a girlfriend), there was no doubt he loved his wife. He would not accept the fact she might die one day from cancer, so he avoided it. And for that, he was forgiven. Right there on the spot, Abraham told him that he was forgiven.

Harold gave him his Hummer and drove back to Houston in that old pickup. He sold the home, quit his job, and leased a two-bedroom condo and reconciled with his wife. After several months of being at home and helping her to get her health back, he decided he wanted to work but not in sales. He took a job as a street sweeper which led to him meeting Theodore. Theodore felt sorry for him and gave him a job. What Theodore did not know was Harold was once a top salesman but chose the work he did now and had a half million dollars in the bank. He lived off the interest. At eight percent per year, forty thousand dollars plus his salary at the front desk went a long way.

His expenses were minimal, and he and his wife lived a more modest life. They still traveled, but the trips were more about rest and relaxation and less about having something to do constantly. He had discovered the simple life.

Phineas McNabb

12

Back in Greensburgh, Theodore and Mr. Wimples made their way to The Motel. It was a three-story building that had been recently renovated. Externally, it had a nostalgic look to it that dated back to eras gone by. The building had a white brick front to it. There was a glass window on the first floor with the words painted "The Motel" and there was a wooden door that had a gold doorknob or latch as you would. On the door was the phone number to the motel. You walked up two steps to enter the building. Above the first floor were exactly four windows per floor spaced about 5 feet apart.

Inside there was very little room other than the front desk. Everything was wood, the floor, the paneling of the walls and the cubby holes in the rear of the attendant at the front desk. This place was renovated beautifully but gave the impression of something out of a Humphrey Bogart movie. Each cubby hole had a key in it for looks although the motel itself did use electronic cards for entry. Based on the gas station and the motel, it looked as if the town was trying to go back in time to an era that had long passed.

The attendant was Ruby Grayhill, who had relocated to Greensburgh some years ago. She was about five foot five, in her forties, blond and was of medium build. She had on a pair of jeans, a nice Ralph Lauren polo shirt, and some black ballet flats. She had straight white teeth and seemed to be really put together. Her demeanor and everything about her said not from around here.

"Good afternoon, sir. How can I help you?"

"Theodore, I mean Ted Hightower and my friend, Mr. Wimples. I would like a room, please."

"How long will you be staying with us, Mr. Hightower?"

"Please call me Ted and I should be here for tonight only. Do you by chance have a suite available?"

"Ted, all our rooms are suites. I have something on the third floor that might interest you. You okay with a King Bed? And we don't allow smoking in the motel."

"A King Bed works fine. My friend and I have been traveling for quite a while now and he's tired."

"Very well, Mr. Hightower. If you don't mind me asking, what's with the Teddy Bear?"

Rich Men Have No Friends

"Mr. Wimples. Oh, he belongs to my daughter, and I promised her he could go on my next business trip with me. Her name is Amy."

"Wow, what a lucky guy. Welcome, Mr. Wimples, I hope you enjoy your stay."

Ruby took his credit card, checked him into the hotel, gave him his key and Theodore proceeded to head to his room. "Which way is the elevator, Ruby?"

"Oh, we don't have any elevators here. The steps are down that hall there and at the rear. Not too bad, just 48 steps in total. You seem to be a pretty fit guy so you can handle it."

"Great, a motel with no elevator. This really is the Twilight Zone."

"Good one, Mr. Hightower. Please enjoy your stay."

"Yea, okay. Oh, one more thing, what should I get at The Diner. Any recommendations?"

"Everything on the menu is good, Mr. Hightower, Myrtle is an excellent cook. She used to run the cafeterias at the plants before they closed them down. Really was a shame, she enjoyed that job and loved the people."

"Okay then why is this town so quiet? And how do you stay in business?"

"C.J. looks out for us, Mr. Hightower. He just keeps telling us all to keep the faith and it will all work out. Since he arrived in town, this town has life again. He literally brought it back from the dead. Greensburgh was on its last legs. When the plants closed, this town went from over twenty thousand people to about two thousand now."

"Who is C.J. Is he an investor, a local developer? I might have an interest in getting in contact with him."

"Lord no, he is the Pastor of the Greensburgh church. He moved here about five years ago. Burned out in Houston, used to be one of those megachurch preachers and decided to simplify his life. At least that's what he told me. Really nice fella, and quite the talker. Never meets a stranger, and always trying to spread the gospel of the simple life. But you better go, Myrtle closes right at six o'clock so she can go home and watch……."

"Jeopardy, I know. The fella at the gas station told me. Thanks for your help."

Theodore and Mr. Wimples made the trek to the stairs, climbed the three floors, and proceeded to their room. Small town America had not

Phineas McNabb

rubbed off on him yet, but he had been cordial to this point. He had no choice. A bearded guy was riding around Texas in his Bentley, and he was stuck in nowheresville, or so he thought.

Rich Men Have No Friends

13

Five Years prior to becoming the Pastor of the Greensburgh Church, C.J. would spend his last few days at Greater Gospel in Houston transitioning the church out of his watch and into the care of an assistant pastor. And all because of a conversation that he had with Sister Leakes that had been followed up with Deacon Jones, a long-standing member of Greater Gospel and a friend of the family for many years.

"What's going on Deacon Jones, did you get the air conditioning situation worked out?"

"I did, and it looks like it will only cost seventy thousand dollars, not the one hundred we originally thought. The maintenance guy said he could use some of the old parts and hold off on replacing the unit for now. Thinks we have at least another two to three years. God is good."

"This is true, Deacon, so true. Deacon Jones, I have a question for you. Do I come across as a prosperity preacher, you know one of those preachers that folks perceive as being about money and opulence versus being a faithful servant spreading the word?"

"I can answer that for you but what prompted this question. Your assistant said you had a visitor right before you called me in to your office."

"Yes, a sister Leakes came to see me and had some concerns."

"Sister Leakes, oh yes, very nice young lady. Life took her down some rough roads, but she is a fighter. Single black mom who never gives up becomes corporate lawyer. Beats the odds despite having three kids and some deadbeat dads who are not stepping up to the plate. Our brothers must do better. If you are going to lay the pipe, you must finish the job. Sorry, Pastor, that's more than you asked me."

"No, Deacon, you are right. There are a lot of good brothers out here doing the right thing but not enough of them are stepping up to remove the perception. We need to keep working on that through our DADS program. Anyway, she shared something with me that really concerns me. You have a few minutes?"

"I have all the time you need, Pastor. What's on your mind?"

Louis would explain the conversation with Sister Leakes, her concerns about tithing and being asked to help with the air conditioner, the loss of sense of community since the church moved, and most importantly her perception that she as well as the congregation was not sure if the money being taken up went to the church to do good things or if it went to the Pastor to keep up his lifestyle as well as keep up what she thought was too much with the new church.

"I knew this would happen, I just did not know when or who would say something. Louis, you know I love you like a son, but you have been slipping for a while now. Not in your efforts to spread the gospel, or all the good things you have done for the community, but in how you went about it.

It was not your father's dream, and I am not sure what he would say if he were here. On the one hand, he would be proud of you, but on the other hand, he might scold you for your actions. Not what you did, but how you went about it."

"I don't understand, Deacon. Everything we have done to date has been paid for in full. We have no debt and the church's money has been invested and is getting a great return. If we stay on path, this church will be self-funded long after you and I are gone on to glory."

"I understand that, Louis, but the church does not know what you and I know. You wanted the members to be fiscally responsible and understand the meaning of tithing which is simply showing the Lord that you are willing to sacrifice willingly a portion of your larger blessing, in this case money, right?"

"Well, yes Deacon. I am just simply trying to teach them financial discipline. A lot of folks don't understand that if they start tithing ten percent when they start working, and save ten per cent as well, then they will be blessed two-fold. And even if you are a non-believer, the same principle applies. You learn to give back, in this case, to help your fellow man or woman, and you learn financial discipline, saving for a rainy day so you can buy a home, put kids through college, or make it through a lay off until you find a job."

"Right, all good points, but let's get back to their perception. Because you see, Louis, they don't know you are paying for everything and saving the money they contribute. They don't know you created a rainy-day fund for them as well as the church so that it can continue to thrive and grow.

They don't know that you are not only making a large contribution to the church but in fact you are tithing ten percent of the interest from your portfolio. They don't know that you give fifty percent of your book royalties to the church as well. And I agree with you that they did not need to know. If they were aware of that, then we might not get any contributions. Unfortunately, people like free stuff and if they know you are treating, they tend to put their wallets up. So, there you have it. But's that not where the problem started, Louis. What car did you drive to church today?"

"Come on, Deacon, let's not start that again. I drove the Rolls, why?"

"How much did that car cost you, Louis?"

"Two hundred thousand. But I used my own money from the interest on the money I had when I first came to the church. You know that."

"The suit you have on today, how much and go ahead and throw in the cufflinks, Italian shoes, and the watch and bracelet as well as t-shirt, shirt, and underwear. Oh, and don't forget the cologne." They both laughed.

"Come on, Deacon, this is ridiculous. Are you serious?"

"As a heart attack. How much, ballpark it for me."

"Suit was five grand, shoes five hundred, watch thirty thousand, and all the other stuff, let's throw in another five hundred, so what's that, thirty-six thousand all together."

"Louis, are you listening to yourself? Between your car and wardrobe, you came to the church today wearing and driving the equivalent value of a nice middle-class home, or the salary of three middle class workers. Now let me ask you a question, what is the average salary of the congregation?"

"I don't know, Deacon, we have a large membership. But I do know that my friends and our largest donors all make good money and live in nice homes. Many of them wear better suits than me."

"Louis, I am not talking about all the people you know that sit on the first couple of rows of the church. I am talking about the average member, the one who wakes up every day and goes out and tries to make ends meet. Or is a single parent like Sister Leakes trying to be the breadwinner and raise three kids. How much?"

"Okay, for the sake of this conversation, Deacon, let's say fifty thousand dollars per year."

Phineas McNabb

"Okay, we will agree on that as our starting point. Now, I want you to think about that fifty thousand dollar a year member. What are they making, after taxes, maybe thirty-five to forty thousand dollars per year?"

"Keep going, Deacon."

"The point I am trying to make, Louis, is you are giving a bad perception to a congregation that does not come from your world and may never live in that world. In a best-case scenario, if they continue to receive the Lord's blessing, they might crack six figures per year as a family.

And even if they do, it will take them thirty years to make three million dollars. How much did you make on your last book deal with Harris and Grumaker, that fancy publishing company that markets your books?"

"They gave me a five-million-dollar advance, and I gave half of that to the church. You remember."

"You are right, so you gave a lifetime of earnings in one check and the church appreciates you for that but again look at the optics, Louis. You are dressing and living like a CEO, an investment banker, or someone who should be on the Forbes 400 list. What you are not doing is dressing like someone who is humble and working on behalf of the Lord. What I am saying is the optics don't look good. You deserve to live good and dress nicely and take care of your wife and kids like everyone else, but you are not a CEO, investment banker, or on the Forbes list. You are a preacher, plain and simple from Third Ward, a very prominent African American community in Houston that is slowly being gentrified and losing its identity. In the meantime, you moved us out to the suburbs where the community is diverse and while that is good on the surface, it goes against everything Greater Gospel was founded on."

"So, you don't like the changes we made, Deacon. You were in the room when we voted for every building, every change, and every decision we have made to date."

"You are right, and I voted no most of the time, son."

"What, I thought it was one of the other church board members, not you."

"Louis, do you even know the members of your church anymore? I mean, you have over ten thousand members, a board of twenty people,

53

most of whom hold important titles in the community or in the entertainment or athletic world, but none of them with exception of me have ever lived in Third Ward or stepped foot in the old building."

"What do you mean, you were the no vote each time?"

"From day one, Louis, from the first day you wanted to move to this campus. A campus, just listen to that. Who are we, Silicon Valley, downtown in the oil or banking district? I mean are we a church or a business, Louis?"

"We are both, Deacon. To survive, you must grow your membership, provide the right amenities and preach a message that resonates with the current climate, both politically and culturally."

"Says who, Louis. Who told you that?"

"Well, there have been multiple studies done, marketing strategies developed, and algorithms run that changed the way churches are run these days."

"Is that what changed them, Louis? Or did you just want to get back in the game?"

"What game, Deacon. I take my job very seriously. I am a man of the Lord just as my father before me and his father before him. I want to spread the word to as many people as I can and try to make a difference in the world. That has never changed."

"When's the last time you did a funeral that was not for someone famous, politically connected or was not a large donor to the church? Think back to the last time you did not delegate that to one of the ten assistant pastors you have, all of whom are fully capable of fulfilling their duties, but not the person who stands up in front and asks people to join the church every Sunday."

"Well shame on them, Pastor, if they are coming just for me and can't follow another Pastor who is fully capable as you said. If I tried to meet every request for my services, I could not do it if I wanted to."

"We agree, Louis, but my question was when is the last time you did it for the member who makes that fifty thousand dollars we were talking about?"

"I don't know, but I am sure you do."

"You haven't Pastor, you have not. And that is not your fault. You are only one person, but again optics. What did you think of Sister Leakes?"

Phineas McNabb

"Great woman. I admire her for what she has accomplished, and the church needs members like her."

"Louis, she has been trying to see you for over two years now. And your assistant kept telling her your schedule was packed for six months at a time. She lucked up Monday because you happened to be here, and your schedule was open. Do you know why that happened?"

"No, Deacon, but I did find it strange??"

"Louis, I cleared your calendar. You were supposed to be golfing with the Senator, and that pro golfer, I forget his name. I called them and told them you were tied up with a member and would not be available today."

"Why would you do that, Deacon?"

"Because that is my job as your right hand. And mind you, I did the same thing for your dad prior to you."

"I know Deacon, I know. Deacon tell me something. Other than you, how many of the original three hundred or so members are left from the old church in Third Ward?"

"You are looking at all of them right now, Louis. Oh yeah, and sister Leakes."

"Are you serious? Never mind, I know as a heart attack. So how do I change this, Deacon?"

"You can't. That ship sailed a long time ago. You either have to tell the church the truth about where the money is coming from or it may be time to............"

"To what, Deacon?"

"To resign, Louis. I mean if you keep trying to be a full-time Pastor and a part time investor slash big baller as you folks say, this won't work. You can't serve money and the people. It won't work. And this church is too large for you to maximize your full reach. What you have done is commendable, but we should have never gotten this big. All these capable preachers you have on the payroll waiting for their chance to lead the way. We could have put churches all over the city in the old communities as well as the new ones.

You pay your assistant pastors well, but you are not maximizing their full potential. And more importantly, the members are not getting the full benefit from you or them. And if you resign now, many of them may leave. And if they do, then that tells you all you need to know."

"I don't understand, Deacon."

Rich Men Have No Friends

"How many members did your father lose on average when he was preaching, not to relocation from Houston or death. Those two things were beyond his control."

"I don't know. I don't remember him losing any members. Or it was so few, I don't recall."

"Right, membership stayed right around three hundred never getting past four hundred which allowed him to service both the church and community in a good way. And when folks would visit the church, he would steer them to a church near their homes and in their own communities. He would convince them that as a church member, you want to be in your own community doing everything you can to grow it and strengthen it through fellowship, and good stewardship."

"I get it Deacon. My heart was in the right place, as were my intentions, but I let the spotlight get to me. Kind of like in that movie. There is a line that says be careful of the cameras and spotlights. They can become as addictive as a drug. I guess I got caught up and hooked on a life that I gave up many moons ago. But Deacon, every sermon, every donation, and every investment decision were in the best interest of the church."

"Let's agree to disagree, Louis. It was well intended, but you benefited in ways that were not planned when you took over. Your dad was a well-known and respected man locally, nationally, and in some other parts of the world for his charitable endeavors. And he met a lot of famous people as well. But he lived modestly, drove a nice but modest car, and he never would have spent thirty thousand dollars on a watch, much less one hundred. He always said a watch was a watch and he did not want the members to see him as anything other than what he was."

"What's that, Deacon?"

"A member of the church, plain and simple. A member who happened to be chosen to lead the flock. They followed him until his untimely death. And they followed you until you changed, not for the worse but into the megachurch rock star who graced the cover of magazines that have nothing to do with church. This is not business, Louis. This is the Lord's house."

"I get it Deacon. Looks like I have a lot to think about."

"Well, I will take that as your resignation. And Louis, I will be leaving as well. Time for me to go back home. There's a nice church around the corner from the house that I can walk to rather than drive way out here."

"Deacon, there's only one church in that part of town. And that was our building that we sold a long time ago."

"Yep, and they have a new Pastor who has grown the membership and is trying to revitalize the neighborhood as well."

"How come I don't know who this pastor is?"

"When is the last time you went to Third Ward, Louis?'

"I don't know, been awhile."

"Right, you have not been home in a while. That's what's wrong with you. You are living in a foreign land preaching to a foreign crowd, and they needed you until now. Now it's time to go home. You need to decide where home is. But Louis, don't wait too long. You have a gift, and that gift needs to be shared."

"Yes sir, Deacon. And Deacon?"

"Yes, Louis?"

"Thanks. I really appreciate it. I would not have made it this far without you."

"Louis, you would have made it this far. You would not have gone any farther though. My job was not to get you here, but to get you where you are really needed. My job was to get you home. I promised your father I would do that for him, and my mission is complete."

"Will you come with me, Deacon?"

"No, where you are going, you will be fine. And you will have a new deacon that will be there every step of the way. Now, I need to get moving. We have a lot to do, and a short time to do it in. See you, Pastor. You are a fine man, and the church will be fine. "

Deacon Jones went outside, got into his 1978 black Ford Pickup truck and went home. He would help Louis draft his resignation, appoint one of the assistant pastors to take over the church and he and Louis would keep in contact until the day he folded up his tent to go to his permanent home in the sky. Louis would donate most of his wealth to the Greater Gospel Church leaving with just a little over twenty million dollars. He had cashed out for the second time. Or so he thought.

Rich Men Have No Friends

14

Back at the motel, Theodore climbed the three flights of stairs, proceeded down the hall, slid his electronic key through the opener, and waited for the green light. He would open the door for Suite 3C, and to his surprise, it was a room like nothing he had experienced since grad school before he made his first million. He was expecting a suite but did not know that all the rooms had the word Suite above the number and letter assigned. He opened the door and his jaw dropped.

In his room was a small desk, 20-inch flat screen tv on a credenza, and a king size bed. There were two chairs against the window with a coffee table in between them. There was to his surprise a little fridge in the room that had a note that said help yourself. In the fridge was water, some sodas, and a few snacks, potato chips, candy bars, peanuts. He had in one day gone from a life of opulence to living like regular folks. He was used to staying in suites that were the size of a modest home.

He cut on the TV, saw that it was 5:15 and he left Mr. Wimples on the bed and rushed out the door to go to the diner. He had not eaten anything other than the candy bar and he was starving. "Be right back, Mr. Wimples. Need to get something to eat. Need me to bring you something back? No, okay."

He went down the hall, back down the three flights of stairs, past Ruby and made his way across the street. The street was paved with black asphalt, and it had a dotted white line running down the middle. There were two lanes and space on each side to park a truck or car. Given the lateness of the day, there were not many people in town and things were starting to quiet down.

The Diner was a white one-story building with a glass front. There was a door in the center of the establishment with writing that said, "Welcome to The Diner". He opened the door and went inside. There was a counter that had about 10 bar stools surrounding it. There were four wooden tables that could seat four people each and a long wooden table adjacent to the window that had a long bench in front of it. If Theodore did not know better, the whole town would be trying to go back in time to a different era and a different place. Thus far, The Gas Station, The Motel, and The Diner all looked like a scene from a movie that would have been filmed some forty or fifty years ago.

Phineas McNabb

Theodore went and sat at the counter. From the back came an older black woman in her late seventies who was short and heavy set. She looked like the ladies that worked in the school cafeterias from days gone past. She had a net on her hair, a red dress covered by an Apron that had a name tag that read Myrtle.

"Hey, baby. Welcome to the diner. Now I am going to tell you right now that it is 5:30 and I close right at six. Can't miss Jeopardy. So that will limit your order to either the special or the special. Which one would you like, sweetie?"

"What is the special, Myrtle?" Theodore said it with reluctance because he was not used to eating at places like this. This was not a five-star establishment which he frequented all the time.

"Well, don't sound so eager, Mr. I did not get your name......"

"Hightower, Ted Hightower."

"Mr. Hightower. The special today is grilled chicken, candied yams, string beans, cornbread, and a side of chocolate cake. That also comes with my homemade tea. All that for $5.99."

"I'll take it, Myrtle. Myrtle?"

"Yes, Sir."

"What is a candied yam and what is a string bean?" Myrtle laughed and shrugged her shoulders at Theodore.

"Why sweetie, that is what you city folk call a sweet potato and a green bean. That sound more familiar to you."

"It does, and how do you know I am from the city?" He had dressed down and was driving a pickup.

"You don't know what a candied yam is nor a string bean. They don't put that on the menu at those fancy restaurants you go to. Let me get that for you now." She looked back at Theodore and laughed again.

The food was brought out, and Theodore reluctantly dived in. He had not seen that much food in one sitting and was not used to being served on a paper plate and drinking from a Styrofoam cup when he went out to eat. Given his day, he was starving and ate everything on the plate and washed the chocolate cake down with the tea.

"Myrtle, that was actually very delicious. Where did you learn to cook like that?"

"Mr. Hightower, I have been cooking all my life. Since I was ten or eleven years old. Learned it from my mother and grandmother. I am the best cook in this part of the country. I used to run the cafeterias for the plants before they closed. We fed over three thousand people on any given day. The previous owner would serve breakfast and lunch for a flat one dollar per meal. For ten dollars per week, you could get two meals. It was one of the ways of letting the employees know they appreciated them. I sure hated when the plants closed."

"What happened to them?"

"They say some big shot guy was involved and bought out the company and then shut the whole thing down."

"Big shot guy."

"Yes, you know those guys who lay people off."

"Oh, you mean investor."

"Yeah, one of them. They just buy and sell companies with no regard for the people, all to make a dollar."

"Why do you say that, Myrtle?"

"Mr. Hightower, I had a lot of friends in this town, some newly made and others that I had gone to school with all my life. I worked at the plants from when I was 18 until the day they closed. I was just a cook, then the supervisor of cooks, I took pride in that job. It gave me pride in myself, and my community. I loved interacting with the people and being a bright light in their lives when they came through my cafeterias. When the plants closed, all that went away. My friends, my job, and the sense of community that we loved and enjoyed. Some moved back to Houston or relocated to other parts of the country. And some tried to make it here. Anyway, the rug was snatched right from under us."

"Did you not get a severance?"

"I did get a severance, except for one thing, Mr. Hightower."

"What's that, Myrtle?"

"A severance is a temporary band aid. A lay-off is forever. And when you can't afford to leave or in my case don't want to leave the only place you have ever called your home; the severance runs out and you're stuck fending for yourself. And the town loses its soul. The best way I can tell it to you is like losing a relative. But that investor, as you call him, would not know that. He or she are businesspeople, and I am all for making a living but not at the expense of hard-working God-Fearing people. I had no problem with the jobs being created in those other countries but why close us down? We were three of the most profitable plants in the company. That was what the big boss told us every year. Go figure. Anyway......"

"Myrtle, sometimes those decisions are made for the benefit of the shareholders and the people who own the company. It's not about hurting anyone but yes, it is about making money."

"Mr. Hightower, I am all for anyone making money. I mean C.J. helped me to get this dinner going so that I can make a decent living. It's when you are making money just for the sake of making money that I have a problem."

"I don't understand, Myrtle. What do you mean just for the sake of making money?"

"These big shot guys......."

"Investors......."

"Whatever, these people who are not from around here make decisions that affect whole towns. And for what, bragging rights to claim who is the richest man in the world or who has the biggest boat or house? And I will bet you ten dollars and a cup of coffee that the richest man in the world is not even happy most of the time. Don't know who your friends are, can't lead a normal life, and not able to spend all that money if they lived to be two hundred years old. And instead of giving that money back, they will just pass it to kids and grandkids who will probably squander it all away. And money will never bring back a loved one or fix a broken heart. "That touched a nerve, but Theodore could not let on who he really was.

"Wow, Myrtle, you really despise rich people, don't you?"

"No sir, I have nothing against rich people, middle class people or poor people. What I have a problem with is hoarding money and not using it for the greater good. I mean seriously, what can one buy with a hundred billion dollars? I read somewhere that the richest man in the world is worth over two hundred billion dollars. He would never be able to spend all that money even if he tried. I bet you he has every toy and house he could ever dream of. And I will bet you every one of his wives was prettier than the last one. I mean, come on, give me a break. and in the meantime, this town will never be the same."

"Myrtle, don't forget your Jeopardy show." It was five minutes until six.

"Lord, have mercy, where did the time go. Mr. Hightower, I need to run. Really nice to meet you. How long you in town?"

Rich Men Have No Friends

"I am here until tomorrow. My truck is at the gas station."

"Well, if anyone can fix it, Ken can. He knows those Ford trucks all right."

"Wait, Myrtle, how did you know I was driving a Ford."

"I heard it backfire when you came into town, Mr. Hightower. Gotta go now, let yourself out."

Theodore left the diner and decided that he would go back to his room. It was getting late, and he was tired. This had been a long and exhausting day. At that point, he heard a loud bang followed by another loud bang. Coming from behind the diner was a 1978 Black Ford Pickup truck. And who should be driving it but Myrtle. He panicked as he thought that Myrtle took his truck until he looked across at the gas station and saw that his truck was in the bay with the garage door closed.

"Must be a popular truck around these parts. Go figure."

Theodore walked back across the street to the motel, opened the door and there was Ruby.

"So, how was the food?" Theodore was back at the hotel and was catching Ruby before she ended her shift at the motel.

"Ruby, it was very good. And Myrtle is quite the character. Does not hold back. Tell me something. Why would a preacher take this much interest in a town and more importantly how is he able to get the money to assist all these businesses? Is he taking it from church funds? And even if he was, the kind of money needed to renovate one business much less several is nothing to sneeze at. How is he able to do that?" Theodore wanted to know this C.J. fella badly now. Preacher or no preacher, he liked a man or woman who could make money.

"Mr. Hightower, you bite your tongue. C.J. would never ever take from the church. He always tells us that the Lord led him to Greensburgh, and the Lord makes a way. I don't question the blessing, Mr. Hightower, I just thank the Lord for it. You know?"

"I guess, I am all for the blessing, but I sure would love to know the brains behind it."

"Mr. Hightower, I don't know where you are from but round these parts, we believe in the power of prayer. And we also believe that God helps those who help themselves. C.J. is bringing this town off life support and he is a man of the Lord. Don't know what else to tell you other than he was sent straight from Heaven. Kind of like the angel in

62

the movie It's a Wonderful Life. You remember that movie, don't you?" Theodore remembered it all too well.

"Yeah, I remember the movie. Jimmy Stewart was quite the character. But you know that was just a movie, right?"

"To you maybe, Mr. Hightower. But in my family, it has been a Christmas tradition as long as it has been coming on TV. Good story about how the small guy becomes the wealthiest man in town and the wealthiest man in town becomes the poorest."

"But that's not realistic?"

"Why not, Mr. Hightower?"

"The wealthiest man in the movie never lost his money so how could he be the poorest man in the town."

"Do you remember the end of the movie, Mr. Hightower?"

"I do but refresh my memory."

"George has lost all the money and does not know what to do. He is mad at his kids, screaming at everyone, and pretty much has lost his mind. But then his friends, all the people who he helped along the way contributed all they must to save the savings and loan. Then his childhood friends who are now successful in their own rights call and agree to give him whatever he needs to keep his business afloat. Remember that?"

"Yeah, I do vaguely."

"Well, if you ask me, he was the wealthiest man in town. Great family, loving friends and a business that did something for the greater good of the townspeople versus increasing his net worth. You see, Mr. Hightower, the richest man is not the richest man after all. Money can't buy happiness and it will sometimes complicate what should be for all of us a very simple life. Anyway, good night, Mr. Hightower, I must go pick up my baby from daycare."

"Good night, Ruby."

Theodore headed up the steps, and he entered his room. He greeted Mr. Wimples who was looking at the evening news. "Hello, Mr. Wimples, how are you doing? Anything big happen in this town while I was gone." Mr. Wimples just stared straight ahead.

"Do tell, they are thinking about getting a third stop light. I heard the same thing." Theodore laughed. As he headed over to his window to look out over the town, he saw Ruby and what would she be

Rich Men Have No Friends

driving? A black 1978 Ford Pickup truck. "What is it with these trucks?"

Since Theodore had met Abraham earlier in the day, things were happening that he did not quite understand. Abraham, the town of Greensburgh and that feeling of going back in time, the Ford Trucks being driven by almost everyone he encountered, and some plants closed that had basically decimated a city. And who was this guy C.J.?

As for Amy, she was still gone, and he was still grieving. He did not know exactly how he ended up here, but he also was not complaining. He was off the grid, had not checked his cell phone or opened his laptop. He was living a simple life. But for how long?

He looked out the window, and across the street was a place called of all things The Bar. It did have lights and there appeared to be a few people inside and a few cars parked outside on the street. It was seven o'clock and he was not tired yet. He was not sleepy yet and could use a stiff drink. He was there until his truck was fixed. Might as well make the best of it.

Phineas McNabb

15

Christmas Eve (Forty+ Years Ago)

Theodore's mother was now married to her third husband, and one of four stepdads that Theodore would have. He lived with his older sister, mom, and stepdad in a poorer part of town. They had a small red brick one story one thousand square foot home with three bedrooms and one bathroom. His mom was a small-time drug dealer who also used, and his stepdad worked at the local factory and loved a good shot of single malt. He had been recently laid off for coming to work late for the tenth time after being too hungover to wake up in time. This Christmas eve was rough because money was tight, and his mom was using so much of her product in addition to selling it that she sometimes owed her supplier more money than she brought in at times.

"Who turned the TV to this? Wrestling is on, turn the channel! NOW!!!"

"Let the boy watch his movie, you know how much he loves that Jimmy Stewart movie!"

"Woman, if I need your opinion, I will ask you for it, otherwise, shut up and get me something cold to drink."

"Screw that, get it your damn self." Theodore's stepdad stepped towards his mom, raised his hand as if he were going to hit her, and she pulled a gun from the drawer and put it to his head.

"Put your hands on me, and that will the last thing you do on this earth. Now I will get your drink, but you need to calm down."

Theodore's stepdad walked past him, picked up the TV and threw it to the ground. The console TV broke into, the screen lay in the floor shattered into what seemed like a thousand pieces of glass, and just like that it was not a wonderful life after all. Another deadbeat dad, another scene around the holidays.

"That's a stupid movie anyway. No such thing as angels. I don't get this whole God thing anyway. God did not keep my dad from beating the snot out of me when he drank and did not bring my mom back when she decided she did not want me anymore. Angels are like Santa Claus, they don't exist. Look under the tree. Don't expect that to change by tomorrow, Theodore. Santa lost our address this year. Sorry."

Rich Men Have No Friends

"Mom, is that true? There is no God and there is no Santa Claus." His mom by that point had taken another hit and was off into lala land, where people go who get high to escape the real world and all its challenges and problems. "Mom, is that true?" Theodore started to cry uncontrollably.

"Come here, son." His stepdad had calmed down at that point and wanted to drive home a point to Theodore, you know one of those lessons that a young child should not learn from a drunk man on Christmas Eve.

"There are two kinds of people in this world. There are those who take and those who give. Those who give get taken advantage of and those who take keep taking until they can't take anymore. I gave ten years to that plant, and yeah, I was late a couple of times, but I was a good worker. But the takers, the people who own the company, took my job. Get it, givers, and takers."

"Yes sir, givers and takers."

"So instead of watching movies about some angel that does not exist and praying to a God that you can't see, you had better start growing some and learn how to take. Because you know what?"

"What, Sir?"

"The takers are having a great Christmas right now and their kids will have toys and clothes and good food tomorrow. While we will need to start looking for a new place. The givers get screwed over and the takers get to see another day. Understand, Theodore."

"I understand, Sir." Theodore would go back to his room, open the drawer, and pull out the bible that his grandfather had given him before he died. He would then walk over to the trash can and throw it away. And as for Santa Claus, he never spoke of him or God again. He was now officially a taker and had no time for being a giver. He had crossed over to the other side.16

Shelley was leaving the office after what had been a long and exhausting Monday. Her boss was out of pocket, she had very few instructions except to put things on hold until he returned in a week, and she had not gotten over the death of Amy. A little girl that she had come to love like her own daughter was now gone. This had not been a good day for her.

She gathered her things, shut out the lights in her office and headed to the elevator. She got on, pressed one and was there in less than twenty seconds. She stepped off the elevator, and as she was walking past Harold, he reached out to her.

"Shelley."

"Yes, Harold?"

"Mr. Hightower left this for you as he was leaving." He handed her an envelope with the note that he had shared with Abraham earlier in the day. She took the note, opened it and proceeded to sit down on the couch in the foyer to read the note. She read it for the first time and did not quite know how to interpret it. Why was Theodore leaving her with complete and sole authority? Why did he want her to know his will was in order? Why did he want her to renovate the space? What was going on? Surely this was not a suicide note.

He was stronger than that. That could not be it. I mean Amy had taken a toll on him, but he seemed okay when they talked earlier although he had given his car away. She also took note of the comment about Pierre cheating with his wife and his fondness for her as a friend. A tear came down her cheek. All these years he had never made her feel like anything more than his assistant and Amy's buddy when he ran late.

"Here you go, Shelley." Harold handed her a tissue. At that point, Pierre exited the main elevators and proceeded to walk towards Shelley.

"Shelley, everything okay. We have not seen you today and one of the staff said they saw Theodore leaving earlier today in his car. Is he okay? I mean how is he holding up."

"He is doing fine, Pierre. I mean as good as someone would be doing given the circumstances, you know."

"I do. And he was such a great dad to Amy. I would not wish that on my worst enemy."

"Hey, Pierre, you have known the boss since grad school, correct."

"Well, yeah."

"You had my job at one point?"

"I did, Shelley, what are you getting at here?"

"Oh, nothing just wondering. And I agree with you, I would not wish that on my worst enemy either. Although, you know the saying, keep your friends close and your enemies closer."

"Yeah, Shelley, that's a stupid saying?"

Rich Men Have No Friends

"I could not agree more, Pierre, unless of course you are the enemy. Funny how that works out, keep your enemies closer. Well, anyway, you have a good night."

Pierre looked at her dumbfounded. He did not know that Shelley knew about him cheating with Theodore's ex-wife. And he lacked her street smarts to know that she had just made him tell on himself. Shelley had to go. She had to see Jess Witherspoon first thing Tuesday morning. She went out to the garage, went to the second floor, and got behind the seat of her 1978 Black Ford pickup truck and drove away.

Phineas McNabb

16

C.J. had spent this Monday like he spent every Monday at the church. Cleaning up after the Sunday service and going over his notes from the sermon. He also would put together his thoughts for the studying he would need to do to prepare for next week's sermon. He also took the time during the day to do other things that were not church related but mattered to his well-being. After he closed and locked the church, he made the short walk to his home which was located about a block from the church.

His wife, Sarah, would always greet him at the door with a hug and a kiss. He would remove his coat, if the weather called for it, and place his keys on the table in the foyer to their home. That was his routine every day.

"Hey, honey, how was your day?"

"It was great, how about yours, C.J."

"It was great, we have a visitor in town. A Mr. Ted Hightower. I have not met him yet, but they tell me he's hurting and really could use some help. No one knows anything about him, but they say he came into town driving one of Abraham's trucks. Myrtle and Ruby said he is a nice guy; they believe he is from Houston. Can you believe this man did not know what a candied yam was or string beans, baby?"

"Yes, I can. You know we get so far in life, and we forget where we came from."

"I guess, anyway long day for me tomorrow so I am going to call it a night. Good night, honey."

"Good night, C.J."

C.J. had learned his lesson in Houston. He and his wife had purchased a modest four-bedroom home that was located about a block from the church when they moved to Greensburgh. They had downsized both in home, car, and wardrobe. There's a lady in Houston who made a killing on e-bay as they gave her all the clothes, and purses, and shoes, and watches. Rumor is she made over one hundred thousand dollars selling the stuff and moved to Cary, North Carolina. The only luxury they had now was he would go into Houston to get their wine, which they drank in moderation. Other than that, they settled into their new home and were living a normal life. They had

Rich Men Have No Friends

been in Greensburgh for five years now, and no one knew that he was a multimillionaire several times over.

Just like he had done for Greater Gospel, he was funding projects, renovating the church, and revitalizing the town with his own money. As far as the citizens were concerned, he had some old friends back in Houston from the banking world who were doing him a favor and assisting the locals in rebuilding their city. Some of the current businesses were financed as well as other businesses that were open or being brought back to the town. He was rebuilding Greenbsurgh, one brick at a time.

To some degree, he was gentrifying Greensburgh, except this time it was for the greater good of all the citizens, not just a few. And all the businesses could cater to everyone, not just those with money. He was reinventing small town America and if it went right, he might be able to convince investors to do this in other small towns across the country. Still the dealmaker, he was still a mover and shaker. This time though it was behind the scenes. He would not ever again let the left hand know what the right hand was doing.

Phineas McNabb

17

It was about seven o'clock in the evening when Theodore decided he would take a walk across the street to the bar which was named The Bar. This oversimplification of all the business names had to mean something and he was determined to find out before he left. He tucked Mr. Wimples in, cut off the TV, and headed out the door. "Good night, Mr. Wimples." He proceeded down the hall, noticed that there did not appear to be anyone staying at the motel tonight but him, and headed down the stairs. He made the trek down the hall and to the check-in area where he had met Ruby earlier that day. As he was going through the lobby, he noticed something on the wall. It was a framed cover of a magazine.

It was a Fortune Magazine cover. Fortune Magazine is an American business magazine known for its Fortune 500 designation for the most successful companies based on revenue. Anybody who knew anything about business and was successful read Fortune.

On the cover of an issue from years past was Ruby. Except her name was Ruth Brenshe Grayhill. Her family controlled a vast real estate portfolio and was synonymous with the Grayhill Hotels and Resorts. She apparently had been named a rising star by the magazine and was rated as one of the most powerful businesswomen in America under the age of thirty. Based on the date of the magazine, that had been as recent as within the last fifteen years. Theodore would look further into it once he was at the bar.

He crossed the street, which at this point was quiet, with little to no traffic, and walked up to the front of The Bar. The Bar had a red brick front and two swinging doors like something you would see in a western movie. Beyond those swinging doors were two glass doors that allowed you entrance. Above the swinging doors were the words The Bar. On the glass doors were the words The Bar and right below that it said no one under the age of twenty-one allowed. Theodore proceeded inside.

It was like your typical bar. Ten brown high wooden tables with stools that could each sit about four people. The bar ran two thirds of the length of one wall and had about fifteen stools in front of it. At the rear were the bathrooms and right in front of them were two pool

Rich Men Have No Friends

tables. Both pool tables were made of black marble with red tops for playing. Appeared to be expensive pool tables for a little town like this. Coming from the speakers was some jazz music and the floor was hardwood flooring with a black and grey hue to it.

The bar was actually very nice inside and fit more to the standards that Theodore was used to. The bartender behind the bar was a tall slender Hispanic man, about six foot eight inches tall, black hair, and long arms with large hands. He had on a blue polo shirt, some jeans, hi-top sneakers, and a blue apron that had THE BAR sewed into the chest area. Behind him were four large screen TVs all showing sports of some type. They were barely audible as he kept them all on mute to allow folks to talk and listen to the music when they visited the bar. He was washing glasses when Theodore entered the bar.

"Let me get a vodka and tonic, please!"

"Sorry, mister, we don't have vodka."

"Okay, then let me have a gin and tonic."

"We don't have any gin either."

"Well, what do you have?"

"We have Coke, Sprite, Root Beer, and non-alcoholic beer. What would you like?"

"Nonalcoholic beer. Who drinks that? And what is your name, sir?"

"My name is Jesus (Haa-suus) Juan Romero. Folks round here just call me J.J. for short."

"Nice to meet you, Juan. My name is Ted, Ted Hightower and I am staying over at the motel until my truck gets fixed. Hey, are you the guy getting all the financing done for the local businesses?" Theodore was getting excited as he was finally meeting the guy everyone had been talking about, or so he thought.

"No, that is C.J., and he is not here tonight. He is probably at home by now eating dinner with his wife."

"Okay, and you did say your name was J.J., correct?"

"That's me. Now what would you like to drink, Ted?"

"And you really only have non-alcoholic beer?"

"That's all we have, Ted."

"Then let me have a cold one of those."

"Coming right up."

Phineas McNabb

J.J. poured the drink and placed it in front of Ted. Ted pulled out his phone and tried to Google Ruby given the magazine cover, but the service was spotty, and he finally gave up. It would have to wait until he spoke with her again.

"Ted, if you would excuse me, I need to go to the back for a second. Please make yourself comfortable."

"Hey, do you have anything to eat around here?"

"No, we don't serve anything other than the snack mix you see in the bowls around the bar and on the tables. Myrtle does all the cooking, but you must get over there by…"

"Six o'clock because she loves Jeopardy. I am aware, met her today, had a good dinner." They laughed.

As J.J. went back, Theodore had a sudden thought. He had heard the name J.J. Romero before. This name was familiar to him for some reason, either through business or just from memory. He pulled his phone out and checked it. Service was barely working but he had three of four bars. He typed in "*JJ Romero, Greensburg, TX*" and the page quickly filled up. The first thing he saw was titled "NBA Champion retires with no explanation". The Second title was "It's just not fun anymore" and appeared to be a quote. The third line read "Champion leaves game in his prime". Was this that J.J. Romero? By then J.J. had returned from the back. Theodore put his phone down.

J.J. was a six-time NBA champion, had been the most dominant player in the league in his heyday but had abruptly quit the game at the ripe old age of twenty-nine. He walked away from a contract and endorsements that paid him over thirty million dollars a year. That had been almost seven years ago, but he still looked like he could play with the best of them. He, for reasons unknown to anybody quit the game, sold his home, all his cars and jewelry, and moved to Greensburgh. There was no farewell tour, or parties held for him.

During the sixth game of the finals, his team was playing at home and was down by eight points with two minutes left in the game. He rallied his team back and there were five seconds left on the clock. His coach called a timeout. After the timeout, the ball was inbounded to J.J. who dribbled right, then left, faked his defender, stepped back and drained the prettiest three point shot ever. Bottom of the net, no rim.

Rich Men Have No Friends

The crowd went crazy, fans rushed the floor, and his team had won their sixth title in seven visits to the finals.

In all that rushing of the floor, J.J. quietly slid right through the crowd. He grabbed a hat off someone's head, picked up a coat off a chair, grabbed his warmup pants and made his way down the hall from the second story of the stadium right above the seats that are the priciest leading to the ground floor where the prices were ten thousand and up for a finals game. He went outside, hailed a cab and no one would ever see him again.

There had been rumors the first couple of years that he had lost his mind, and that people thought they saw him in this 1978 Black Ford Pickup truck. Those rumors were promptly squashed when he finally called into a national sports show and explained why he had left the game and why he did not want to play anymore. After that, no one ever asked about him again.

"Are you the J.J. Romero that once played in the league?" Theodore was excited to meet someone he had admired as both a businessman and a sports fan. He also was a minority owner of the team that J.J. played for and never understood how he could walk away from all that money.

"I am him, but I prefer to maintain a low profile now. I would appreciate it if you did not tell anyone you saw me, Ted. I am off the grid and want to stay that way."

"No problem, I like to maintain a low profile myself. And can I get another one of these cold beers.?

"You sure can." J.J. poured the beer, poured himself a soda, and came around the bar to sit next to Theodore.

"So, J.J., why did you leave the game?"

Phineas McNabb

18

"Ted, I left the game because it was not fun anymore and I met this fan right before the finals that night and it affected me in a way that I had not experienced my entire life. And you are talking about a kid who grew up poor, whose parents immigrated to this country, and was able to realize the American dream beyond his wildest dreams. Yep, meeting that fan that night right prior to the game stuck with me and that's why I left."

"No way, man. You meet a fan, they say something to you, and you decide you don't want to do something you love anymore. I don't believe it. What did they do, attack you or something? Did they try to hurt you?"

"Ted, they did hurt me, but not like you think. This fan on that night humbled me in a way that changed my life forever. It made me evaluate what was important to me and for that reason the game just was not fun anymore for me. The sport I loved was reduced to a thing that had greatly impacted this fan."

"J.J. what did they say?"

"Do you remember what happened after game five a couple of nights before, Ted?"

"Yes, you lost the game but were still up in the series three games to two. One game and the championship is yours."

"Right, but you don't remember the incident after the game that made national news, do you?"

"Not really. What happened?"

That night, a twenty-nine-year-old young black man by the name of Granville Jenkins was leaving the stadium with his son. Granville was wearing a jersey for the team that J.J.'s team was playing, and his son had on a kid's jersey with J.J.'s name on it. J.J. was his favorite player and he had watched him exclusively during his short nine years on earth.

Granville and his son were confronted by three men who were rooting for J.J.'s team. They had drunk one to many beers and were mad about the game five loss. They confronted the man and his son.

"Hey, what are you doing wearing that jersey out here, punk?"

"Man, come on, he is with his son, and he has on a J.J. jersey. It's all good."

Rich Men Have No Friends

"I don't care, I want this jackass to answer my question, why are you wearing that jersey?"

"Look, I don't have to explain why I am wearing this jersey. I am with my son; I would like to go home, and you need to go sleep off your beers."

"Who are you talking to? Do you know who I am, son?"

At that point, one of the drunken men swung at Granville. He ducked and knocked the guy out cold while holding his son's hand.

"Look, fellas, I don't want any trouble, I just want to get my son home. It was a good game and you guys have a chance to close this thing out in game six. Can I just take my son and......?"

Before he could finish his sentence, out of nowhere came a baseball bat and a loud thump followed by what sounded like the cracking of bone. Granville fell to the ground, blood was coming out of his head, and his son was on his knees crying in a pool of blood. Some locals who happened to be coming out of the stadium chased the men off and called the police and an ambulance.

"Wow, J.J., I do remember that story. What I don't understand is how that affected you?"

Theodore and J.J. were continuing their conversation and J.J. was beginning to tell him what happened prior to game six of the finals that would forever change his life.

"Ted, two nights later we have game six of the finals. I am walking down the tunnel when I see this kid whose father had been attacked a few nights before. He is with his mom, and they are with a representative from the other team. He has on my jersey, so I speak to him."

"What's up little man?"

"Nothing, sir, how are you?"

"Do you know who I am?"

"Yes, sir, I do. You are J.J. Romero, my favorite player."

"So, who are you rooting for tonight?"

"My dad, sir."

"Your dad?"

"Yes sir, my dad."

"Who's your dad?"

"Granville Jenkins, sir."

"Then why don't you have on his jersey, son."

Phineas McNabb

"Because he does not play basketball anymore. But my uncle does."

"Who's your uncle"?

"Frankie Jenkins, sir."

"Frankie Can't Miss Jenkins is your uncle."

"Yes, sir."

"But wait, you said you were rooting for your dad."

"Yes, sir, I am because he is in the hospital right now and his head is hurting really bad."

"What happened to him."

"Some of your fans hit him in the head with a baseball bat, sir."

"Wait, what? What happened to your dad and what do you mean my fans? What's this kid talking about?" At that point, J.J. was caught off guard and did not know how to process the information.

The child's mom and the representative explained that three guys all wearing Romero jerseys were drunk, did not like the fact the father was wearing the jersey of the other team and confronted him. What they did not know was that Granville was the twin brother of Frankie Jenkins and was there to see his brother play. He was late going to the parking lot because he had stayed over after the game for his son to meet the players. By the time they left, most of the fans had gone home. The fans who confronted him had not even been to the game that night but had seen it at a local bar and were simply in front of the stadium trying to get an autograph from J.J., their hero. The dad was in the hospital recovering but had almost died on the way to the hospital and during surgery.

J.J. was so shaken up by that story that he went inside the stadium and asked to speak to the owner of the team, Bernard Finkle, who liked him and recently signed him for a hundred-million-dollar extension.

"Bernard, we can't play this game tonight. We need to postpone it for a couple of days. Do you know who that fan was who was hurt the other night? It was the brother of Frankie Jenkins. We can't play this game. We must show the fans and the world that human life matters more than the money and this game."

"J.J., we can't do that. You know that, and besides, I believe the fans would want us to play the game to show these knuckleheads that they don't run this city, nor do they represent this team."

Rich Men Have No Friends

"Bernard, I understand that but what about Frankie. I know that I would not be able to play my best game if that were my brother, and might I say twin brother which is a different set of dynamics altogether."

"J.J., look, Frankie is a professional and so are you. I talked to the owner of the other team, and he said that Frankie is going to play tonight so we need to get going. There is too much at stake tonight and a lot of advertisers as well as the network will lose a lot of money if we cancel this game tonight."

"How much money will be lost, Bernard?"

"What?"

"How much money will be lost tonight?"

"I don't know the exact figures but for our team alone, ……"

"What about that dad, Bernard?"

"J.J., look, I feel really bad for the dad. I would beat the crap out of those sons a bitches who did this if I could, but I can't. Life goes on, son. That's all I can tell you. Now, are you suiting up or not?"

"I will be there tonight, Bernard, but after tonight, I am done. I quit. This game is not for me anymore. I struggle with business decisions being more important than human life."

"That's not fair, J.J. No one hurts more for that dad and that little boy than me. And I am sorry that Frankie is affected as well. Assuming we win, this is not how I want to win, you know that. But the show must go on. This is bigger than you and I. A lot of decision makers and millions of dollars on the line. And the fans would be devastated if we postponed this game. You know that as well as me."

"What does that say about our society, Bernard?"

"Nothing, J.J., it does not say anything. It's the world we live in, and you and I can't change that."

"Maybe I can change that, Bernard. You have been nothing but a great owner and almost like a dad to me. But after tonight, I have laced up my sneakers for the last time. I'm out. I can't play this game anymore. Won't be the same."

"J.J., let's get through the game, and lets you and I get together in a couple of days to discuss this further. I will make sure the dad gets the best care possible and I will set up a scholarship in the son's name. How about that?"

Phineas McNabb

"Sure, Bernard. Every little bit helps. See you after the game. Go Sharks." J.J. would never talk to Bernard again. He would call the national sports carrier and tell them the story of that night and why he walked away from the game. His jersey would be hung in the rafters the next season.

And as for Frankie Jenkins, he scored fifty-eight points that night. He and his brother were both twenty-nine, so he scored fifty-eight in honor of their bond. He would call J.J. a few days after and thank him for trying to delay the game. His team would win the championship and repeat the next two seasons. With J.J. gone, he was now the best player.

"Wow, J.J., that's what caused you to leave the game. What happened to that fellow was not your fault. You let some jerks cause you to quit the game you loved. And the fact they would not cancel the game?"

"No, Ted. I left the game because it was not fun anymore. I had more money than I could dream of, I had won six championships and life was good for me. But the incident with the dad gave me perspective. If the game could go on that easily and a man almost died, then what did that say about what was important to me. Money, fame and championships or human life. Which was more precious in that moment, and which did we value the most?"

"I am sorry, J.J. but I don't see your point. Three drunks caused that, not you."

"Ted, three drunks with my name on their back wearing a one-hundred-dollar jersey. They were so caught up in the team that they had no regard for human life. As if they were defending my honor and the team's honor. We are talking about basketball, a game, Ted. A game that every kid plays and loves. And that game has become such big business, that we can't even stop long enough to smell the roses and appreciate human life. I understand capitalism well, I benefited from it. What I don't understand is greed. And those are two totally different things."

"How are they different, J.J.?"

"Ted, capitalism would have delayed the game for a night, showed some reruns of a favorite TV show, and made sure that dad was okay. Greed made the show go on, and had the dad died, I would have been hoisting a trophy over my head while Frankie rushed to the hospital to see his brother for one last time. I would not have been able to live with myself had that happened."

At that point, the thought of Amy entered Ted's mind as he has blocked her out most of the evening and was beginning to get to a good place mentally about her death. This story from J.J. was one more reminder that money could not fix this one. Had the dad died, the show would have gone on, but a son would have been without his dad the rest of his life.

"Anyway, it is time for me to close this place up. I really enjoyed talking to you tonight. I have not told that story in a long time, well except for Abraham and C.J."

"J.J., can I ask you a question. Is it because of those three drunks that you don't serve any alcohol in the bar?"

"Yep, don't see the point. I have no problem with anyone drinking responsibly in their own homes and when they are out. But not to the point it affects human life, you know?"

"I do. Good night, J.J., nice to meet you. J.J. a quick question for you."

"Go ahead."

"If you had stayed…...?"

"Yes, Ted, we would have won more championships. I say this with humility, but I was unstoppable, you know. Nothing like God given talent and hard work. We would have won until I retired. At least that is what I believe when I play with the locals and pretend, I am back in the league like I did when I was a kid. And you know what, Ted?"

"What's that, J.J.?"

"The game is fun again playing with these local guys behind the church. I am still as competitive as ever, but there is no money, no television, no shoe contracts, endorsements, and unnecessary groupies. It's just me, nine guys, two hoops and a basketball. As it should be. Good night, Ted."

"Good night, J.J."

As Ted left the bar, he noticed hanging up on the wall were two jerseys. One had G. Jenkins on it and the other had F. Jenkins on it. And J.J.s jersey was nowhere to be found. He had those jerseys as a reminder of times past, why he left the league, and what mattered most in life. Human life.

Phineas McNabb

    As Ted crossed the street, he approached the motel, sat down on the steps and for a moment, Amy came to mind. He had tried not to think about her this evening, but J.J.'s story had brought perspective back to him again for why he was taking a break from work. He looked up in the sky and all he could see was stars in the distance. "I wonder if my little angel is okay." The man who did not believe in angels had just called the only love of his life an angel. Right then, he heard a loud pop and then another loud pop.

The bar was closed, and all the lights were out. What should come from behind the bar? A 1978 Black Ford pickup truck and J.J. was behind the wheel. He honked at Ted and headed home.

    Ted did not know what to think. On the one hand, he was happy to be in this small town and all its peace and quiet. But what was the deal with these trucks. And why did everyone have one? Or at least the people he encountered. It did not matter. They were all very nice and cordial to him so maybe they just liked black trucks made by Ford in 1978. He made his way upstairs, took off his clothes, and fell fast asleep. It had been a long day in Greensburgh, Texas.

Rich Men Have No Friends

19

It is Tuesday morning, exactly 24 hours since Theodore left his business, and turned everything over to Shelley. The sky in Houston is gray, thunder is coming every forty seconds, and lightning is flashing across the sky. It is 7:30 and rush hour is in full swing. Shelley is trying to get ready for work. She did not sleep well last night so she is a little fatigued this morning. She lives on the twenty ninth floor of the Rotillion, a forty-floor building about twenty minutes from the office on a good day, today it will take about 30 minutes.

She makes her way to the kitchen and turns on the gas stove to make herself a cup of coffee. Being an old-fashioned person, she puts water in a silver kettle and places it on the stove. She likes her coffee black, no sugar, no cream. As the former owner of a coffee shop, she never saw why people needed so many variations of coffee, and the need for it to be hot, cold, chilled, and so on. Coffee was coffee, plain and simple. She had made a nice living doing that until the franchise across the street started to offer lower prices and put her out of business.

She picked up her cell phone. No calls from Theodore. Hope he's okay. She dialed the number of Jess Weatherspoon, Theodore's lawyer. The phone rang four times and then he picked up. Jess has been Theodore's lawyer for the last fifteen years. They met at a fundraiser, hit it off for some strange reason, and Theodore asked him to come on board and be a part of what is now HenPot Industries, a company that dabbles in everything from oil and gas to furniture to peanuts. HenPot started at Theodore's kitchen table and grew from there. He would take his one hundred million dollars and initially dabbled in the stock market. He invested a million here and a million there. When he saw the potential returns, he decided that he not only wanted to invest, he wanted to have a larger piece of the pie.

Theodore became a buyer of companies, rarely holding on to them. He would do his vetting, buy a company that he thought was undervalued, slash and burn, and then sell at a profit. Sometimes he would hold a company if the stock was doing well and use the increased value as leverage to do other deals. His slash and burn exercise always started with the elimination of staff. Theodore had determined a long time ago that there was no harm in doing this. Not a day went by, and no more than a week at the least, that some company was announcing that it was laying off a percentage of staff to save costs. He figured that if companies all had that kind of associate or employee float, he wanted to get in on that.

He created an algorithm that would study the breakdown of a company's staff, focusing on the middle managers and up specifically. His goal was to find the company who had low ratios of workers to leaders and executives. Given the history of other companies he had studied, he would plug in a number, say four percent, and it would say how many people he could lay off immediately. After all, if a company could lay off two hundred people with little or no notice to the street, then there would be fluff in every company.

If that equated to say four hundred people making an average of fifty grand per year, then his savings after severance in the first year would be potentially ten million dollars based on a six-month severance and twenty million in the second year. Add a zero to the staff and you add a zero to the savings.

The formula was simple, buy the company by himself or with a group of investors, lay off a percentage of the higher paying people, then announce to the street that the company was more efficient and watch the stock price go up. As soon as it hit his number, then he would sell the company. If the stock was at forty dollars, and because of his action it went to fifty dollars, he stood to make ten dollars for every share he owned. Since he owned most of the shares as the largest investor, then you multiply that by ten dollars, and he would make hundreds of millions or a billion or billions. The whole concept was to buy, lay off, and sell for a profit. No invention, no new patent, no new efficiencies. Just lay off the people, convince the street the company was more efficient, and sell for a nice profit. He became known as the "Numb Investor". He was numb to the impact on the people, or the communities that the companies were located in. He did not care. There was no Santa Claus, and there were no angels.

But there were companies to buy and money to make. He would expand that model when outsourcing became the hip thing to do. Outsourcing meant taking a job that cost x in the United States and shipping that job to another country where it cost half of x or less than that. Outsourcing would allow him to include the front-line employees in addition to manager and executives. He was determining who could

Rich Men Have No Friends

go and what jobs could be shipped overseas resulting in savings in both salary and brick and mortar space or real estate.

Gone were the days or creating companies that did good for the local community by creating jobs and giving the town and its citizens a sense of pride in knowing that they had built this good, and it was Made in the USA. All that mattered was the bottom line, the stock price, and the increase in his net worth. He was now officially a taker.

Phineas McNabb

20

It is Tuesday morning and Shelley is to meet with Jess Witherspoon, Ted's lawyer, about the note.

Jess became his point man in making sure that nothing fell through the cracks and was also charged with public relations. His only job was to spin the story for Theodore so that he did not look like a noncaring corporate raider, although that was exactly who he had become.

Once it was time to take the personnel action and more importantly sell the company, he would back out and Jess and Shelley would step in. All he did was count the cash and move on. On the rare occasion when he held onto a company, he would appoint a new CEO through Shelley and place his own people on the board. For the companies that he sold quickly, he would force his people into key board positions that helped move his cause. If there was even a rumor that he might be looking at a company, it would cause panic within the organization and the stock price would see an immediate slight uptick. After all, he was the richest man in the world.

"Good morning, Jess. This is Shelley."

"Hey, Shelley, I was expecting your call. How are you doing?"

"Well, I don't quite know. Mr. Hightower informed me that he was taking a hiatus from work, it was supposed to be for a week but now I understand that it could be indefinite. So not quite sure how to absorb all of this. Anyway, I would like to come to your office and discuss a note he left me. I would rather not do that over the phone."

"I agree, what time can you be here?"

"I can come straight to your office prior to going to work. You available at say, nine?"

"Nine works fine, see you when you get here."

Shelley prepared her coffee, finished getting ready and grabbed her keys and headed out the door. Traffic was not as bad as she thought, and she made it to Jess's office in time for the meeting. His law office was a small boutique shop located across the street from Theodore's office. He had moved there five years ago based on a request from Theodore to be closer to him in case he was needed quickly. He had one client now, HenPot Industries. And he had a team of ten people all dedicated to his work for Theodore.

Rich Men Have No Friends

The office was located on the tenth floor and took up half the floor. There was a receptionist at the front door who greeted all visitors and across from her desk was a glass enclosed door that required her to push a button under her desk to let you in. Directly in front of the glass door beyond her desk was a conference room that seated 20 people. It has a nice brown mahogany table. At the end of the table on the wall was a sixty-five-inch television with smart technology for doing presentations or having a virtual conference call.

Shelley knew this office well as she sat in for Theodore for all deal closings. She and Jess were the faces of HenPot. There was always some lower-level staff member who thought she was the big dog. She will be let in by the receptionist and go to the conference room. Jess was meeting her there.

"Good morning, Shelley." Jess would walk in right at two minutes to nine. He was six-foot-tall, jet-black hair and clean shaven. He looked like Clark Kent without the glasses. Very athletic build, former captain, and quarterback of his college football team. He had made a lot of money formerly as a mass tort lawyer. He lost most of it trying to dabble in too many deals, trusting a partner who did not know how to keep information confidential, and trying to get too big too fast. Theodore had rescued him from himself, paying him a fee to close every deal, and a bonus if he closed ahead of schedule.

In the past two years alone, Jess and his team had made over one hundred million dollars in attorney fees. He was another loyal subject just like Harold and Shelley. Theodore only had one rule. If Jess talked to anyone about Theodore's business, he was fired. If someone on his team talked, they were to be fired immediately.

"Good morning, Jess. So, what the heck is going on?"

"Shelley, Theodore called me from California when he was out there for Amy's funeral. Such a sweet girl. She did not deserve that. Anyway, he called me and told me to put the wheels in motion for you to take over the company. He said he needed some time off to process what had happened and did not want any distractions to bother him. He also updated his will but assured me that he wanted his affairs in order and not to worry about his mental state.

He said while he was not handling her death well, he was coping the best he could. And that was that. Nothing else, nor anything that I can share with you that will help alleviate any concerns you might have.

Phineas McNabb

As of your signature on the documents I have with me, Theodore is chairman in name only, but you are the new chief executive officer of HenPot Industries. Your role as chief operating officer is to become vacant until further notice. You can hire someone to assist you, but they can't assume your role, nor can they move on the fiftieth floor. His return date is unknown at this time, but he did leave open the possibility that could happen. Any questions."

"So basically, it is business as usual?"

"Not exactly, Shelley. Theodore wants the company to continue to invest in any new opportunities and continue to grow the current business. Except now you are the decision maker. The buck starts and stops with you. You find the opportunities and take the same actions Theodore would if it looks right. You sell when you think the time is right and your job is to do no harm. If you make money great, if you break even, that's okay too. Just don't lose any money. Your job is to keep Theodore as the richest man in the world. That he was very clear on. He does not want to be number two, understand?"

"Wow, Jess. His daughter just died, and his primary focus is being the richest man in the world. I mean with all due respect, is that really the priority right now?"

"For him, no. But for you as the leader of his organization, that is all that matters. Keep the ship afloat, keep it moving forward. If you can make him money, great. But keep the ship steering in the right direction. Got it."

"I am not built for this. Being his assistant was a great assignment, despite how blunt and to the point he was at times. But being responsible for his money, and his companies is a whole different ball game. That's the pressure he dealt with, not me."

"Shelley, who has attended all the conference calls? Who has been the face of the organization at every closing on behalf of Theodore? If you really think about it, you have been here every step of the way. He finds them, hunts them down, and you and I are there for the kill. Theodore does not like blood on his hands. When it is time to cut staff or sell the company or a division that is underperforming, it is either you or me or both of us who meet with the current chief executive officer of that company. HenPot is nothing more than a pass through or the holding company for all the subsidiaries that it controls at any given time. You have been doing the heavy lifting along with me the entire time. Theodore just provides the money and expertise when needed. Now that will be you, except you are here to make him money, and spend it where appropriate. No pressure."

"So, I don't have to clear any decisions through him, Jess?"

"How would you? He has turned everything over to you. He can insert himself at his discretion and veto a decision he does not like. But short of a call from him to you to intercede, it is your company now. And yes, if he does that it can complicate matters, but I don't anticipate him doing that. He does require that you keep me on staff and consult with me as always, but only he can stop a deal that meets the litmus test he has always applied through the algorithms already in place. So, you ready to get to work? And you will need to tell the team. And we will need to notify the street as is required by the regulators and SEC. Now, the hard part."

"What's that, Jess?'

"We will need to give everyone the impression that with Theodore still in the role of Chairman, no decision is being made without his blessing. And he won't be attending any board meetings. You will continue to do what you always did, be his voice on the ground."

"So, I am supposed to lie and give the impression my decisions have his blessing."

"No, we could go to jail for that. What I am saying is that if asked, you are to notify the team, our current CEOs, the analysts who follow HenPot, and any of our shareholders that you speak on behalf or Theodore as you always have. Except now you will be making the decisions and defending them as well. Basically, the assumption will be if asked the question is Theodore aware, your answer is yes. And if we need to get his blessing, he will make himself available or sign off on the necessary paperwork. His goal is to keep that at a minimum. Given how he has run things for the past ten years, and our roles, this will work. You are the decision maker, and I am his attorney. You make the decisions, and I make them happen. If you and I are not in cahoots with each other, his money is not impacted. And that is what makes it business as usual. Understand?"

"Not really, but I get it. Nothing illegal, unsafe, immoral, or unethical about it from where I sit. We are basically acting on his behalf except he has given us full control."

"Correct."

Phineas McNabb

"Well, I better get to work." Shelley was headed back to the office.

Rich Men Have No Friends

21

It is Tuesday morning, and the sky is blue in Greensburgh. It is a balmy sixty-four degrees outside with a slight wind from the east. The birds are chirping, and the town is starting to come awake. It has now been almost twenty-four hours since Theodore left Houston on what was supposed to be a hiatus from work to think things through. Ken was walking across the street from the garage to notify Ted how his truck was coming along.

"Good morning, Ruby."

"Good morning, Ken, what brings you over here?"

"I wanted to tell Ted that I should have his truck ready by tomorrow just like I promised. I saw J.J. and he said that this Ted fellow is an okay guy. Said they talked until closing last night. Well, anyway I'm going to get breakfast. You want anything?"

"No, I am good. Made breakfast this morning prior to coming to work. Egg whites, veggie sausage and a bagel with a nice cup of tea."

"Umm, umm, Ruby, that sure sounds good. I should have had you bring me a plate. See ya later!"

"Bye, Ken. I will give Mr. Hightower the message."

As the sun had risen in the sky that morning, Theodore had woken up and made himself a cup of coffee with the coffee maker in the room. He sat down in one of the two chairs, set his coffee down and looked out the window. The town was awake first thing at sunrise.

Ken had opened the gas station; Myrtle had opened the diner and Ruby had come through the door about seven. These folks were at work as if business was booming, but other than them opening their businesses, the streets were still very quiet. A few cars passed by; a couple honked at Ken, but it was peaceful. The sun was rising, and the sky was as blue as it could be.

Theodore took his shower and dressed, got Mr. Wimples up, made the bed and cut on the TV. There was nothing of interest, so he cut the volume down low. As he looked out the window, he decided to do something he had not done in over forty years. He walked over to the desk by the bed and opened the drawer.

There in the top drawer was a Bible, the book he had thrown away many years ago. He looked at it but did not take it out of the drawer. He stared at it for about two minutes, then he closed the drawer again.

Phineas McNabb

He did not know what made him open the drawer but a conversation from years past made him close the drawer back. There are no angels, Santa Claus, or God. He remembered he had asked about his angel, Amy, the night before without hesitancy. He had not said my little girl, my beloved Amy, he said my little angel. And that was still on his mind that morning.

"Mr. Wimples, what do you think? Do you think our Amy is an angel? I mean, I don't believe in angels but if there were angels, based on the requirements to be an angel, then Amy would surely fit the profile, don't you think?" He smiled at Mr. Wimples who was now sitting in the chair opposite him.

"I agree with you; she would be an angel. For the sake of our morning conversation, which I appreciate, we both agree that if there were angels, our Amy would be one of them and she would be the prettiest angel in Heaven, right. Right. Now let's just keep that between the two of us, okay."

Rich Men Have No Friends

22

Shelley had left Jess's office and went straight back to HenPot headquarters. She had sent a message ahead to tell the team to gather in the main conference room on the 49th floor. She wanted to tell them the news as it was being released simultaneously to all who had a need to know. She was the new CEO and the team needed to get back to work.

Everyone had been working on strict orders to do nothing until Theodore returned from Amy's funeral. Keep working on all current situations, but don't do anything new until further notice. Many had temporarily stopped working on anything that was classified as a new project. All were highly educated analysts, having met the requirement of having an undergraduate degree in a STEM major and a graduate degree in a specialized discipline that gave them expertise in areas that HenPot would potentially invest in. And they had to be right out of school. While others believed in hiring only those with experience, Theodore thought differently. He wanted new hires with little to no experience, with very few exceptions. At least ten of the twenty people on staff were original hires that had been with him for almost the entire time that HenPot had been in existence.

Shelley entered the office around 10 that morning. She walked past the main floor where everyone sat in the exact same desk, with the exact same chair, and the exact same computer and monitors. It was not about the title, and size of anything at HenPot. It was about making money, period. If you needed to know how many inches your desk was, or how big you monitor, or what your title was to put on business card to give to an old friend at homecoming who was going to put it in a drawer as soon as they got home never to be seen again, then you were in the wrong place. If you wanted to be on a team that wanted to succeed and ensure everyone made a good living, you were in the right place.

"Good morning, team. I will be very brief. Effective immediately, I am the Chief Executive Officer for HenPot industries. All decisions will be made by me. All ideas are to come to me, and I will tell you how to proceed if there is an interest in the project. What's the difference about this? I am glad you asked. Nothing, it is business as usual. My role will be expanded slightly to cover for Mr. Hightower, who will still be involved. It allows him the time he needs to process what has happened recently. Anyone asks you; we are still in business. Anyone asks you why the change in my title, you tell them it's the natural progression of the organization and I had been acting in the role for a while now. Got it!"

"I have a question. Why you?" It was Pierre.

"I don't understand your question, Pierre, why me?"

"I mean, you are the assistant to Mr. Hightower, and I as well as others here have always respected your role, but why you. Some of us have been here a long time, made this company a lot of money, and were not even considered for the role."

"Pierre, we can take this offline."

"No, Shelley, I think everyone here needs to know why you. Being CEO of this company will set you up for the rest of your life. Given the success and track record of the organization, you will make more money than you could ever dream of. Again, some of us have been here longer than you."

"Okay, Pierre, I will answer that for you although I warned you to take this offline. You know what makes me uniquely different than those CEOs you are describing that will make a ton of money. I am not chasing money. I just found out about this change this morning. And as for money, it never came up and I did not ask. I don't do things for the money. I do them for the opportunity. Money just naturally follows or, so it has been for me all my career. That help, Pierre?"

"I guess."

"Pierre, come see me after this meeting. Everyone else, thanks for your hard work and understanding during this time. Now let's get back to work. Oh, and one more thing, Mr. Hightower does not want any more cards, flowers, or any type of communication about his daughter sent or relayed to him. I am asking you in a very blunt way to stop. Let him have his time. Thanks."

Pierre followed Shelley back to her office and closed the door.

"What are you doing, sleeping with Ted?"

"What did you just say to me and remember who I am as of ten this morning."

"I have known Ted since we were in grad school together. And yes, we hit a rough patch many years ago. But he has always paid me well,

Rich Men Have No Friends

you make me feel like I am your number two on the floor when you are out so what gives. How did a friend, colleague and basically the third in command does not get a forewarning this was happening but learned about it with everyone else?"

"Pierre, what happened with you and Mr. Hightower, Ted as you call him?"

"What do you mean?"

"What happened? I have always been curious. He puts you on the forty ninth floor, I take your place, and he gives me clear instructions to keep you around if you performed at the level expected of someone with your talent, education, and background. He told me that you all were partners on many of the patents that made him his first hundred million. He also said that you made quite a bit of cash yourself. What exactly happened to you and Ted, as you call him. And why didn't you start your own shop when you were demoted?"

"Because he looked out for me when we were in college. That is why I have never left. We were like brothers. I was smart, but not like Ted. We partnered on those projects, but he did all the work. He gave me credit for helping him but a lot of the nights he was up late trying to get something to work, or finalizing a project, I was with some girl, drinking more than I should, and sleeping through my first class."

"Then why did he take care of you. That would be out of character for him."

"Shelley, I don't come from money. I scratched and clawed my way to grad school. My mother abandoned me at birth. I don't know who my dad is, and I floated from foster home to foster home being mistreated, abused, and treated like nobody. The only thing I had going for me was my grades. I shared this with Ted when I first met him, and he shared his story with me as well. When we were in college, he did threaten to kick me to the curve one day when I did not do the work I was supposed to do."

"So, what happened. Why didn't he let you go? I would have."

"Because, Shelley, I told him I had nowhere to go. If I flunked out of grad school, I was done. And after the life I had lived, being a regular guy making regular money was not appealing to me. I was on the brink of going over the edge and Theodore knew that."

"What happened next, Pierre?"

"He told me that if I tried and did not miss any more key meetings or project assignments, he would help me. And that he did. I ended up making over ten million dollars and thought I was set for life until……"

"Until what…."

"I met a girl, we got married, she left me after six months, and all the money was gone."

"What do you mean all the money was gone?"

"She stole it, disappeared off the map and I never saw her again."

"Wow, Pierre. You have had some back luck but that still does not explain why he moved you to the forty-ninth floor. Something is missing from this story. "Shelley already knew the answer.

"Shelley, let's just say that I did not obey one of the top ten."

"What?"

"Thou shall not covet the neighbor's wife. I broke one of the top ten."

"I don't understand, oh, I get it. One of the four wives and you……"

"Yep, and it broke Ted's heart. That coupled with his other struggle, and it was just too much for him to handle."

"What other struggle?"

"You ever hear Ted talk about God, Angels, or Santa Claus."

"Never noticed, plus that's not something that is normally discussed in the workplace, Pierre."

"How about Santa Claus?"

"Ted is a grown man. Why would he talk about Santa, wait a minute, that explains why Amy was never here for Christmas but always for Thanksgiving. I never noticed until now."

"Shelley, Ted, and I come from a place that shapes you, molds you, and if you are not careful hardens your heart to the point you struggle with right and wrong. It's not that you don't want to care, it's just that you don't. There are two people in this world that can struggle with compassion for others, those who have always had everything and wanted for nothing and those who have had nothing and finally get everything they could ever dream of. In both cases, they both get everything and forget what love, compassion, and empathy are about, you know what I mean."

"Kind of."

Rich Men Have No Friends

"So that is why I still work here, plain, and simple. Ted has only looked out for three people his entire life. Me, his mom and of course Amy. Amy and his mom are gone now so the one person he would normally lean on is a person that he has not spoken to in over ten years. And I don't blame him."

"Pierre, thanks for sharing that with me today. You can go back to your desk now."

"Thank, Shelley."

"One more thing, the next time I tell you to take something off the floor, please do that. Because if I fire you and I will, you will have hurt your friend for a second time. Got it."

"Got it, Shelley. And thanks for listening."

Pierre returned to his desk. Shelley closed the door to her office, walked over to the window and a tear came down her cheek. "Mr. Hightower, I hope you are okay. And yes, your Angel is in Heaven."

Pierre would return to his desk. Shelley did not know it, but Pierre was worth over a billion dollars himself. Theodore had set up the company from day one to always pay Pierre one percent of whatever Theodore made. Pierre had asked him to manage his money for him given the experience of the first marriage, and the millions his wife stole from him. Theodore had done that for him to date, despite the transgression he had committed to hurt their friendship. Two billionaires who had not spoken in over ten years loved each other like brothers. No amount of money could fix that.

Phineas McNabb

23

C.J. was awoken by the sound of his alarm. It went off consistently every weekday at five thirty in the morning and six on Saturdays. Sunday, for whatever reason, he did not need an alarm. He woke promptly at five to be at church by six. Today was Tuesday, so his alarm went off at five thirty on the dot. He got up, kissed his wife on the forehead and began his normal routine.

He put water in his kettle and placed it on the stove. He let Nellie, his cocker spaniel, out to go to the bathroom, opened all the curtains, blinds in the house to let's God's light in and checked his phone for messages. After he did that, he fed Nellie. Nellie would then go sit down and look at him for their next move. He would shower, put on his clothes for the day, and his favorite pair of sneakers. He would then take Nellie for a short walk through town. They would not go more than one mile as that took about thirty minutes and made Nellie smile. When they returned home, he would go to his study and say a prayer and then spend time studying his bible. Must always be prepared to save a soul and get ready for his Sunday sermon.

Once he had completed his morning routine, it was seven o'clock in the morning. He then put on breakfast for him and his wife. Most days it would be egg whites, veggie sausage, and toast or a bagel. On some rare mornings, he might make some pecan or walnut waffles or pancakes.

And if he was really in a good mood, he might put on some grits and bacon. He did not mind fixing breakfast as that was their quiet time together before he headed out to conduct church business. Like clockwork, his wife would come into the kitchen right at about seven twenty and he always greeted her with the same line, one he had been saying since they left Houston and the big house.

"Good morning, pumpkin! How did you sleep last night?"

"The same way I have slept every day since we moved to Greensburgh."

"And that is?"

"Like a baby. I slept like a baby, sweetheart. Now to the important stuff. What's for breakfast this morning?"

"Well, I thought you might want some pancakes this morning, with a few pecans mixed in. How does that sound?"

Rich Men Have No Friends

"Great, what's the occasion. You only fix pancakes or waffles when something big is going on. What did you do, and I mean that in a good way, C.J.?" He put the food on the table, they said a prayer and he began to explain his new mission to her.

"There's this new fellow in town and he's hurting bad. Lost his daughter in a tragic accident. Poor thing was only five years old. Gone before life even started for her. Anyway, Abraham contacted me and told me that he would be coming this way. Arrived yesterday afternoon. Truck is in the shop, and Ruby, Myrtle, and J.J. said he appears to be doing okay though he has not talked to any of them about his situation. More of a listener than a talker."

"C.J., that's a smart man if he is a listener more than he is a talker. You know they say the sign of a mature man is the amount of time he spends listening than talking. Sounds like a guy who takes in information and processes it before speaking. That's interesting."

"Okay, let's not go figuring the guy out before I have a chance to meet him. But I agree with you. You don't become the richest man in the world by talking all the time. The less you say, the more you keep your competition at bay. Learned that when I was in the business myself."

"Did you say the richest man in the world? As in Theodore Hightower, the richest man in the world."

"Yes, Sarah, but how do you know who Theodore Hightower is? He leads a very low profile."

"Read about him in People Magazine when he married that actress, Isabel, Isabel something. Anyway, he married her, she wanted a public wedding and somehow it got out that he was the richest man in the world. They had a daughter, named Amy. She should be about four or five now. Wait a minute! Is that the little girl that died in the pool a couple of weeks ago? I heard about it from some of the ladies at the church. That's a real shame, little girl had her whole life in front of her."

"She did, Sarah. So now he is riding around in his truck with her teddy bear, Mr. Wimples, and that has become his primary source of comfort to keep him from going over the edge. He also does not believe in God or Angels, or Santa Claus. You know that I don't ever try to force my faith on anyone who does not want to receive it, but I also want them to have faith in something other than the material trappings of this earth. I am excited to report that he had a breakthrough last night. He called his daughter his little angel. I did not expect that this soon. There is hope with this fellow. My challenge will be convincing him there's more to life than money."

"Well, if anyone can do that, Louis Cletus Johnson can do it. After all we have been through since you took over your dad's church, you are a good source of credibility for Mr. Hightower. Now the question is will he listen to you?"

"That is the million-dollar question. You know my struggles, Sarah. Every time I am in Houston, I pass the luxury car lot or drive by those nice homes downtown. And I will admit that I do sometimes miss that life and the satisfaction in knowing that my success was rewarded. But then I remember the perception and the optics of those I am trying to influence and inspire, and I quickly realize that I don't miss those things at all. Nice to haves but not fulfilling my needs, but my wants. And right now, I want to make a difference and I need to see Mr. Hightower before he leaves town. He left Houston with no known destination and Abraham was able to get him to take a detour to Greensburgh. Hope it works."

"It will work, C.J. Look at J.J, Ruby, and Myrtle. Look at what you have done for them. Remember who they used to be. J.J was the best player in the league, Ruby was heiress to the largest hotel chain in the world, and Myrtle was bitter towards anyone who even looked like they had money. Remember that?"

"I do, and I am still working on them. The work is ongoing and never stops. Right?"

"That's right, it is just a matter of getting Mr. Hightower to where they are. You better get going, you have between now and tomorrow to complete your mission. Abraham is counting on you."

"That's right. Let's finish our breakfast first, Mrs. Johnson. I love you."

"I love you to, Mr. Johnson." They finished their breakfast and C.J. headed out the door. He needed to get over to the motel to meet Mr. Hightower for what he was hoping would not be the first and last time."

C.J. made his way out of the house and proceeded to take the short walk about a half a block down to the motel. He made his way inside and there was Ruby, wide awake and smiling from ear to ear when she saw him.

"Good morning, Ruby. How are you doing this morning?"

"Good, C.J., how about you?"

"Excited to meet our new guest. How is he doing this morning."

"Well, I know he's up, curtains were open this morning when I walked up to the front door."

"Good, Ruby. What do you think of Ted?" C.J. had not told anyone in town about Theodore or about him being the richest man in the world. They might find out on their own, but it was not his to share. Ted wanted to maintain a low profile and he of all people understood that.

"Seems like a nice fellow. Doesn't say a whole lot. But he's been very cordial. Myrtle liked him and that is saying a lot. She almost missed Jeopardy last night talking to him. She said it was him who reminded her that she needed to go. She thought that was the nicest thing. And you know Myrtle."

"I do know Myrtle. And for her, that is saying a lot. She will never forgive those rich guys as she calls them for ruining her town. And I just now am getting her to come around to the fact that business decisions are not always popular, but life goes on. Life goes on, and ultimately everything normally works itself out. At least that has been my experience. Are you missing the hotel business, Ruby? Are you missing the Grayhill experience and the exposure that comes with it?"

"I do miss it. I miss the people that I met daily, I miss the limousines, the chauffeurs, the maids, the nannies, I miss it all. I miss having someone at my beckoning call. I miss buying something just because I could, even if I already had ten of them in the same color taking up space in that two thousand square foot hole that I called my closet. I miss my food being made for me; I miss all that. But you know what I don't miss."

Ted had decided that he was hungry and made his way downstairs. As he was approaching the front desk area, he overheard the conversation between C.J. and Ruby. He decided to stop in the hall, hoping they did not notice him. He leaned against the wall and listened to the conversation. They were not aware that he was already downstairs.

"What's that, Ruby?"

Phineas McNabb

"I don't miss all those things because they just filled a void and did not allow me to have the peace of mind, and happiness I was so trying to get."

"Do tell, Ruby."

"Well, Pastor, here I was the third youngest billionaire heiress in the world. And I had no relationship with the one brother that meant all the world to me. A brother that had been estranged from me and the family for over ten plus years. A brother that was out in the world struggling while I was living it up with people who did not care about me. They only hung around me for my money and the business opportunities. They were not my friends. Not my real friends, and you know how I know that?"

"How did you know that, Ruby?"

"Because they never asked me about my brother, yet I always spoke highly of him and how much I missed him. I had the best private investigators looking for him. And yet no one ever asked me about him. What kind of friends do that? Not the kind of friends who understand that there is more to life than being a hanger on and wanting to get a little bit of the spotlight when the spotlight is not even worth it. "

"And why is the spotlight not worth it, Ruby?"

"I was in every magazine, and on every major news network doing interviews. I always made it a point to talk about my brother and most of the time that part of the segment was cut out or it was at the end of the clip. And then I would get fake sympathy from people who just wanted to know more about my opulent lifestyle than my brother. Anyway, to answer your question, I am just fine now. I have a good team, they take care of my affairs, and I get to live in this nice town with you and the other fine folks of Greensburgh. I get to keep my toe in the water running this simple little motel and I have never been happier in my life. Does that answer your question, Pastor?"

"It does. Now let me go get Mr. Hightower for you." Ted came out of nowhere as if he had just walked down.

"Here I am. Good morning, Ruby. How are you?"

"I am good, Mr. Hightower. Did you have a good night's sleep? Is your room to your liking?"

"I had a great night's sleep as did Mr. Wimples. Coffee this morning was excellent and looks like we are going to have a beautiful day today. I'm starving, thought I would go across the street and get some breakfast before I go check on the truck."

"Well, Ken stopped by and said it still is not going to be ready until Wednesday. But I have someone I would like for you to meet."

"Who's that?"

"C.J., our Pastor you have heard everyone talking about. This is Pastor Cletus Johnson, leader of the Greensburgh church and the towns benefactor."

"Whoa there, Ruby. I am just a guy who has a few friends in the right places that understand I'm just trying to do my work for the Lord." Theodore then spoke up.

"Nice to meet you, C.J."

"So, where you headed, Mr. Hightower?"

"Well, I am hungry, and I need some breakfast. Thought I would try Myrtle out again. The dinner she made me last night was actually very good. Not sure what I ate, words were foreign to me, but I ate it all up."

"Myrtle has that effect on her customers. Not a drop of food left behind. Hey, Mr. Hightower, do you mind if I join you for breakfast? I mean I already ate this morning with the wife, but I can always use another cup of coffee."

"Well, I was going to try and catch up on the news on my phone, but I guess we can do that. Sure, why not? If you are the brains behind the revitalization of this town, I have some questions about how you are doing that. You ready now?"

"Ready when you are. After you, Mr. Hightower. See you later, Ruby."

"Bye, C.J. Enjoy your breakfast, Mr. Hightower."

"Thanks, Ruby. I will."

Ted and C.J. headed across the street to The Diner. They were about to embark on a journey together that would greatly change both their lives. The question was, would it be for better or worse? The richest man in the world meets the top investor from a lifetime ago. The joining of these two individuals could either change their corner of the world or create a monster capable of ruling the business world for many years to come. And solidify Ted's legacy as the richest man in the world for many years to come. As they were walking across the street, Ted sent a text to Shelley:

get me everything you can on a preacher by the name of Cletus Johnson. Also find out who is helping to finance the businesses. What banks are involved and are there any investors involved as well. Need this information ASAP. Confidential, eyes only, highest level of discretion needed. Will call soon.

    Ted was back on the prowl. Nothing about Greensburgh said this was an investment opportunity but something about this C.J. fellow and the people he had encountered said that something was up. Rich basketball player, heiress to a hotel fortune, and a cook from one of the largest plants in the U.S until they closed. And a mysterious preacher who was able to get financing to rebuild a town. What the heck was going on and how could Ted get in on the action if there was some money to be made. He still had not learned his lesson. He was still on the prowl. Could not help himself.

Here everyone thought he was changing. Nope, he was a hunter and C.J. and the others were ripe for a kill. The only question was what was their price? There was always a price. And Ted always came up with the money to pay for it. His Angel was in Heaven. He and Mr. Wimples had agreed confidentially on that. Time to move on.

Rich Men Have No Friends

24

Shelley had not had a chance to check her e-mail, voice mail, or phone messages. She had felt a buzz when she was meeting Jess, which was a reminder that she had a text message. As she sat in her office still processing her conversation with Pierre, she looked at her phone. She had a message from Theodore. He had not gone away. He might be on a hiatus, but he could not totally let go. He was the richest man in the world, which made him the best businessman in the world. And for that reason, he was always working.

She read the message and called Big Jim of Big Jim Investigations. He was a former FBI agent, served in the Army's elite Special Forces Unit, and if anyone could find someone or find out their history, Big Jim was the guy. Six feet tall, two hundred pounds, from Boston, and third generation soldier and agent. Take no prisoners, no BS kind of guy. Not one for small talk, and normally got right to the point. Shelley dialed him on his cell phone, he did not answer, she left a message.

"Big Jim, Shelley here. Boss needs a favor. Our normal fee. I have the specifics. Will e-mail them to you now. Please call when you get a chance."

She started to work, lot to be done, spoke with Jess a couple of times and began her normal routine although there was nothing normal about her routine today. She was being entrusted with more money than a lot of small countries had at their disposal. She did not want to screw this up. At that point, her phone rang. It was Big Jim.

"Shelley, Jim here. Hey, I got your information. You know who this Cletus Johnson is, don't you?"

"No why would I know him, Jim?"

"This guy is Pastor Louis Cletus Johnson, who used to be the Pastor of the Greater Gospel Church, one of the largest and most prosperous mega churches in the country. Prior to being a preacher, graduated from Harvard with a combined JD/MBA, he was top partner at French-Helliman, first African American to reach the position of partner. Took one-hundred-million-dollar fund and made it worth one billion. Left the business abruptly due to the tragic death of his parents in a car accident in Baton Rouge at the age of twenty-nine. At the time he walked away he was personally worth somewhere north of seventy million dollars by most estimates."

"Are you serious, Jim?"

"As a heart attack, Shelley, but the story gets better."

"How does it bet better, I am already in awe, shock and somewhat surprised. Keep going."

"He gives up ninety percent of his wealth at the time to take over his dad's church in Third Ward. Had a total of three hundred plus members, well known in the community. He moves the church to a large campus. No one knows where the money came from. Becomes a best-selling author and is making money hand over foot. Never could let go of the past life. Church becomes popular with some of his athlete friends and entertainers from his time in the investment world. Then everyone whose anyone in Houston wants to be a member of his church, grows to over ten thousand members. And he walked away. For reasons unknown to anyone, he resigned and moved to Greensburgh. Gave up his house, which I understand is worth over three million currently, sold all his cars, and gave all the clothes, and jewelry to a lady who made over one hundred thousand on e-bay. This guy gave everything away again and moved to Greensburgh."

"What about his net worth, Jim? What is his net worth now?"

"No one knows, Shelley. It is the best kept secret in Houston. He moved all his money and whoever has it ain't talking. You know better than me how that works. Your boss is the same way. People estimate his net worth, no one really knows. People should stop making assumptions based on what they read. Anybody who is that rich would never tell anyone about it unless they don't understand how the world really works."

"What do you mean, Jim?"

"Shelley, people with real money and who understand how this world really works don't talk about their money. They will neither confirm nor deny their net worth. You know what I'm saying.?"

"I do."

"Well, anyway, that's your guy. He is the real deal. Not sure how you folks know this guy or what Theodore is up to, but he would have probably been Theodore if not for his parent's untimely deaths. He was a Rockstar, the Michael Jordan of the investment world. I will send the file over to you now. I tell you what, I see why Theodore is the richest man in the world."

"What do you mean, Jim?"

"This preacher fell off the grid. No one knows what happened to him. He left no forwarding address and dropped his first name so that he would not be found. No one is looking for him, I mean the guy is clean. But he fell off the map, and I believe he wants to keep it that way. Given his current occupation, I think we should respect that, Shelley. I am not the most religious person in the world, but I also have the utmost respect for those who do the Lord's work. If not for people like him, where would we be? I give you and Theodore credit. You have found a diamond in a deep mine that no one knew existed. I mean everything this preacher touches turns to gold. Not my business but tell Theodore to be careful with this guy."

"Be careful?"

"Yes, I like money as much as the next guy. But this one is a little different."

"What do you mean, Jim?"

"This guy went off the grid for a reason. In my background as a soldier and agent with the Bureau, when someone goes off the grid, they are either hiding from something or they don't want to be found. Now to his credit, he is just up the road in Greensburgh, and people probably know he is there. But for whatever reason, they are not bothering him. I hope Theodore respects that and does not try to exploit this Preacher. He has successfully walked away from the riches and the lifestyle that comes with it twice now. He may not be able to do that a third time. Just be mindful of that, Shelley."

"Got it, Jim, anything else."

"Nope, sending over my bill now."

"I see the e-mail. I will have a check in the mail to you tomorrow."

Shelley was at a complete loss now. Was Theodore grieving or on some secret mission? Had he been looking for this preacher all along? Had another agency found him and the funeral delayed him going after the guy. Was the timing of his daughter's death just a smokescreen to go see this guy? Surely, he was not that heartless. The only way to know was to figure out had Amy's death affected him or was he just back to business as usual. Mr. Wimples? Was that just a distraction to take everyone off his scent. One person knew and he was not talking.

Phineas McNabb

He was in Greensburgh meeting with the only person that might have dethroned him had he stayed in the business, Louis Cletus Johnson. Shelley was speculating a lot. And through all that speculation, she was right and wrong. Only time would tell.

Rich Men Have No Friends

25

It is still Tuesday and C.J. and Theodore are at Myrtle's getting breakfast. They are both here to have a conversation about something that is on their mind. The challenge is that they have different agendas and neither of them is aware of the other's motive.

"Good morning, Myrtle. What's good today?"

"Everything, Pastor. You know not to ask that question up in here. Might give our visitor the impression that I can't cook. Now you wouldn't do that to me, would you." They smiled.

"Why, no ma'am. Anyway, a coffee for me and whatever this gentleman wants."

"I'll take the special, Myrtle."

"Ted, I am starting to like you even more. One special coming right up."

Myrtle brought out the coffee and the breakfast as Ted and C.J. had small talk about how Ted had ended up in town and what his plans were once his truck was fixed.

"So, Ted, what brings you to this part of the country? We don't get a lot of visitors other than supply trucks, and relatives of the locals. This is not your normal pass-through and we are more than a few miles off the freeway." C.J. already knew the answer to his question, but as a good preacher, he knew that he would need to gain the confidence and trust of Theodore before he could talk about the death of Amy.

"Well, I met this guy and he suggested I try out the town. I told him I wanted to get off the grid and he suggested Greensburgh. Glad I took him up on his offer." Theodore did not want C.J. to know who he was yet. He wanted to gain his trust and confidence as well. This chance encounter of the preacher and the rich man was about to reveal itself for what it really was. Or so they both thought.

"What do you think of Greensburgh? Nice little town, not a lot of traffic, pretty laid back."

"That it is, C.J., is it okay if I call you C.J. or should I call you pastor."

"C.J. is fine."

"C.J. what's your story? How does a preacher in a small town like this have so much business acumen, I mean how did you start the process of bringing back this town and why did you want to do it?"

Phineas McNabb

"Ted, I had a calling to come to Greensburgh. I met this guy and he convinced me this was the perfect spot for me. Once I got here, I decided I would never leave. It's just right for me. Reminds me of a time from the past, before the world got out of hand."

"How exactly did it get out of hand?"

"It got out of hand when the material trappings of this world became more important than looking out for our fellow man. We have enough resources in this country to feed, house and cloth every person in this country, yet we have homelessness, stagnant wages, gentrification hitting every major city and this obsession with having more money than we really need. I am just tired of it and decided to try something different."

"What's that?"

"What if we had the ability to make goods in this country and reinvest the profits back into rebuilding this country, one business at a time, one brick at a time, and make this country the country it was once? Not the shell of itself that it is now but truly a country where one looks out for each other, providing opportunities to live wherever you choose to live and bringing back a sense of community. You know, a place where you know your neighbors and they know you. Where you all can have a conversation that means something versus a bunch of sound bites, living on social media and always being in hurry to get to nowhere."

"C.J. I am not sure I follow you. I have a great life, and I don't want anything. And I would not trade it for anything in the world."

"You would not trade it for anything, you sure about that. Ted, what brought you here in the first place?"

"I don't follow."

"What brought you here? Why Greensburgh?" C.J. was trying to get Theodore to talk about Amy.

"I came here to meet you, Pastor. I wanted to meet Louis Cletus Johnson, the Rockstar of Wall Street, I believe that's what you were called over twenty years ago. I wanted to meet the man who gave up his fortune twice and turned it into over one hundred million dollars. I wanted to meet the guy who still trades and makes a good living of it but does not want to do it full time given the possibilities of becoming one of the richest men in the world. I wanted to meet this guy."

Rich Men Have No Friends

Theodore pulled up his phone and showed C.J. the picture from Forbes magazine that his father had in his office.

"Ted, we need to take this conversation to another place. I need to know how you got this information, assuming it's true and I am not saying it is. I need to know how you know so much about me and more importantly, how did you get the information about my financials?"

"C.J., I am the Richest Man in the World. There's very little I don't know. And I am here to offer you a job. That's why I came to Greensburgh. I want you to come to work for me. You won't have to leave this little paradise you have built for yourself. I just want you on my team. And you will be a billionaire inside of the next two or three years and you can build all the cities you want, although I think it is a far-fetched idea myself."

"Ted, what about the truck and Abraham?"

"The truck. I traded my car for the truck so I would not stand out when I arrived in town. I know everyone else drives the same type of truck. I assume that's a thing around here though I don't understand it. As for me, I can buy another Bentley. I am here in town on business, and you are that business."

C.J. for the first time in his life since moving to Greensburgh was at a loss for words. Theodore did not know who Abraham was nor did he care. He did not understand the significance of the truck. His time spent with J.J. had impacted him but had not affected him as the richest man in the world. He was here on a business trip, and nothing more. He was grieving for his daughter, but he was handling that with Mr. Wimples. And Mr. Wimples was all the therapy he needed.

Amy wasn't coming back, and there was no Santa Claus and there was no God. He had bounced back quickly because he never left. He had played everyone again. And that is why he is the richest man in the world.

"Ted, you really don't know who Abraham is, do you?"

"Yeah, some random guy that I met at a convenience store who had his net worth increased by over two hundred thousand dollars when I gave him that car and my watch."

"Ted, Abraham is ……never mind. Let's walk over to the church."

"C.J., we can finish this conversation at the church, but you need to know that I am not a religious man. A man convinced me a long time ago that the only person I can depend on is myself and no one else."

"Well, Ted, I hear you and I am really sorry about that."

"Sorry for what."

"That a man could convince you that life was so bad for you that all you believe you have on this whole earth is yourself. I would be lonely if I thought like that. Almost like being in the middle of the desert with no water. That attitude can make a man thirst for the one thing that he needs to survive in this world."

"And what's that, C.J.?"

"Life, Ted. A full life that makes it all worth living. But anyway, I said I was not going to preach to you. Ready to go."

"Sure. Myrtle, the food was great. See you for dinner."

"See you for dinner, Ted. And remember......."

"I know, be here before six because you have to go watch Jeopardy." They all laughed. Ted and C.J. got up and proceeded out the door to walk over to the church. What in the world was going on here? C.J. was at a loss. He saved souls, but he had finally met his match. Not only was he not saving a soul, but he was being asked to come back to the dark side. Although based on his net worth, it appeared he never really left. He and Ted had one thing in common. Money. And as for Amy, his little angel was in Heaven. A Heaven that he did not believe in but a place that was worthy of his daughter.

Rich Men Have No Friends

26

Shelley forwarded the information from Big Jim to Theodore and proceeded to get back to work. Around noon Tuesday, she was preparing to leave and go to lunch, and her cell phone rang. She did not recognize the number, so she ignored it. She picked up her purse and headed downstairs. As she exited the elevator, her phone rang again. It was the same number. This time she picked it up.

"Is this Shelley Winslow, assistant to Theodore Hightower?"

"This is Shelley Winslow, who am I speaking with?"

"This is Carol Hightower, Theodore's sister. And I need to get in contact with Theodore. I am in town, arrived last night and I need to see him as soon as possible."

Shelley was completely at a loss. Theodore seldom mentioned his sister in any conversation they had. And if he did, she did not remember it which meant he and his sister probably did not have a relationship that mattered.

"Carol, I can't get you in contact with Mr. Hightower. He's out of town right now with no expected return. How can I help you?"

"Shelley, I need to see Theodore. I heard about his daughter, and I need to see him."

"Carol, I am afraid that is not possible. I have strict orders from Mr. Hightower, and I can't break them for anyone, including family. I'm sorry."

"But I am his sister. Are you serious right now?"

"Carol, I tell you what, I was getting ready to go to lunch. How about we meet and let's talk. I will relay anything you want me to pass to Mr. Hightower before the day ends. I just can't put you in contact with him. Those are his wishes."

"Okay, Shelley, let's meet. That is crappy that I can't contact my own brother, but I will meet you."

"What hotel are you at? I will pick you up and we can go from there."

"I am the Sentarion. You know where that is?"

"Yes, you are a couple of blocks from the office. I will be right there." They both hung up. Shelley immediately made another call.

"Big Jim, I need you to do me another favor and this one is off the record. I will pay you myself, no invoice, got it."

"Got it, and congratulations on your new role. Don't envy you, but if anyone can do it, you can. Ted trusts you with his life. Now, what's up?"

"I need whatever information you can get me on a Carol Hightower. She just called me and claims to be the sister of Mr. Hightower. He may have mentioned her in passing but he has seldom talked about her, so I need to know who she is. Given the situation with Amy, want to make sure that she has no agenda or motive for wanting to contact Mr. Hightower. And again, we never had this discussion."

"Got it, I will get right on it and call you as soon as I have something." Shelley went outside, started her truck, and went to pick up Carol. The ride over to the hotel only took about ten minutes. When she pulled up in the front of the hotel, a petite white woman was standing in the front. She was beautiful, not a hair out of place.

She had on red lipstick, long black hair, glasses, and diamond earrings. She was wearing a red dress that said classy, professional but in casual Friday sort of way. She was wearing some short red pumps, looked like Prada or Gucci. And she was carrying a Black Brahmin bag that had an alligator skin look to it. Given the way she looked, and who Ted was, why had he never mentioned this sister before. Shelley pulled up to the curve. "Carol Hightower?"

"Yes, but I don't have any money for you, sweetie. I am waiting on someone." It must have been the truck. The CEO for the wealthiest man in the world was driving a 1978 Black Ford pickup truck. And his sister appeared to be living a pretty good life. She was taken aback by the truck and thought Shelley to possibly be a panhandler looking for a handout.

"Ms. Hightower, it's me, Shelley Winslow. I am here to take you to lunch."

"No way, let me see some ID?"

"Seriously?"

"Yes, show me some ID. Ted would never have his top person driving around in a truck like this."

Shelley reached into her purse, pulled out her wallet, and pulled her driver's license as well as a business card for HenPot Industries. "Does that put you at ease?"

"Well yes, but what's with this truck. I mean, I read articles about Ted but is he really this cheap? He must not pay you anything. Poor thing."

"Carol, why don't you get in? And he pays me very well. Just not that caught up in what I drive. I just need transportation plus this truck has special meaning to me. Given to me by someone who changed my life."

"I guess, does this truck pass inspection, I mean, is it safe?"

"Carol, are you coming or not? I have a lot going on right now and you called me, remember?"

"You are right. Let's go to lunch." She opened the door, surprised by the creakiness of the door as it opened, stepped up and sat down. She looked for the seat belt, put it on, and she and Shelley headed to lunch. Shelley was anxiously driving to the nearest lunch spot as she wanted to know who Carol was and why she was in town.

Phineas McNabb

27

Later that Tuesday, C.J and Ted arrived at the church and were sitting in C.J.'s office. C.J. had re-created his father's office for a third time. He had all his accolades and accomplishments on shelves and nailed to the wall along with all his dad's things as well. He had long put away the Forbes cover for obvious reasons. He made it a point to remind himself of where he had come from and the legacy he was trying to carry for his dad. He was keeping his promise. And he was still living his dream. And he saw nothing wrong with that.

"C.J., let's cut right to the chase here. You were worth a little north of twenty million or so when you left that big church in Houston. Now you are worth five times that. I have one of the best teams in the world and we are not getting those kinds of returns. You are investing at the right time it seems and have not had to buy a company or immerse yourself personally in the inner workings of the companies you invest in, or so it seems. I mean how does a full-time preacher do that?"

C.J. pushed a button under his desk. The wall of fame that he built for he and his dad opened and behind it was four big computer monitors, flat screens that could be used both as TVs and computer monitors. He then pulled a keyboard from his drawer and a mouse. He typed in a password and all four monitors brought up information that only the most skilled investor could understand. And Ted was just that guy.

"What in the world? What kind of set up is this?"

"Ted, I monitor companies right here in this office. You see, in a small town like Greensburgh, there are not a lot of interruptions throughout the day. I have the occasional visitor and I have an alarm system set up that lets me know when someone enters the building. Two hours every day, I monitor the stock market from here in my office. And I have a team of five individuals who don't know they work for me in Miami. They don't know they work for me as I have a friend who is the quote boss and owner in name only. I set up a limited liability company in Florida when I first left the business and my fraternity brother from college oversees it for me. I can trust him, and he has never exposed me."

Rich Men Have No Friends

"C.J., I did my homework on you. There is no record of this company." Ted had not really done his homework but was working on inside information from a bank in the Cayman Islands where they both had accounts set up.

"No, Ted, you received some inside information on me. Someone who I can't trust at the offshore bank I deal with is in your pockets. They shared with you that this guy multiplied his account five times over in a short period of time and you wanted to know this guy. And he was right, except he did not tell you where the money was coming from. And that is because I set up the company purposely to keep the money trail discreet."

"Okay, C.J., but how are you making all this money?"

"Book royalties, Ted. Book royalties and smart, conservative investing?"

"What book royalties? You have not written a book since you left that church in Houston. I know because I had my people check."

"Ted, you ever heard of a pen name?"

"I have but......."

"I use a pen name, started writing books that were purely fiction, with religious undertones, and they are doing well. I created a publishing company, and the royalties from the books are pumped into the limited liability company in Florida. The royalties are deposited into an account for the investment company, and the team in Florida invests the money for me. My team came up with this algorithm that predicts the future success of a new company based on current activity. I get in, and when the company takes off, I cash out and the money is eventually pushed to my offshore account where your snitch works. You see, you did not do your homework. You took a hunch and ran with it. How did that work out for you?"

"Looks like my guys were right about you."

"How's that, Ted?"

"You would have been the richest man in the world if you had stayed in the game fulltime?"

"Ted, that was never my dream, to be the richest man in the world."

"Then why the elaborate set up and how do you explain the one hundred million, Pastor? I mean why would a preacher need one hundred million dollars. And given your current situation, you don't need a million to live in this small town that is still living in a time from the past. I mean who wants that?"

"Everyone, Ted, everyone. You want it, you just don't know it yet."

"Yeah, right. You can keep this town. I mean the people are nice. But I don't get it. You, Ruby, and J.J. are at the top of your games and just walk away for what? I don't get it."

"A simple life, Ted, a simple life. Where money is used in the right way and not just hoarded and stacked up to be the best baller ever, or the richest heiress under forty, or in my case the most successful pastor because I have the biggest house and the largest congregation. I have real friends now and we live a simple life."

"You are missing one thing, C.J.?"

"What's that, Ted?"

"You all became rich or inherited riches before you moved to this nice little town you're trying to build. So, keep your save the world speech. You are all rich and can leave anytime you want. I don't know why you each walked away from your situations but save me the simple life speech. Your lives are simple because you each are set for life. And why is that because you have more money than you could have ever dreamed of. I mean, hell, you still make money, and your net worth increases every day. What makes you different from me?"

"What makes me different, Ted?"

"Yes, C.J, what makes you different? You and I both make money, and a lot of it. The difference is I know who I am, and I make no excuses for who I am. I was taught a long time ago that there are givers and there are takers. Well, I am a taker and proud of it. The alternative sucks, frankly, and I never want to live in that world again. Living check to check, dysfunctional family, clawing and scratching to survive, no thanks. You can keep that life."

"And why do you think people claw and scratch to survive, Ted."

"Here we go with this. Let me guess, because of Capitalists and the rich folks who figured it out."

"No Ted, I am actually a big fan of capitalism. I just don't like greed. I don't like greed Ted. Greed is why I left Houston and moved to Greensburgh. I keep trying to leave the greed and it keeps finding me."

Rich Men Have No Friends

"Look, C.J., I am here to offer you a job. Very simple proposition. You join my team in whatever capacity you choose. You tell my people what your people are getting ready to do. We mimic your investments, and everyone gets paid. I am just putting a lot more money on the table, get it."

"That won't work, Ted. My investments are made very discreetly. You start putting the kind of money you have on the table, and these companies will freak out. They see the Numb Investor coming and my investments won't pay off in the long run."

"You don't know that. I may help your positions."

"I tell you what, Ted, let me think about it. This is not what I thought we were going to be discussing today. I thought we would be talking about...."

"My daughter. Look, Pastor, my Amy was all I had in this world. She's gone and I am dealing with it in my own way. The same way you dealt with the loss of your parents. You and I are uniquely alike in that we move on. Life goes on for us. Grief is not something that keeps guys like you and I down. We are hunters, and in this case, companies are the prey. You invest in them, I buy them. Matters not how you do it, we are chasing the same thing. Money, and to think differently would be lying to ourselves. The camel has a better chance of getting through the needle than you or I in getting into that Heaven you preach about, C.J. That is our reality. This is bigger than you or me."

"Ted, I need time to think about it."

"Okay, C.J. I am just trying to help you realize your dream while I realize mine."

"And that is, Ted?"

"To be the first Trillionaire. That's right. I am bored with being the richest man in the world. There are no more toys, houses, or wives that I want. But no one has the distinction of being the first trillionaire. And with your investment mind, my team and money, being a trillionaire is a real possibility and will finalize my legacy. And as for you, you can save the world however you choose to and become a billionaire in the process."

C.J. had a real problem on his hands. He was not prepared for the conversation that had taken place today.

Phineas McNabb

28

(Two weeks prior to Amy's Passing)

Theodore was sitting in his office studying financials when his cell phone rang. He had been reading the Wall Street Journal and had been working on finding a new deal for him to do. His most recent deals had netted him a nice small profit, but he was not getting the returns he was used to. He had put the word out that if anyone had a new idea, new talent, or a way to increase his net worth, to get in contact with Shelley. Somehow, the person calling was able to get his cell phone number and call him directly.

"Hello?"

"Mr. Hightower, please."

"This is Mr. Hightower."

"Mr. Hightower, Granger Barfield in the Caymans, sir. I was informed that you are seeking some information about potential new investments."

"Not sure where you heard that, but all conversations go through my assistant, Shelley Winslow."

"Understood, Mr. Hightower, but I don't think you want this information to go through her. I have information that quadruple your wealth."

"Keep talking. Granger don't waste my time and lose this number after we get through with this conversation. You have five minutes."

"Understood, Mr. Hightower. I have been tracking an account here and in reviewing the past five years, it has gone from being worth somewhere north of twenty million to over one hundred million dollars."

"Granger, so what. People's accounts increase all the time."

"Yes, Mr. Hightower, but this account belongs to the Rock Star of Wall Street, Louis Cletus Johnson."

"Who did you say it belonged to?"

"Louis Johnson, the first African American partner at French-Helliman. Guy graduates from Harvard, goes to work for firm, leaves abruptly never to be seen again. Turned one-hundred million into one billion during his short tenure there. He has done it again, except with his own money. And this is the second time he has done it."

Rich Men Have No Friends

"I don't follow, Granger."

"Louis Johnson, who now goes by Pastor Cletus Johnson, or C.J. gave away his entire fortune when he left French-Helliman. He was worth about seventy million at the time and gave most of it to charity. Well, he became a famous preacher there in Houston, turned his church into one of the most successful churches in the county to the tune of over ten thousand members from a start of three hundred. Built a large complex, sold millions of books and became rich all over again only to cash out once more."

"What do you mean, Granger, he cashed out again."

"He gave over half his fortune to the church. Kept twenty million and had it put in this offshore account. I guess he did not want anyone to know he still had money given what happened at that big church."

"What do you mean, Granger?"

"Well, I did some research through a friend of mine, and he said that when Louis left the church, it was rumored that the people in his congregation thought he was stealing from the church to support his lifestyle. You know expensive cars, lavish two-million-dollar house that is now worth more than three million, the best suits, watches, and shoes. They did not know where the money was coming from to support his lifestyle, so they assumed he was stealing from the church. Or so the rumor mill says. It goes back to that saying no good deed...."

"I am not following you, Granger."

"Mr. Hightower, if you look at Theodore's history, gave up sixty-three million to go be a preacher at his dad's old church, turns it into a megachurch that is totally self-funded with no debt. I had my people check on the church finances and they never borrowed a dime. Then he gives up half his fortune or twenty million dollars a second time. Cashes out at twenty-nine years old and second cash out was in his late forties. That alone is ninety-three million dollars. Now add that to the hundred million he has now, add on some conservative interest to the original seventy million of say eight percent annually on average and he would be worth over five hundred million today. This guy did not steal from the church. He was the church.

He was the preacher, treasurer, largest donor, and trying to do everything in his power to serve the Lord just as his dad did. Did he have another motive, chasing money? Well, that was between him and his God. All I know is becoming a preacher cost him money but did not make him poor. The church was wrong about this guy. Extravagant, maybe. Did not want to let go of a lifestyle he had gotten used to, yes. But he was not a thief. He was the best thing that ever happened to that church."

"Okay, Granger, so what's the main point here?"

"The main point is you have a man who is conflicted, trying to serve a God he truly believes in and trying to make money just because he is good at it, and it comes natural to him. He has a hobby that does not necessarily line up with his current career or calling as he might say. But if someone could convince him to come back to the investment world, he would make them a very rich man."

"Granger, you are a smart guy. And thanks for the information. I will have one of my people get with you to send you a token of my appreciation. What happened to his dad, Louis that is?"

"Both parents died in a tragic accident in Baton Rouge, Louisiana. Ran into the back of a semi on their way to visit him supposedly. Don't quote me on that."

"Thanks, Granger, and have a nice day."

Just at that moment, the phone rang. It was Amy. "Hello Daddy!"

"Hello, Angel. How are you?"

"I'm fine. Daddy?"

"Yes, Amy."

"Why do you call me your angel?"

"I don't really know, honey, but when I hear your voice and I think of you, I feel like you were an angel sent to me. Now daddy needs to go, important stuff to take care of."

"Okay, Daddy, how is Mr. Wimples?"

"He's fine, I have him working on a big project."

"Daddy!"

"Honey, I need to go. Tell mom I said hi. Love you!"

"Love you too, Daddy." Theodore hung up the phone not knowing that his conversations with Amy would soon be a thing of the past. And as for the Angel comment, he really believed she was his angel. She had taught him how to love again, and care for someone other than himself. That would change in less than two weeks' time.

Rich Men Have No Friends

Phineas McNabb

29

In a little under twenty-four hours, the world had turned upside down from Houston to Greensburgh. The richest man in the world had everyone thinking he was grieving. Fact of the matter, he was on a reconnaissance mission. Not only was he chasing a diamond in a mine that no one knew about, but he was chasing the Rockstar of Wall Street. And he was doing that without anyone's knowledge.

He did not want anyone to know that he had found the Louis Cletus Johnson, once the darling of Wall Street, up and comer, the preacher's kid from Third Ward, the Morehouse man who made his way to Harvard. He had found Jim Brown, except Cletus Johnson was not an actor. He was the man, still getting those remarkable returns that he had achieved at French-Helliman. Guys like C.J. come along rarely. There's only one Michael Jordan, one Babe Ruth, one Bill Gates, well, you get the point. These guys are born with unique gifts and talents that others can only dream of. In every case, it's God given talent, hard work, right place, right time, and a little bit of good luck. Put that all together and you have a recipe for more money than you could ever dream of. C.J. was one of those guys.

Ted headed back to his hotel. It was time to go back to Houston. In the meantime, Shelley was meeting with Carol Hightower in Houston. Who was Carol Hightower and why was she in town?

They drove to the Picket Fence, a small homegrown diner around the corner from the hotel Carol was staying in. They valet parked the car and went in.

The Picket Fence was unique. Upscale restaurant with a down home feel. The building was white, and the front of the building had a white picket fence in front of it. When you enter the restaurant, everyone wears a white and black plaid apron, white short sleeve button down shirts, and black khakis. They all wear mule clogs like the nurses in the hospital wear. The tables are all square shaped with black and white plaid tablecloths on them. There is a bar that looks more like an old counter from drug stores of the past. It has two flat screen televisions on the wall with the news on one and a sports channel on the other. Their specialty is their chicken fried chicken and chicken fried steak. Side of mash potatoes and gravy, zucchini, and squash vegetable medley, and some of the best iced tea you could ever want.

Rich Men Have No Friends

They served breakfast from seven to eleven, lunch from eleven to four, and dinner from four until closing, which was ten on the dot.

Shelley and Carol went in, sat down and the waiter brought them both a glass of water. Shelley ordered for both her and Carol. She went with the chicken fried chicken special as did Carol. They conducted small talk until their food was brought out.

"Shelley, I am worried about Theodore, or Teddy as I have called him all his life. The loss of his daughter is going to take a toll on him. He won't be able to handle it. It's just a matter of time."

"Why do you say that, Carol. I can call you Carol?"

"Sure, Carol is fine. I know because I was there the last time, he lost someone who was close to him."

"Who's that, Carol?"

"Our mother."

"Your mother? Ted never talks about his mom. And you say it affected him."

"It did and drove a wedge in our relationship that has not nor may never fully recover."

"I don't understand."

"Shelley, Teddy and I grew up on what some would call the wrong side of the tracks. Where people go and no one cares about them and leaves them to the wolves. The land of food deserts, high interest rate loan sharks, liquor stores, and check cashing places. Where you watch your back constantly and everyone has the same net worth as you. Zero. Where the only hope used to be the church before the church and all the good people left the community to go to the suburbs and greener pastures. It's great to make it, Shelley, but we tend to forget about the people we left behind. And so, for Teddy, the only person or thing that mattered to him was our mom, God rest her soul."

"Wow, Carol, I have never heard this story before."

"And you never will. Teddy is not ashamed of where he comes from, he just does not discuss it with anyone. Always been that way, just felt it was better that way. A sort of therapy for him. Anyway, eat your lunch. How much time do you have?

"All the time in the world. I can move some things around. Give me one second." Shelley notified her assistant to cancel her meeting that was scheduled for after lunch. This was the most important lunch she would have had this week.

Phineas McNabb

"You see, Shelley, our mother was a drug dealer and she used. She had quit school in the seventh grade, had Teddy at seventeen and me at nineteen. We did not ever meet our dads and mom did not do a good job of picking her boyfriends or husbands. One night she was sitting at the kitchen table, I believe it was Christmas eve. She and her boyfriend had a fight. I remember because he broke the TV that night and Teddy was devastated. His favorite movie at the time was It's a Wonderful Life. The movie gave him hope because he believed that there was an Angel out there like Clarence that would come to his rescue one day. And when mom would get a new boyfriend, they would take a liking to Ted, but they could not deal with mom. She was a handful, I must say. I raised Teddy because she was never there for him."

"I don't follow. What does a movie have to do with who Mr. Hightower is today? And how does this relate to Amy."

"Well, that night for reasons unknown to me, Teddy said that for the rest of his life he was going to be a taker. I also found his bible that our grandfather had given him in the trashcan. He told me that there was no Angels, God or Santa Claus. Here he is barely ten years of age, and he is being told that by boyfriend number whatever."

"What happened?"

"I went in his room, and I took the bible out of the trash can. I tried to talk to him, but he would not listen. When that TV broke into a million pieces and whatever else happened in that room, it changed him. He became a handful to manage, always getting in trouble, would fight anyone at the drop of a dime. And did not take stuff off anyone. But while he was a rebel, he was also one of the smartest and athletic boys at our schools. Excelled at everything but stayed a loner. Did his job but would not get close to anyone."

"What happened to the bible?"

"I have it, use it to this day."

"And Teddy's mom."

"When Teddy was in grad school, he was starting to do well. He would send money home to mom and begged her to leave the part of town we were living in, but she would not do it. She always said these were her people and she wasn't leaving them. She had toned down the drug dealing and was using a lot less."

"So, what happened to her?"

125

Rich Men Have No Friends

"One night, she was driving her van on of the tracks as they call them. Mom was trying to get the prostitutes off the street. Ironically, she saw nothing wrong with dealing but thought that the selling of women's bodies was not right, particularly if they were doing it against their will. You know if they were being trafficked. So, she went to get this young lady, they had agreed on the time and place. When mom got there, her pimp was there instead. He took mom to an old, abandoned building and she had some drugs with her that she intended to sell. He used them to kill our mother. It looked like an overdose to the police and that was that. The investigation ended with the conclusion that our mother had died from an overdose."

"And the pimp."

"No one knows what happened to him. He was found at the bottom of the river by some kids with a two hundred-pound barbells chained to his feet."

"Okay, but how does this relate to Amy?"

"Shelley, Teddy loved our mother. He never held it against her that she was a drug dealer or used. That was his mother, and he would fight anyone who talked about her, so he did a lot of fighting until the kids figured out that he liked a good fight. They gave him the nickname Numb-Numb. Because he was numb to other people, had no feelings towards them. He was a taker now and the only person he gave to was mom and he helped me as well."

"So, Carol, why don't I ever hear Teddy, I'm sorry Mr. Hightower talk about you. He never mentions you and I don't think I ever heard Amy talk about you."

"You are right. When Teddy was home for mom's funeral, he told me that someone was going to pay for her death. Well, by that time, my life had changed, and I mean for the better. I was getting my Ph.D. in divinity and well on my way to becoming a servant for the Lord. I tried to explain to Teddy that he needed to let it go and mom was fine now. Her body was here, but her soul was gone. I also explained to him that God was aware, and this would work itself out."

"He became angry, told me he never wanted to hear about God or Angels again. He told me I was wasting my time studying religion and I would find out one day, it was just a matter of time. Anyway, I am working for the Lord today and I must say I have been very successful. I have a large congregation, my services are streamed worldwide every

Phineas McNabb

Sunday, and I have been able to spread the Gospel. That has been my way of dealing with what would have otherwise been a tough world to live in, giving where we come from and what Teddy and I have been through. So, what's your story, how did you end up with Teddy.?"

Shelley would not tell her much except she met Teddy at her coffee shop that went out of business, and he gave her a job as his personal assistant, and he eventually made her his most trusted adviser. Carol would ask about Pierre, and she would tell her that he was still with the company, but not much else. Teddy or Theodore had a very strict rule, not discussing his business to anyone, and that meant family and HenPot. No exceptions. None. They finished their lunch and Shelley took her back to the hotel. As they were pulling up to the front door, Shelley asked her one last question.

"Carol, what made you want to serve the Lord and become a preacher?"

"Teddy. It was Teddy, Shelley."

"But he is not a believer. You yourself said he threw that bible from his grandad in the trashcan."

"And remember, Shelley, I took it out of that trash can. That night I was so sad for Teddy that I went back to my room, and I laid on my bed. The next thing I did was open that bible. I started reading and well three hours later, I was hooked. That book helped me understand my circumstances, that my life was not over yet, and good things would eventually happen for Teddy and I as long as we did the right thing and looked out for our fellow man. Now I know that Teddy is the "Numb Investor" as those analysts like to say, but he has a heart. He just does not know how to show it. And when God sent him his little Angel, I thought there was hope for him. With her death a couple of weeks ago, he may never come back to the light again. That's why I wanted to see him. Not to preach to him, but to try and get him to understand that Amy was a message to him that he needed to change."

"He struggled with that, Carol. He did not make her birthday party because he was out on town on business. Her death, while untimely, is further complicated by the fact it was her birthday party and he was not there."

"And this time, Shelley, he can't go after the killer like he did mom because knowing Teddy the way I do he would think he were chasing himself. And I worry that he may be asking himself, had he been there

127

would this have happened? And frankly no one will ever know. But I am sure that deep down inside he is blaming himself. And it is eating at him, no matter how he portrays himself publicly as the richest man in the world."

They finished lunch and Shelley drove Carol back to her hotel.

"Carol, nice to meet you. Let's stay in touch. If you don't mind, I will tell him you called but I won't share our lunch or our discussion. Mr. Hightower has Mr. Wimples and me at this point. If you are right, he needs someone in his corner."

"I agree, nice to meet you, Shelley." Carol went into the hotel, and Shelley headed back to the office. "That explains a lot." Her phone rang. It was Big Jim.

Phineas McNabb

30

It is still Tuesday, a little later in the morning, but it has not reached noontime yet. Theodore is getting impatient.

Theodore had had his fill of Greensburgh and made a change of plans. He headed back to his room and started to pack everything when he noticed something. Mr. Wimples was gone. He searched high and low, opened every drawer, and Mr. Wimples was gone. He opened the door to his room, looked in the hall, and he ran downstairs.

"He's gone. He's gone. Mr. Wimples. I can't find him." Ruby came from her small office located behind the front desk.

"What do you mean he's gone?"

"He's not in my room! Who did you let go in my room?"

"No one, Mr. Hightower. You are our only guest, so I was going to ask you when you returned if you wanted me to have someone clean your room, that someone being me. We don't have many guests. I normally take care of the room. I can assure you that no one was in your room. Are you sure you did not take Mr. Wimples with you since you have been here?"

"No, I left him in the room while I ran my errands, got something to eat and met with C.J. this morning."

"So, he's been there the entire time. I don't know what to tell you. I will keep a lookout for him for you Ted, I can assure you that Mr. Wimples is here somewhere. And when I find him, I will let you know, okay."

"Yeah, whatever, he was just a stuffed toy anyway. I need to go. Can you check on my truck and if it's not ready, I can call for a ride?"

"Ted, I will check for you. Why don't you go to your room and pack?"

Theodore went to his room, packed his belongings, looked again for Mr. Wimples and had no luck. Just then, the phone rang in the room.

"Ted, your vehicle is ready and waiting for you in front of the motel." Theodore headed downstairs and as he went to checkout, he looked out the front door and there was his Bentley. All shined up and ready to go.

"What the hell?"

Rich Men Have No Friends

"You said you were ready to go, Mr. Hightower. And we don't want to hold you up. And Abraham wanted his truck back. Something about not liking your car after all. He felt you would not appreciate his truck. And Abraham does not give his truck to anyone. He values them too much. And wants people to have them who appreciate them. Oh, and here is your watch and your clothes are in this bag. You are welcome to change back. Have a good day, Theodore. I wish you nothing but the best and you are welcome to stay here anytime you like. We always have a room for you. Should I tell C.J. you are leaving?"

"You can tell him anything you want. Let me get out of this one stoplight town. No beer in the bar, everything with a generic name. You people are from the planet nowhere. And frankly I don't understand and don't care. Why did you leave the hotel business anyway? You were destined to become one of the richest women in the world, if not the richest. And now you are in this small town wasting away and denying the business world of your expertise. I sold all my shares in your company when they said you went off the grid. And glad I did; I would have lost my shirt. So, what gives?"

"Sit down, Ted. Give me a few minutes and then you can leave, and no one here is going to hold you up."

"You have ten minutes. I gotta go."

"Oh, and Ted."

"Yes?"

"Two stoplights. We have two stoplights." She smiled and Ted gave her a look.

Across the street, Abraham was sitting in the 1978 Black Ford Pickup Truck he had given Theodore. And sitting beside him all buckled up was Mr. Wimples. And Ted did not notice because he was talking to Ruby.

"Let's go home, Mr. Wimples. I hope Mr. Hightower has a change of heart. Otherwise, there's a little girl waiting for you. She has missed you and would love to see you." And they drove off down the street and took a right and headed back to Abraham's garage.

31

Shelley was riding back to the office after meeting with Carol. Her phone rang. Traffic was light and the sun was beginning to shine. The day was turning into a beautiful day.

"Shelley?"

"Hey, Jim. What's up?"

"What are you guys doing over there, getting ready to get in the megachurch business. I like money as much as the next guy but investing in churches, not sure the Big Guy would like that and by Big Guy, I mean the man upstairs."

"Jim, what are you talking about?"

"Carol Hightower, known as Carol Hightower-Smithers, one of the most well-known and renown ministers of her lifetime. Resides in Tampa, Florida, has a twenty thousand membership in a nondenominational church that ministers to anyone who seeks to understand that you must have faith in something other than this earth or at least that what her website says. Minister of The Church of Our Last what some call the Cool Church. COOL represents the first letter of each word in the name of her church."

The Church of Our Last was founded on a street corner by Carol many years ago. She decided when she graduated divinity school she would go back to the old times of preaching to the masses where they were. She took to the streets. She found while doing that there were a lot of more homeless people, beggars, prostitutes and in some cases immigrants who had come to the country to chase the American dream.

These were not bad people but had had a turn of bad luck in some cases or had reverted to whatever they had to do to survive. She saw them as the last people on earth since no one seemed to care about them and that prompted the name of the church. She was also inspired to preach on the streets by the scripture which indicated the last would be first and the first last, for many are called, but few chosen. She would be recognized by the major news outlets, then a Christian network found out about her, and the rest is history.

"What is it with Mr. Hightower and preachers suddenly? Jim, this man has never mentioned church or God the entire time I have known him. He sends me to all funerals and weddings that impact his

Rich Men Have No Friends

business relationships with the business world. Now we are knee deep in preachers."

"I hear you, Shelley, but anyway here is the scoop. Carol and Mr. Hightower have not talked much since their mom's funeral. She has mentioned it in her sermons more than once. She loves him, that's obvious, but other than that, she is his sister and that's that.

"That's what she told me as well."

"Shelley, there is one thing you must know."

"What's that, Jim?"

"She and Mr. Hightower were exonerated. They were found not guilty."

"For what, Jim."

"Killing the pimp that Mr. Hightower thought was responsible for the death of his mother. Apparently, they were seen on the dock the night that this pimp disappeared. He was found by swimmers a few days later with two one hundred-pound barbells chained to his feet. No one knows what happened, and there was no one that could say that they had pushed this pimp in. Coincidentally, the only witness left town and now lives in Connecticut. She's gotta be in her early forties because that was over twenty years ago. It's almost like they hit the lottery."

"What's the name of this witness, Jim?"

"Why, Shelley?"

"Just wondering, that's all. I like reading about people who win the lottery. It's a past time of mine."

"Susan Flannery. Her name was Susan Flannery."

"And...."

"Her number is 856-456-9001."

"Thanks, Jim and Jim..."

Not a word, Shelley. Jim was very loyal to HenPot Industries, but his only point of contact was Shelley, and he would keep this one a secret for the rest of his life. He then picked up his phone as his vehicle was in the shop and he needed to check on it. "Yes, this is Big Jim, checking on my truck, a 1978 Black Ford Pickup. Is it ready yet?"

Shelley was getting in deep. There's a saying that goes something like what happens in the dark will come to the light. She knew that Mr. Hightower was a little different, almost eccentric to a fault. But the death of Amy was exposing her to a side of him she had never known. And she was determined to find out who her boss was. Who was this man that she had spent the last ten years with and what made him tick?

Rich Men Have No Friends

32

It is still early Tuesday, and while Theodore is checking out of his hotel. C.J. returned home to speak with Sarah. He wanted to talk about the offer that Theodore had made to him. He wanted to get her blessing this time. Previously, he had acted on his own only sharing the minimum information possible to clear his conscious.

But today was different, he was about to go into business with the richest man in the world. And the thought of being a preacher and an investment consultant to one of the most powerful men in the world was creating internal conflicts that he could not reconcile. At least, not without Sarah's blessing, which he was probably not going to get.

"No, C.J, absolutely not. You are never going to learn your lesson, are you. Honey, there are some people that just can't be helped. And after all, he's the richest man in the world. He can buy all the help he needs. Why you? I don't understand."

C.J. was now caught between a rock and a hard place. He had never lied to Sarah. He did not always share everything as it related to his finances, but he did not lie to her. It was time to come clean. They were in their living room. The house was modest, but she had put her touch on it.

In the living room were matching Carolina Blue couches they had delivered from a boutique furniture store in Houston. At the end was a nice comfortable oversized white chair with a matching white ottoman in front. That was C.J.s favorite seat. There was a coffee table in the middle and a nice throw rug that covered the area above the hardwood floors. The living room was two stories high with six big windows that allowed for natural sunshine to come through. There was a big entertainment center with shelves on each side, and doors below made of deep brown wood. In the middle was a 65-inch TV that was primarily used to watch sports. He had come home for lunch to tell her about Theodore's proposal to work for him on a consulting basis.

"Sarah, I have to tell you something, okay. And I don't want you to get mad at me."

"Well, that makes me mad already. C.J. when you tell someone don't get mad, they normally do. Remember Adrian and Adrianna." She was referring to their children who were now grown. Anytime they would say don't get mad, that normally meant they had done something. He smiled but she was not in the laughing mood.

"I do, First Lady, but it's important you hear me all the way out."

"Go ahead." She was at this point running her fingers up and down on her knee starting with her thumb and working her way back to her last finger and then starting the process all over again. She was not a happy camper. As a mom and wife, she knew this would not be good.

"I have a company in Florida and Thomas has been running it. All the paperwork is clean, and it can't be traced back to me. Additionally, I have continued to write under a pen name, Franklin Williams. Since we left Greater Gospel, I have written and self-published five best sellers. What started as a past time turned into a thing. I was writing thrillers with religious undertones while not disrespecting God or the word in any way. It was my way of trying to reach the unchurched and the churched who don't come to church. You know how important that is to me."

"Keep talking. That's actually a good idea but how did we end up with Theodore Hightower and you taking a job with him?"

"Well, you remember me telling you that I gave the money away and kept enough to keep us afloat until we moved and started a new church."

"Don't tell me you kept the money. Louis Cletus Johnson, you are going to burn in...."

"Hold on Sarah, I did give half of the money to the church. Except I, I mean we had twenty million dollars left over."

"Twenty million dollars. What happened to seven million? And you mean to tell me we have twenty million dollars in the bank. I go to the bank all the time. And there's never more than one hundred thousand dollars in that account. I assumed you were transferring some of the interest for us to live off."

"One hundred million, Sarah. We have one hundred million dollars."

"Are you serious?"

"As a heart attack. Sarah, I have always invested our money but did not let it interfere with church duties. It was my investing that allowed us to build Greater Gospel to the large church it became, paid off our homes, helped the congregation in times of need, and that is why the church is debt free to this day. I am doing the same thing here in

Rich Men Have No Friends

Greensburgh. There are no bankers involved, I am using our money honey to build this community. I am doing the right thing."

"How many times are you doing to keep telling yourself that, C.J. And how did Theodore find out about you?"

"I keep all the money in an offshore account, and Thomas and I set up a process that allows money to be funneled to our account via the company in Florida and it's all legal and on the up and up. I pay taxes on the distributions which are about one hundred thousand dollars to our personal account and then the other money is funneled straight to the businesses and no one in town is the wiser. They just don't know it. "

"And the motel and the bar, what about them."

"Now that's J.J and Ruby. They have their own money and did not need my help. I mean, I put them in touch with my investor, who you now know is Thomas, and they are not the wiser. It's clean, honey and the paper trails are clean."

"C.J., the richest man in the world found you. If he can find you, so can others."

"Sarah, we are not hiding, honey. You act like we are in witness protection. We relocated. I slightly altered my name but that was so I could go on with life. If the folks in this town want to know who I am, they can just Google me. For whatever reason, that has not been an issue for us, and I don't think it ever will."

"And why did you feel the need to invest the money and keep it a secret from me?"

"Because every time I try to walk away, I go back. Never got it out of my blood and I am not harming anyone. And again, it benefits those around me."

"C.J., I love you, but you have got to stop this. You are good at what you do, and I get it. Everything you do turns into gold. I am proud of you, and I am glad you have these gifts from God. But it is time to quit. You are about to hit three strikes and when you hit three strikes, honey, in baseball you are out. And this time the stakes are too high because you don't want to strike out with the man upstairs, do you?"

"Sarah, we will be fine, and I will be fine. He needs me. The man just lost his daughter. And he has no other family other than a sister who he has an estranged relationship with. Have you ever heard of Carol Smithers?"

"Heard of her, I am trying to get her to come to my conference this year. She is one of the most preeminent female preachers in the country, if not the world. But she is related to Ted. Seriously, talk about opposite ends of the spectrum. I mean really. Wow! And how do you know this?"

"When you have money, honey, information is very cheap to get. We all have our ways."

"Well, Mister, I mean Pastor, you need to get in and get out fast. After you finish this little mission of yours with Mr. Hightower, we need to talk about divesting this little side company of yours and this time, the money needs to go. We don't need it and it's not good for a preacher to have that kind of money even if some part of it is being used for the right thing. The optics just don't look good. We keep what we need, put some money in trusts for the kids, and the rest gets put in a foundation to help the church, rebuild this city and help others. Got it!"

"Got it, First Lady."

Sarah was a good woman with a kind heart. C.J. met her at a church function. She was a light skin black woman with long black hair that went down her back. She was about five foot eleven inches tall and could hold her on in a conversation. She also was a graduate of Spellman college, right across the street from Morehouse where he had attended undergrad. Their paths had not crossed in college. But she had returned to Houston and came to a service at the invite of a friend who attended Greater Gospel. He asked her out on a date and twenty plus years later, they were still together. She was his rock but was not a fan of the word millionaire. She wanted to be financially secure but was not interested in being rich. There was a difference. Just ask Ted.

Rich Men Have No Friends

Theodore had not left town yet. He had lost Mr. Wimples. The conversation with C.J. had not gone exactly as planned for either one of them. He was irritated and just wanted to leave. His care had been returned to him and he was standing at the front desk of the motel talking to Ruby. He wanted to know why she would live in this small town when she was one of the richest women in the world and the heiress to the largest hotel and resort chain in the world. He was about to leave town when she offered to explain to him why she decided to move to Greenburgh.

"Ted, you want to know why I moved here, to this small town that was on its last legs?"

"Yes, I really do. I mean you built this nice motel that frankly is an upgrade for a town like this. You barely have any customers. I believe you told me that I was the only customer you had last night. There is no money in it, so what gives?"

"Ted is that all that matters to you in this whole world, money. Nothing else matters to you, does it?"

"Not anymore, Ruby. Not anymore. I mean....... Never mind. Go ahead."

"Ted, I have a brother. His name is Cecil. Cecil and I are twins."

Cecil and Ruby were born some forty plus years ago in Hartford, Connecticut. They were the heir apparent to the Grayhill Hotel and Resort fortune which was now estimated at over ten billion dollars. Ruby would grow up, go off to Stanford, graduate with a degree in Economics and go into the family business. Cecil would leave home at the age of eighteen to go and explore the world. Money meant nothing to him, but he needed it to survive. When he made his last request for money, his parents told him to come home and go to school. He refused so they cut him off. In a fit of anger, he told them he hated them, and no one heard from him again. Not even Ruby.

As the years passed on, Ruby would hire private investigators to find him with no luck. She would also talk about him every chance she got when she was being interviewed. Still no word from Cecil. Until one day about four years ago when she was on a business trip in New York City. She was in town to open what was a renovated and new and improved Grayhill Plaza, a one hundred room hotel that sat in the heart of Times Square. Her team had decided that it was near the holidays, and they would volunteer to work at a soup kitchen in a homeless shelter near the hotel. While she was there a chance encounter with a gentleman would change her life forever.

"How long are we doing this today? I mean I would like to do some shopping before we head to the airport tomorrow. I mean I don't mind doing this, but the homeless are not my issue. You would think that they would figure it out and get back on their feet." Ruby and her assistant were riding in black stretch limo to the homeless shelter.

"Ms. Grayhill, these folks are down on their luck for whatever reason. You are doing this because it is the right thing to do and more importantly, the photo op will do wonders for the opening of the new hotel."

"You're right. It's about the publicity which brings in the clients and ultimately makes us money. I get it. Very well, let's get to it." When they pulled up to the shelter, there were people standing in a line that extended outside onto the streets. There were young and old, all races, people by themselves and there were single moms with kids and whole families to include the dad and mom. It was depressing and normally would bring humility to the average person of a kind heart. Ruby did not understand what she was seeing because she had never been homeless for a day in her life. She was the daughter of one of the richest families in the world, a fifth generation Grayhill, and the money had always been there. As a matter of fact, she had never wanted anything in her life. This was different for her.

She and the assistant went inside the shelter, which was an old brick building that was once an old YMCA. The YMCA closed when the new fitness centers became the rage. This part of the city had been gentrified and for that reason affordable housing no longer existed in this part of the city. No one had ever considered the people who ultimately were put on the streets through evictions, that while legal, were questionable from a moral standpoint. People were being displaced from the only place that they and their parents and grandparents before them had ever called home. They were in fact generational just like Ruby. The difference is they were not rich.

Ruby and her assistant called themselves dressing down this day, but they still stood out. She had on designer jeans, a very expensive blouse, and her shoes said expensive department store. Couple that with the fact her purse cost more than a reliable used car and she stood out like a sore thumb. She realized that as soon as she arrived, but it was too late now. They were put in charge of distributing napkins and drinks. After seeing how they were dressed, the manager of the shelter decided to put them at the end of the feeding line. No need to get their clothes dirty.

"These folks are really bad off."

"Yes, Ms. Grayhill, they are." Her assistant was getting a little irritated because Ruby just kept going on about these people, these people, as if they were somehow less than a normal, decent Americans chasing the same dream she had basically inherited. And then it happened.

In line was a white man, about the same age as Ruby. Beside him was a Hispanic woman, and two children who appeared to be interracial, perhaps the children of the man and woman. He had a long beard; his hair was long as well. He was wearing some old jeans, a plaid shirt and a very old winter coat. The woman had on jeans, a turtleneck sweater, and a long coat. On her feet were some boots that had a lot of miles on them. Both had backpacks. The two boys, who appeared to be about eight and ten, wore jeans, sneakers that had lots of wear, and ninja turtle sweatshirts along with coats of their own. They each had wool caps on. As they approached to get their napkins and drink, the gentleman looked down at the ground and noticed he had dropped his keys. When he picked them up, his face came directly in contact with Ruby.

"Would you like some drink, sir?"

"Yes, Ruby, I would."

"That's good. Is this your family? And how do you know my name?"

"Ruby, it's me, Cecil."

Ruby would drop the drink out of her hand, and it would hit the table, splash onto her jeans before finally landing on the floor. She stood there for about ten seconds in complete shock. What did this man just say to her?

"Ruby, it's your brother, Cecil."

Ruby continued to stare. First came one tear down her left cheek. Then another tear came down her right cheek. And then the slow stream of tears came down her face.

"Ruby, we are holding up the line. Can I get my drink, please?"

"Sure, sure, here is your drink. But...."

"Ruby, this is my wife Isabella, and my two boys Raphael and Roberto. Boys say hi to Ms. Ruby."

"Hello, Ms. Ruby." Ruby was still in shock but had regained her composure.

"How are the folks?"

"They are fine, Cecil. They are fine."

"That's good. Tell them I said hi. Come on boys, let's go sit down. See you, Ruby!"

Just like that, Cecil would walk off with his family, go take a seat leaving Ruby and her assistant in line to complete their work as volunteers. Ruby would watch them the whole time, making sure they did not leave before she was able to speak to Cecil again. While she was working, she looked away, and in an instant, they were gone. She had found her brother, and in an instant, he was gone. She asked one of the shelter managers about him.

"Yes ma'am. I know Cecil and his family. Really good people. Up until six months ago, they were doing fine. The building they were living in has been purchased by the Grayhill Hotel. It is being renovated to be a mixed-use building. My understanding is it will have shops on the first two floors, a hotel on the floors above that and then the top ten floors will be high-end housing for the millionaires that are starting to take over New York. Cecil volunteers when he can to help us out. Really sweet guy."

Not only had Ruby found her brother, but ironically, she only found him because of the eviction. And she was the cause or at least her family's corporation. They had evicted Cecil a second time and did not know it. She would wait another day to see if he showed. He did not. She cancelled her plans to leave and waited another day. She waited and waited. While she waited, the manager of the shelter put her to work.

She began to understand that there was another group of people in this world who were good people but had fallen on hard luck not because of a lack of work, but instead a lack of affordable housing. They were being pushed out everywhere. And then Cecil showed his face early one rainy Friday morning. He came through the door and walked right up to Ruby. She had her back turned to him when he approached her.

Rich Men Have No Friends

"Hey, I understand you are looking for me." She heard the voice but did not want to turn around. She did not want to be disappointed a second time. But when she turned around, there he was in the flesh, her brother Cecil. He looked the same as before, except he had changed shirts, and he had this big smile on his face. His family was not with him. She threw her arms around Cecil and cried uncontrollably. She had found her brother and this time she was not letting go.

They went and sat down at one of the tables that was normally full of people seeking something to eat. It was a little after lunch and the crowd had dispersed until the dinner rush which began at four.

"Cecil, what happened to you? I mean, where have you been all this time?"

"Ruby, are you happy?"

"Yes, I am happy. How could you ask that question? I am really happy today because I found you."

"No Ruby, you did not find me. I found you. You are in my neck of the woods, and frankly, I thought I would never see you in this part of town. Well, until this part of town became potential development property instead of the home of the middle class or us regular folks. But a deal is a deal. Nice place you have coming up. I used to live there."

"Cecil, I can help you."

"That's not the point, Ruby. It's not about moving to another place. It's about a sense of community and knowing your neighbors, Ruby. That building you evicted me and my family from. That had been in Isabella's family for over fifty years."

Cecil would go on to explain that he was working downtown when he met this beautiful pecan tan Hispanic woman who had the sweetest smile, a body with not a curve out of place, and the cutest feet he had ever seen. He met her when she came in the pizza shop he was working in. He had moved to New York, and after his parents refused to help him, he found work. Nothing special, but a decent day's work for a decent day's pay.

Anyway, he would ask Isabella out. She was a waitress at a restaurant around the corner from his place. She lived with her parents in a three-bedroom apartment that they had been paying $150 rent on and it had been transferred to them by their parents before them. They were grandfathered in until Grayhill came along. And six months ago, everyone was evicted, and it was perfectly legal. Grayhill had sold it as an economic stimulant to the mayor and local politicians, for the city and showed how much revenue it would bring once built.

After Cecil and Isabella got engaged, then married, they moved in with her parents and the boys came not soon thereafter. It could feel a little crowded at times, but it was their home. And they were happy.

"What happened to her parents? I mean I saw you and your family the last time you were here."

"They moved to Florida. Her dad has a brother who moved down there years ago after he retired from the police department. "

"So why did you and Isabella stay?"

"Because this is our home, Ruby. This is our home. Not some pass-through place to stay but our home. I mean at least it was our home. The sad thing is now that the area is being developed, it's not a home for anyone."

"What do you mean, Cecil?"

"Our building was one of the last ones to go. And what was going on around us made her parents and Isabella cry on most days when they talked about the old neighborhood compared to the neighborhood now."

Cecil would tell Ruby about the new high-end shops coming in that no one could afford. Ten dollars for a slice of pizza, four dollars for a cup of coffee, one hundred dollars for a pair of shoes. If you wanted groceries, three days was two hundred and that was if you skimped. And the people, they all walked around with their phones out, constantly on social media and when they did talk to each other, it was so pretentious and out of touch with reality. They would look down on the locals as if when are you leaving.

The locals had been colonized again. Except this time, it was their own fellow Americans, not some strangers on a big ship that had come many miles to claim this new land. But for Isabella and her family, it felt the same. He explained that this was not a neighborhood, but instead a high-end out of touch with reality fake paradise where people were pretending to be happy, but he knew they really weren't.

"Wow, Cecil, I am sorry to hear that happened to you."

"What about my family, Ruby?"

"What do you mean?"

Rich Men Have No Friends

"You said you are sorry to hear that happened to me. What about these good folks who help build this city and now are being displaced so that it can become a concrete paradise for the very few who can afford to live here. And more importantly what about my family?"

"I did not mean it that way, I apologize. Cecil, you do know that nothing can be done. These are business decisions. If Grayhill does not move in, someone else will. We won a bid, Cecil. I hate to say it, but you can't stop progress."

"What progress, Ruby? Displace people from the only place they ever called home. Where their kids played stickball in the streets and then their grandkids. Three or four generations all growing up on the same street, going to the same church, working in a lot of the same places. A sense of community and a sense of pride knowing that they were all family, related both in blood and a sense of belonging. Where everyone looks out for each other, and everyone starves, or everyone eats. Where good morning and good afternoon are said with a smile. If we are saying that a sense of community is no longer progress, then you can have progress and give me back Isabella's neighborhood." Cecil had tears coming down both cheeks at this point. "It's just not fair, Ruby, and that is why I left home."

"I don't understand. Mom and dad were good to you. They love you."

"I know that but how many homes do they really need. I mean how much money is enough. Do you know what Grayhill money could have done for this city? It could have renovated those same buildings, upgraded the interiors and raised the rent maybe two hundred dollars per month which would have still made it affordable for us. Grayhill still makes a profit and saves the community. Imagine that. It is possible to be a capitalist, and make money, and give back to the community. What a concept, huh?"

"Cecil, you are right but getting a group of people to think like that, specifically the one with money is going to be tough to do."

"So, you do nothing. Anyway, I need to get to work. Good to see you, sis. Tell the folks I said hi."

They would talk a little longer. Ruby would try to offer her brother some help. He would not take it. While he was working in the pizza shop, he had gone to a coding bootcamp where they teach you how to code. He had taken those skills and become an efficient programmer who made a good living as a freelance remote worker. He and Isabella and the kids were fine.

"Well, if you are fine, Cecil, then why do you come to the shelter for food?"

"Ruby, I help out here as much as I can. The day you saw me I was trying to teach my boys a lesson."

"What lesson could that possibly be, Cecil? I mean, look at this place."

"A lesson in humility, Ruby. Like you and I, I am providing for them best I can much like our parents provided for us without all the opulence and extra stuff we really did not need. So, I am teaching them about wants versus needs. And I brought them here so that they don't ever forget where they come from. Isabella is a nurse now and we were finally able to find a place that we could afford in a nice neighborhood that reminds us of the old neighborhood. The only question is when?"

"When what?"

"When will we have to move again, Ruby?"

"Cecil, let me help you. And congratulations to the family. And thanks for letting me know that my twin brother was married, and I am an aunt. Mighty unselfish of you to let me know."

"Ruby, I could not come back. I just wanted to fade into the woodwork. That's your life, that's not me. I am just a regular guy trying to provide for his family and I love it. Was it tough when we got evicted? It was, I am not going to lie. But I am glad it happened to me. I now know that I can survive in this world without having everything handed to me. You know?"

"Can we keep in touch? I mean nothing mattered more to me than finding you."

"You sure about that, Ruby?"

"What do you mean?"

"Let's just say this. Had you disappeared, not only would I have hired people, but I would also have walked to the end of the earth to find you. I would not have cared at all about some fancy overpriced hotel being built to add to the family fortune, money that can't be spent for a thousand generations."

"You are right, Cecil. But it was selfish of you to have me worrying about you and you were fine."

Rich Men Have No Friends

"You are right, sis, you are right." They hugged, gave each other a kiss on the cheek and would stay in touch from that point going forward. Cecil still wanted nothing to do with the family money or the business.

"There are good people with good intentions all over this country and that's commendable, Ruby. But we have enough housing in this country to house every single person, yet we have gentrification and new developments going up every day, and for what, money? Capitalism is good, greed is not. Gordon Gecko was wrong."

Ruby concluded her story about her brother. Ted was quiet the entire time but had been listening very carefully. Ruby grabbed a napkin and wiped her face where a couple of tears had run down the sides of her face.

"Ted, that is why I am here. It broke my heart to know that my brother was homeless or in his case displaced, and I had somehow been responsible for his neighborhood's demise. It was as if I had taken the soul out of the neighborhood for a façade of a new world that as he said could be perceived as pretentious."

"Please, save me the speech about saving the people. This is America, we are the richest country in the world. If you want to make it, you can. I did. If people knew what I went through to get here, then they would understand that you can make it."

"At what cost, Ted. At what cost?"

"I don't follow?"

"Ted, we are the richest country in the world, right. That's what you said. And you wear that as a badge of honor, don't you?"

"Damn right I do."

"Well, let me ask you a question?"

"Ask away, Ruby. But I really gotta go?"

"Why didn't you say that we are the richest country in the world, the melting pot of the world, where everyone had a fair chance to make a decent living, have affordable housing, a good education, and where we live in humility and look out for our fellow man doing unto others as we would have them do unto us?" Ruby was as agitated with Ted as he was with her as shown in the redness of both their faces.

"Yeah, I mean the rest is implied, Ruby?"

"Is it really, Ted? Or do you make yourself feel good by believing that every time you buy a company, lay the people off, increase your net worth, maintain your status as the richest man in the world with no regard for the impact on the cities and towns that are forever altered. So, which is it, America, the richest country, period? Or America, the land where to your earlier point everyone has a fair chance at succeeding." The cat was out of the bag, everyone knew who Ted was.

"Well, it's both. I don't know. Look, I need to go. Hopefully I will see you again one day, Ruby. You are a nice person and I wish you well."

"See you, Ted. And Ted, I'm sorry about the loss of your daughter."

At that point, Ruby's daughter came through the door. She was a sweet five-year-old girl named Samantha. She was blond haired and had a cute little walk.

Today, she was wearing a pink dress with some cute little white sneakers. Ruby had not only moved to this small town, but she had convinced her fiancé at the time to move with her. And they had a daughter Samantha or Sam. She was the same age as Amy.

"Mommy, mommy. Guess what we did today?"

"What's that, sweetie?"

"We made paper airplanes. And my plane flew a long, long, way."

"Sweetie, I want you to meet my new friend…."

Theodore was gone. Seeing Sam reminded him of his Amy. He had just cracked. The Bentley sped off making a high screeching sound as it pulled off. He blew right through the stop light, one of the two in town and was headed back to Houston. They could have this one stoplight; I mean two stoplight town. Ruby's story had not affected him at all nor had his two days in this town. Or so it seemed.

Rich Men Have No Friends

34

Shelley was now back in the office. The lunch with Carol had been interesting but she needed to get back to work. She was the CEO of one of the largest companies in the world and charged with managing the money for the richest man in the world.

"Why me, Mr. Hightower?" She was asking herself a question that until now had not really crossed her mind.

Shelley was a barista when Ted met her. He had vetted her but nothing about her said assistant to the richest man in the world. She was educated at North Carolina State University in Raleigh, North Carolina. Parents were both retired military and she had been born and raised in a little town about sixty miles from Raleigh. Fayetteville was a military town through and through.

After getting her degree in mechanical engineering from NC State, she would go to the University of North Carolina and get her MBA in Finance and Accounting. And then she would go work for some of the best firms in the country, excelling everywhere she went, getting promotion after promotion. She became a top partner at a prestigious consulting firm and then one day out of the blue, she decided to leave. She cashed out what little money she had and opened a coffee shop.

She was very proud of that shop, Shelley's, she called it. Loved the fact that it was hers and she was the boss. There was no e-mail, no voice mail, no meetings. She had a team of four people, and she was open from six in the morning until four in the afternoon. Her customers did not like the fact she closed early but she wanted both her and her team to have a good work-life balance. She paid them well, twenty dollars per hour and rather than have eight part-time employees, she had four full-time people.

She bonused them at the end of each year. She would keep seventy-five percent of the profits and share twenty-five percent with the staff. She always bonused them the Friday before Black Friday. Made for a good Christmas. But then a new coffee shop was built directly across from hers. It was one of those big franchises. She competed for a long time.

Unfortunately, the other shop kept longer hours and her customers slowly migrated over to the other place. They cut their prices long enough to drive her out of business and then after three years, she closed the shop. Ted reached out to her via a recruiter, and she went to work for him. What started as a part-time gig to have something to do turned into a full-time job. A very good job with good pay, benefits and the trust of the richest man in the world.

What Shelley did not know was that Theodore was the reason her shop closed. Much like his pursuit of C.J., he had done his homework on Shelley when he first met her. She had left such an impression on him as the owner of the coffee shop. He researched her background. Once he found out who she was in a past life, he wanted her on his team.

He had his people buy one franchise under a subsidiary he created outside of his normal organization. Then he had the manager of the franchise figure out what was making Shelley's shop successful. They then extended the hours and pulled customers away given her closing time of four o'clock in the evening. He then studied her prices and lowered his by one dollar. The shop never really made any money, but it drove Shelley's shop out of business. Once that happened, he recruited Shelley to come work for him.

Theodore then closed the coffee shop, fired all the people and paid for the manager to relocate to another part of the country. All in all, Theodore spent a little north of one million dollars to get the services of Shelley. And that would at some point in his future come back to haunt him. He was of the belief that everything could be solved with money. After all, he was the richest man in the world.

Money has a strange way of either being good or bad, depending upon how it is used and for what purpose. Theodore was using it for neither. He was just good at it and did not want to go back to the life he had run from so long ago.

Rich Men Have No Friends

35

We go back in time now to twenty-six years ago. Theodore is in grad school, and he is doing quite well with his patents. He is starting to see real income from his ideas and on his way to becoming a multi-millionaire. He can help his mom out and sends money home to her quite often. On a mild winter weekday near the holidays, he receives a call from his sister. Something has happened.

Theodore was at his apartment in Boston when the phone rang. It was Carol who was working on her doctorate at divinity school on the other side of the country. He did not recognize the number initially as he and Carol had never been close again since the night that he learned the lesson of the givers and the takers. But he loved his sister, he just did not express it, ever.

"Theodore, this is Carol, your sister."

"Hey, Carol, what's up?"

"Mom, Theodore, something has happened to mom."

Theodore knew that his mother had brushes with the law on a much less frequent basis, but her line of work always drew their attention. He had the best lawyer in town on retainer to ensure that she was protected. Once he started making money from his patents, he did two things.

He sent her money and made sure she had a good lawyer. As the judges began to figure out that she was difficult to convict of anything, the police backed off. She was monitored, but it was not worth the taxpayer's money to pursue her any further.

She would change. She still dealt and she still used, but a lot less frequently. This infusion of cash created something she had never had before, a positive cash flow and money in the bank. She dumped boyfriend or husband number whatever and settled down best she could into a normal, but unorthodox life. She met this prostitute one night at a diner who was a "client". The prostitute would tell her about how bad it was on the streets. She would tell her that she was being held against her will to pay off a debt to a local pimp named Silky who had tricked her into prostitution when she first came into town. It was your typical story. Young girl runs away from home to pursue her dreams, ends up with good looking guy, he charms her, then turns her onto drugs, then turns her to the streets to make money for him.

Phineas McNabb

Silky kept a close eye on his girls but on this night, he was at a club on the other side of town. The prostitute's name was Susan Flannery. Susan Flannery was from small town America, a petite young lady about five foot four inches with blond hair. Her teeth were yellow from living a life that was not high on hygiene and her clothes of choice fit the profile of her current role. She had on a short yellow dress with yellow high heels, purchased at a thrift store that her pimp took all his girls, nothing in the store cost more than five dollars per item.

Susan was not a dumb girl as she had graduated in the top ten percent of her high school class. She wanted to move to the big city and try her luck at getting a job and making it on her own. Her original intent was to save up enough money to go to college. Meeting this handsome guy who would become her pimp would change all that overnight.

The night she met with Theodore's mom, her life was about to change and so was his mom's.

"Theodore, mom is dead."

"You're lying, Carol. Mom is not dead. I spoke to her a couple of days ago."

"I'm sorry, Theodore, she is dead. They say it was an overdose."

"That's a lie, Carol. Mom was cleaning herself up. She was not using it like she used to. As a matter of fact she was helping to get these young girls off the street. She's fine. I'm calling her now."

Theodore angrily hung up his cell phone. He then immediately called his mom. The phone rang and then a voice picked up.

"Yeah, who dis!" It sounded like the voice of a black man in his late twenties.

"Who is this and let me speak to Marilyn Hightower."

"I don't know no Marilyn Hightower. Now, how can I help you, partner?"

"I promise you that if I find you, you will regret the day you were born. Now where's my mom?"

"Bitch overdosed several days ago man. I walked by and picked up the phone. Figured she was dead and did not need it anymore. Anyway, partner, I got to go. My girls are waiting on me."

"Wait, what did you say?"

Rich Men Have No Friends

"I said I got money to make. So, if you not trying to get laid tonight, I would appreciate it if you stopped tying up my line, partner."

Theodore knew exactly who he was talking to. He was talking to a pimp. His mother might be dead after all. Had she gotten caught up and been in the wrong place at the wrong time. Only time would tell.

The day of the funeral was cloudy with an overcast. Given Theodore's past life and his mom's line of business, not a lot of people came to the funeral. Except for this one young lady who stood in a distance. Her hair was blond, a little unkept, and she had a light coat and under it was a yellow dress and she was wearing yellow high heels. Theodore noticed her but figured she was someone who may have known his mom from the past.

Carol was dressed in all black, a coat, dress, and shoes. Theodore, being the non-conformist, he was, he came in jeans, sneakers and an untucked polo shirt. He was grieving but did not believe in this whole funeral process. He had suggested cremating his mother, but Carol convinced him that would not be what his mother would have wanted. Neither of them knew what she wanted as death had never been discussed. It was always knocking on the door given her profession of choice, but it had never been discussed.

They had a service at the funeral home. Theodore was nonattentive given his feeling about religion and God. He came out of respect for his mom. Nothing more. They took her body to a cemetery that Carol had found. Given their mother was not aligned with a church, they found a public cemetery that took in anyone with money. And that Theodore had plenty of. As the preacher was giving the last rights at the cemetery prior to lowering their mom into the ground, he asked the two of them to do something that made Theodore angry.

"Carol and Theodore, let's join hands and say the Lord's prayer." Theodore would surprise the preacher but not his sister.

"Man, screw this. Drop her in the ground already. She's gone. Doesn't your bible say the soul is gone and all that remains is the body. So, what exactly are we praying for?"

Theodore walked away and headed towards the young lady who was standing off in the distance. She had something for him.

"Mister, are you Theodore?"

"Yeah, what do you want? Look, I don't know who you are but now is not a good time...."

Phineas McNabb

"Mister, I think you would want this…." It was his mom's cell phone.

"Where did you get this?" He grabbed her arm and given the loudness of his voice; he drew the attention of the few people gathered around his mom's casket. He quickly calmed down.

"My pimp, Silky Tim. He had it, Mister. Your mom did not die of an overdose, he killed her."

"What?"

"He killed your mom for trying to save me, mister. I'm sorry, mister." Susan began to cry and leaned onto his shoulder. He did not know what to do so he took his right arm and placed it lightly over her back. This went on for about forty-five seconds before she regained her composure.

"How do you know this Silky guy killed her. What proof do you have?"

"I overheard him tell one of the other pimps, sir. He told him that this drug dealing bitch was trying to take his money from him and she had to be dealt with. He also told him he made it look like it was a drug overdose. He said he wore gloves, and no one would know what happened."

"Why do you have a black eye, and I'm sorry, your name is…"

"Susan Flannery, sir. My name is Susan."

"Well, Susan, I still don't understand how you know my mom or this Silky guy. How do I know you didn't kill my mom and are now having a guilty conscious? Maybe I need to call the police."

"Please don't do that sir, Silky would kill me if he knew I was here talking to you. I have nowhere to go, and your mom was my last hope, that is why he killed her."

Susan would explain that she met Theodore's mom one night in a diner in the rough part of town, where his mom chose to stay even after he would send her money to get out. Susan would tell the story of coming to Houston with dreams of working and saving up money to go to college so she would not be burdened with student loans and debt when she graduated. Marilyn had promised her she would get her out of the environment.

The night his mom was killed, she had ten thousand dollars on her for Susan to get away from Silky. Silky found out what was happening from one of the other girls in his stable who Susan had trusted with the information. He would meet Marilyn, knock her out cold, put her in his car and take her to an old, abandoned building by the docks. There he would drag her inside the building, shoot her up with some drugs and she would die of what would appear to be an accidental overdose. He would then go back and from that point on, he would beat Susan almost daily for being disloyal to him. She was on the brink of death herself, either from the streets or suicide, but she could not go any further. She was responsible for Marilyn's death and for that she was truly sorry.

"Susan, do you have somewhere to stay right now?"

"No sir, I am hiding out best I can. But you know the streets, hard to hide in broad daylight when you got nowhere to go."

"Can't you go home?"

"Not like this, sir. I can't go home like this. I can't." She started to cry again. If Susan went back home, life would not get better for her. Her small town was dying a slow death itself. Nothing there, all the jobs were gone, and her folks lived on a fixed income through government assistance and whatever they could hustle. Sadly, she was being forced in her mind to choose between the lesser of two dire situations, neither of which gave her the motivation to keep on living.

"I tell you what, I am going to put you up in a hotel until I can sort this out. This Silky guy, where can I find him?"

"Silky can be a dangerous man, sir. He is not someone you want to mess with."

"Let me worry about that, Susan. Let's get you out of here and somewhere safe. How about that?"

"Are you sure? I mean, I don't want something to happen to you."

"Susan, I want you to remember something someone once told me, there are givers and takers in this world. I am going to "GIVE" this silky guy a lesson in humility for "TAKING" my mother's life. Don't you worry about me. I will be just fine." Carol walked up as the casket had been lowered but Theodore was too busy talking to Susan to notice.

"Who is this, Theodore?"

"A friend of moms. She came into town for the funeral and is here for a couple of days. Carol, meet Susan, Susan Flannery."

"Nice to meet you, Susan." Carol knew this young lady was no friend from out of town. Her volunteer work with the local ministry at her school gave her the knowledge of exactly who she was talking to. She knew what a streetwalker looked like from a mile away. Poor hygiene, short dress, no stockings, cheap high heels, and the smell of cheap perfume always gave them away. There was no smell of perfume, but there was the smell of someone who had turned a trick in the past few days and had not had a chance to take a shower. Susan and Carol would cross paths again.

Just then, the phone would ring. It was Silky. He was looking for Susan. Theodore would walk away from the two of them and he would answer the phone. "Bitch, where you at? I have been looking for your ass for three days now. You are really trying my patience. I should have killed your ass when I killed that...."

"Go ahead, say it. Please say it!" Theodore was pissed.

"Look partner, hey, your voice sounds familiar to me. You are trying to steal one of my girls. You don't want to do that, man, I'm telling you."

"Or what, you going to drug me and make it look like and overdose, punk!"

"I knew I should have killed that snitch. She was not making me any money anyway. But she is my property, and you can't just take her, feel me!"

"How about I pay you for her. Say one hundred thousand dollars. Can you meet me?"

"Wait, how do I know you are five-O?" (Five-O was street slang for the police)

"Because if I was five-O, as you call it, you would already be arrested. Think about it, dumbass. If I have your phone and your girl already told me you killed someone, you would already be locked up. How stupid are you?"

"Look here, partner, don't call me stupid. And yeah, your one hundred thousand works. She's not worth it but better you have her then the morgue, feel me?"

"No, I don't feel you. We meeting or what tonight, the old, abandoned building by the docks. You know where it is over off fifth and Conway."

"Know exactly where it is. And look here, man. You better have my money and this better not be a trick or you and the girl will be dealt with."

Rich Men Have No Friends

"I'll be there, don't worry."

"I want my girl back until you pay me."

"Silky, I believe that's your grown-up name, Silky, this is not a negotiation. You are getting paid in lieu of me kicking your ass for what you have done to this girl. So shut up, hang up, and I will see you at twelve midnight. FEEL ME!"

"Whatever. I'll be there. And you better be alone."

"Silky, I will be alone but again, this is not a negotiation."

"I don't even know what that is but whatever..." Both hung up at the exact same time.

Theodore was pissed and you could see the red in his face. Keeping his composure was not a strong point for him right now. Mom is dead, killed trying to do something good, and for a young lady who was young and impressionable and had been misled by a young man from the wrong side of the tracks, or so it seemed. No one would ever know because they were the Last People, those who the rest of the country throws away subconsciously because they are the biggest sinners in the world. They just take. From each other, from the government, from society. They just take and never give anything in return.

What was sad about that thought process, is that Susan Flannery was a giver. She was one of the good guys. She had moved to the big city so she would not be a burden to her parents. She was trying to make it on her own. She had given her heart to a young man who had been led astray early in life. He would chase the quick dollars and his girls were his enterprise.

Susan was giving her body physically and mentally to men in back alleys and the back seats of cars and on park benches. She was being forced to take the ultimate act of intimacy and reduce it to a business transaction. And the price per transaction was twenty dollars.

A priceless act of intimacy that was meant to show love between two people and ultimately bring life to this world was worth twenty dollars, that's it. And Carol knew this all too well as she and Marilyn were trying to get the givers (prostitutes) off the street so the takers (pimps) could stop taking their youth, their hopes, and their dreams away from them. And they were not givers because of the cheap sex. They were givers of a different kind. Young girls trying to make it in the world and give of their talents and abilities to make the world a better place who took the wrong detour and were led down the wrong path.

Rich Men Have No Friends

36

C.J. had thought over Theodore's offer and he was not ready to say yes yet. His conversation with Sarah was weighing on him. No matter how he tried to justify it, he was trying to get back in the game on a more full-time basis and all under the cover of doing good for the people. And that he did. But he always kept more than he needed for himself. Theodore was trying to become a trillionaire and C.J. was trying to relive a time of the past when he was the Rockstar of Wall Street. No one else knew what he was doing, but he did. And that gave him satisfaction. The problem with that is that he knew more than most that money was the root of all evil if not managed for the right reasons, primarily satisfying his needs, and not his wants. As a preacher, he had a different standard he had to live by. He made that choice when he became a preacher. Optics and perception were different for him, and he knew that.

He was sitting in his office, looking at the screens and his investments were doing well. A couple of stocks his company had purchased were up. It had been sixty days since their IPO's (initial public offerings) and he was ready to cash out. He called Thomas, his fraternity brother, best friend and the one guy who had been with literally since the death of his parents.

"Thomas, what's going on?"

"You tell me frat. Making money and not letting the money make me, pastor."

"I hear you. It looks like it is time to sell Teleguise and GuessSims. Both are up over ten each and...."

Teleguise and GuessSims were two technology companies who had recently hit the public market. C.J.'s company had been an early investor, and it was now time to cash out.

"Already ahead of you, frat. Was waiting on you to pull the trigger. That's a nice little haul for a sixty day wait. You know that the account at over one hundred now. To be exact, one ten. You just made a cool ten million, my friend."

"No, Thomas, we made ten million and we did it for the people. That will go a long way with the plans I have for the church."

"C.J., are you serious right now?"

Phineas McNabb

"Dead serious."

"Hold on, let me close my door." Thomas would close the door as he often did when talking to C.J.

"C.J., don't you think it's time to wind down? When you started this, your goal was fifty million, then seventy-five, then one hundred. At what point is it enough. I mean I know you have good intentions, and you are doing good work in Greensburgh. And your track record for giving away your fortune should never be questioned as you have done it twice. But don't you think this is enough. "

"Thomas, I love you like a brother, but don't tell me how to manage my money. I pay you well to run MY COMPANY and you do that well, but let's remember who runs the show. Don't get it twisted, friend."

"Wow. Man, what has gotten into you. First, don't talk to me like that. And secondly, you know I don't care about the money. Didn't care when we were kids, did not care when you were the so-called Rockstar of Wall Street and I only do this because of the good work that comes from it to help people. And more importantly, don't make me come to Greensburgh and kick your ass, excuse my French, PASTOR!" Thomas had known C.J. since they were freshmen in college, and other than his dad and mom and of course Sarah, he was someone C.J. respected and revered like a brother, a big brother. Thomas never cared about his money or status. He was just C.J. to him.

"You're right, Thomas. My bad, how's the wife and kids?'

"All good man. Now what did you really call me for? You could have e-mailed me the sell instructions so what's on your mind."

"Theodore Hightower."

"Yeah, what about him. You read an article or something, got a trade on your mind involving one of his companies."

"No, I met him and spent the better part of the morning with him today."

"You serious? You met with the richest man in the world, the one hundred-billion-dollar man."

"Yeah, and he wants us to help him on his quest to be a trillionaire."

"Get the f, I mean get out of here! Theodore Hightower wants to hire us!"

Rich Men Have No Friends

"That he does, Thomas. On a consulting basis, we send him trades, he executes when we do basically mimic our actions and we make a small fee for the advice. Say two percent of whatever he makes, basically a finder's fee."

"I don't know man. You know once you get in bed with guys like that, you don't get out. There's a sort of mob mentality that comes with it. You remember what happened when you left French-Helliman, don't you?"

French-Helliman was not happy when he resigned. The top guy at the company tried to talk C.J. out of leaving since he was now their billion-dollar man. When he explained that he had made a promise to his dad, the top guy told C.J. there was no money in preaching. C.J. explained it was not about the money, but a promise and a calling to his dad.

The top guy was disappointed in him and made him leave his office and the company that day. And C.J. later found out that the owner tried to blackball him in the business. And just like that, he had gone from being the Rockstar of Wall Street to a disgruntled employee who was unreliable and left abruptly with no logical explanation, or at least that is what his old boss was telling anyone who would listen. His big boss was thinking about the money the organization could potentially lose versus what was in the best interest of C.J. Good employee gets bad reference again.

"Like yesterday, Thomas. Glad I went into preaching because I could not have ever gone back into that life. Talk about going from superstar to the child no one wants. If it ain't about money, then it ain't worth talking about with those guys."

"I hear you. C.J., seriously, man, it's time to get out. You don't want to deal with this guy. Getting in is easy, getting out is like trying to break out of prison. You don't break out."

"But some have broken out, I mean folks broke out of Alcatraz. Only the strong survive, my friend. Anyway, giving you a heads up. I will let you know."

"Take care, C.J. and really think about his before you do it. Tell Sarah I said hi and tell her I agree with her."

"About what?"

Phineas McNabb

"That you should not do this and it's time to wind down. I got you man, to the end, but it's time to wind down." They laughed, and then proceeded to hang up.

Rich Men Have No Friends

37

We are back to the time when Theodore's mom died twenty-six years ago. The funeral is behind him now and he has arranged a meeting with her killer. He is about to become the taker that no one wants to be. The taker of life.

The docks are very quiet at night. Al the ships are in port and most if not all the employees have gone home. Midnight is a time when no one should be hanging around, particularly the old, abandoned buildings that are not currently being used. These are the buildings of companies of the past who have long closed their doors. Probably belonged to a company that had been bought out, merged with someone, or ran out of business. It matters not to Theodore at this point as he is a grad student who is just starting to understand the real value of money and not yet the shrewd investor he is about to become.

Silky pulls up in a green Cadillac four door sedan. Windows are darkly tinted, and the music is blaring with the bass making the car bounce at every move. The rims on the car are shiny spokes much like from the gladiator days. Silky is smoking a mini cigar. He is a young black man in his late twenties. He is six foot five inches tall, wearing expensive shoes and expensive jeans. He has on an expensive designer blue long sleeve shirt and on the outside of it he is wearing a big gold chain that has a pendant on it with the words Silky on it. He is wearing a blue baseball hat with a capital S embroidered in the middle of it. He has an athletic build about him and is quite the charmer given his profession. He is on a mission tonight. He wants his money. Theodore offered to pay him one hundred thousand dollars for the freedom of Susan.

Theodore arrives in a rental sedan as he was only in town for the funeral. He stopped by his mom's house to get his weights, two one hundred-pound dumbbells and some chains. He had some jeans and a green sweatshirt and black sneakers. He does not have the money with him. He never intended to pay Silky a dime.

The two of them meet in the abandoned warehouse. The light from the full moon is shining into the top windows. This warehouse was used years ago to store merchandise that was being sent overseas and to take incoming as well. The company that used the warehouse has long gone out of business. The inside is empty, and they are standing in the middle of the warehouse looking at each other.

"What's up, pardner? I don't appreciate you taking one of my girls without my permission."

"Look, we are here for one reason and one reason only, to finalize a deal!"

"Yeah, well whatever, you feel me. Do you have my money? Because if you don't have my money, then…"

"Then what?"

Silky reaches to pull for his gun and as he does, Theodore pulls out a gun, one that belonged to his mom.

"I would not do that, Silky."

"Well look here, we got us a street brother. What part of town you from carrying a gun like that?"

"I'm from the part that does not take kindly to people pulling guns on us." Theodore was using everything in his power not to drop Silky on the spot.

"So, you really are a pimp. Man, I thought you were some idiot trying to save Sue Bird's life." (Susan had been given the nickname by Silky.)

"But here's the problem, bro. I need my money and I am tired of talking. So, the money…."

"Silky, I need you to pull out your gun slowly and put it on the ground."

"You serious right now? We made a deal."

"Dead serious, put the gun on the ground and turn your back to me."

"Man, you are tripping. I am going to pull it out now and place it on the ground. Look man, I just need my money."

"And you will get your money after I frisk you and make sure you are not trying to double cross me. Now turn around."

"Whatever, bro." Silky had been set up and did not even know it.

Silky turned around, Theodore slowly walked up behind him. In an instant, he took his gun and with the butt of it he pulled back his right hand and knocked Silky out cold. He then pulled Silky out of the light and rolled up one of his sleeves. He was going to die tonight just like Marilyn.

Rich Men Have No Friends

In the meantime, Carol was trying to find Susan to find out what she and Theodore had talked about. She knew that Susan was someone of interest to Theodore but not because she was from out of town. She went back to the streets of her old neighborhood and found out who Susan was. One of the girls on the track had heard from Susan and knew where she was staying. She was put up in a hotel on the other side of town near Cypress, a small town outside of Houston. Earlier in the night prior to the encounter between Silky and Theodore, Carol would go visit Susan. She would explain what happened.

"Susan, what did Theodore say to you before I walked up on the two of you."

"He said he would take care of it. Why?"

"What do you mean take care of it?"

"He was mad after I told him Silky was bragging about killing your mother."

"What do you mean? Killed my mother?"

"Silky killed her, and I believe you brother is going to get his revenge."

"Why do you say that?"

"He told me to meet him at the warehouse tonight by the docks. He told me to be there at fifteen minutes after midnight."

"Susan, where is this warehouse you are talking about, can you take me there?"

"I can. You have a car?"

"I do, I will pick you up at eleven thirty."

Meanwhile, later that night at the warehouse, Silky was taped to a chair. His hands were taped behind his back and his legs were taped to the front legs of the chair. Theodore was angry and he wanted answers. He had put just enough drugs in his system to make him nonthreatening. In his hand was a hammer, and he was going to get his answers one way or the other.

"Silky, why did you kill my mother?"

"Who? Man, I don't know what you are talking about." Theodore moved the hammer from his right hand to his left hand. He balled up his right hand and punched Silky in his mouth. Having always been an athlete who could still bench over two hundred pounds and could deadlift a house, the blow was as powerful as the hammer itself. Blood flew out of his mouth and a tooth went flying across the concrete.

Phineas McNabb

"Tell me again, Silky, why did you kill my mother?"

"What are you talking about, I came here about Sue Bird. You said you would pay me one hundred thou and that's all I know."

"Silky, I am not a pimp. I am Theodore Hightower, son of Marilyn Hightower, the woman you killed over a woman that is not your property. You of all people should know that."

"What does that mean, Theodore?"

"How can you, as a man of color, claim that you own someone?"

"Man, please, don't you dare do that. I am an employer who provides a service. These girls love me. I give them what they need."

"No, Silky, you take what you want. You, my friend (said with sarcasm) are a taker. And takers don't have any compassion or sympathy for those they hurt."

"Listen to you, Mr. Holier than thou. And what makes you so sure I am a taker, pardner?"

"Because, Silky, I am a taker. Except the difference between you and I is that I take for good. And I never lose. So, time's up. Why did you kill my mother?"

"I already told you, it was business, man, it was never personal. All I can tell you is that your mother was bad for business. So, do what you gotta do."

At that point, Theodore hit Silky so hard that he passed out. He then loosened the tape, and he took Silky to the dock. There he had two one hundred-pound dumbbells waiting with some chains. He attached the barbells to Silky's feet and wrapped them in chains. He stood Silky up on the edge of the dock and he woke him.

"Silky! Silky! Wake up, you piece of shit. Wake up! "Silky was groggy, but he was able to open his eyes. Theodore was holding him up.

"Look man, I'm sorry about your mom. I thought she was just some low-level drug dealer messing in my business. It was never personal." Theodore's eyes were watering over. And Silky now understood the seriousness of what he had done.

"She was my mother. And you reduced her to a business transaction. She was my mother. You took something from me and now I must take something from you, Silky!" At that point, Carol and Susan were running down the dock towards Theodore and Silky. Carol would try to stop him.

Rich Men Have No Friends

"Theodore, what are you doing?" Theodore was holding Silky up by his shirt, but the weight of his body was pulling him to the water. There was a thirty-foot drop to the water which was not shallow.

"This piece of scum killed our mother and shopped Susan like a piece of meat. The world won't miss him. He needs to go."

"Theodore Hightower, if you do this, you will never be able to live with yourself. This is not the way to handle this. You have a witness; he can be tried in a court of law." Carol was talking about Susan.

"Really, Carol. Let's talk that through. Low level pimp kills a small-time drug dealer and the only witness, no offense, Susan, is a prostitute who has an axe to grind. He'll be out in a week. This is the only trial he needs. Carol, go home."

"Theodore, this is not the way to do this. You know better. You are not this guy. Please, I am begging you."

"Listen to your sister, Theodore. Listen to her." Silky was baiting Theodore.

"Silky, I only have one more thing to say to you."

Silky spit in his face and said his last words on this earth "F%$k you, Theodore!"

"Silky, I understand you had to do what you had to do, I mean its business, right. You did not know it was my mom. Well, this time, man, It's not business, it's personal." Theodore let go and as Silky's body dropped and the weight of the barbells took him straight down and he made a splash in the water. He sunk to the bottom. He squirmed and tried to undo the chains, but eventually he ran out of breath and his lifeless body stood over the weights and he died.

Several days later some divers would find Silky at the bottom of the water with the weight of the dumbbells holding his body upright. Theodore and Carol would be questioned as they had the most motive to kill Silky. Susan was rumored to know something from the girls on the track. But she was able to say that she was not there that night and disappeared soon thereafter. Rumor, was she relocated after coming into a small fortune that would buy her a house, a car, and a new life.

As for Carol and Theodore, this would forever cause a rift in their relationship. Thou shall not kill was more than just a scripture to Carol and Theodore was in no mood to be lectured or preached to. They would not speak again for a very long time.

Phineas McNabb

38

As the day wore on Tuesday, things were not going as planned. Theodore is back in his Bentley driving towards I-10 to head back to Houston. His trip has not gone as planned.

Theodore was not happy. He had planned this whole thing. He was not trying to take advantage of his daughter's death. He really was grieving, and Mr. Wimples was helping. He had determined that he had to get back to work to get over the death of his daughter. Sitting around and thinking about it was not good for his mental state. And he was on a new quest. Theodore Hightower, the first Trillionaire.

Theodore stepped on the gas, got the car up to sixty-five miles per hour and turned on the cruise control. He turned on the radio to a channel that played some contemporary jazz and let the roof down. He put on his shades and put Greensburgh behind him for now. He would give C.J. a couple of days to call him. He knew that his offer was too good to pass up. In the meantime, he was headed back to Houston.

As he was headed towards the highway, he saw a truck up in the distance. A black 1978 Ford Pickup. And kneeled changing a tire was a man. A man with overalls on, a short sleeve shirt, a baseball hat and boots.

It was Abraham. And in the truck was Mr. Wimples, patiently waiting for the tire to be changed.

Theodore put his foot on the brake to cut off the cruise control. He pulled over in front of the truck and put his car in park. He was tired of seeing these pickup trucks and wanted some answers. He felt like he was being haunted or followed. Either way, what was the deal with these pickups.

"Aren't you the guy who I traded my car with for this truck?"

"I am that guy, Abraham Jacob. And you are Theodore Hightower, the richest man in the world or so he thinks."

"What does that mean, Abraham?"

"It means what I said. It is not my intentions to confuse you, I speak the truth. You are the richest man in the world who does not have a clue about how poor you really are. You see, you measure your total net worth by the size of your bank account, your assets, your material things and the people you control and a ranking on a list. And while no one will ever criticize your hard work and your pull yourself up from the bootstraps attitude, you are missing the one thing that truly shows your true value, your true net worth."

"What's that, Abraham?"

"Theodore, you are one of the smartest men in the world. Many call you a genius. And when one is given a gift, one should share that gift and do things that benefit the greater good of the whole world, not just the one percent. You see, men have prospered for hundreds and thousands of years. Did you know that Solomon was the richest man in the world and considered the wisest man in the world?"

"Abraham, isn't that the guy who had over seven hundred wives and three hundred mistresses?"

"Someone's been reading, Theodore."

"No, Abraham. Small talk at the country club amongst guys."

"Well, anyway, Theodore, you have so many gifts that could benefit so many people. Yet here you are back in your car, and on your way back to the big city while you make another deal for money that you don't even need. That sound about right."

"I don't get you people. Black pickup trucks, successful people who all move to a small town to do what, give up their lives, all that they worked for and for what. To have a simple life. And here's the irony of that. While they are in that small town, the whole world does not get to benefit from their talents, their abilities, and their influence. J.J. inspired many kids, male and female that they could make it to the NBA. Ruby was an inspiration to little girls who could dream about being her one day. And C.J., an African American makes partner at the top investment firm in the country, if not the world. Then takes a small-town church and turns it into a megachurch that converted over ten thousand people to a religion that I don't understand, and frankly don't believe in. Abraham, explain to me how going off the grid benefited anyone but the three of them? Was it the simple life or guilt that took them out of the game? You see, the difference between them and me is I admit I am a taker, they don't."

"Don't let me stop you, Theodore, go on."

"Well, look at J.J. Where was the holier than thou talk when he was signing a multi-million-dollar contract, plus a multi-million-dollar shoe contract. And the impact of those two things. Tickets that his normal fans can't afford and jerseys and shoes that cost the average person almost half a week's work. But I'm the bad guy. And Ruby, she was gentrification before it became a thing. And where did all those people end up. Homeless, involuntarily relocated, and in some cases uprooted from their homes. And I'm the BAD GUY!"

"So, Theodore, as the richest man in the world, what do you propose they do. Continue to live a life that is all about money and nothing else."

"You see, Abraham, that's where your blind spot is, no disrespect."

"None taken but go ahead."

"You see, a man once told me that you can either be a giver or a taker. And it just seems to me that the takers live much better than the givers and have larger bank accounts. And after they get those large bank accounts, they can give back. I mean, I have a foundation that provides scholarships to needy students in Houston and my foundation feeds over a thousand families every Thanksgiving."

"And that makes you feel good, does it Theodore?"

"No, it does not make me feel good. It makes me a smart businessman. And I am happy to do it. I have never complained about the efforts of my company to be philanthropic but if I listen to you, I should be doing more, and I could do that if……"

"If you were the first trillionaire?"

"Well, yes, what's so wrong with that?"

"Theodore, we live in a world that has advanced in so many ways. The only catch is that this was not part of the original plan."

"And what plan is that?"

"That the technology, and all the advancements would lead us to where we are today."

"Which is?"

"On the brink of an international collapse. One that if not managed could lead us to the end of the world as we know it. You see, a trillion dollars can change the world. And if a guy like you were to sacrifice your riches for the greater good of the world, imagine the impact of what that would do to others who are just like you. You might get people to change. I mean you move whole markets by just buying three shares in a company. You let it leak that you have an interest in a company, and the stock goes up."

"What do you propose, Abraham, that I give it all away. And how do you know it will do anything?"

"I don't but I think it's worth a try."

Rich Men Have No Friends

"Abraham, I tried this before, I mean I looked into it and it just does not work."

"How do you know that?"

"My old neighborhood. I thought about revitalizing my old neighborhood when I first started making money. And you know what I found out. That it never works. I mean you save a few, but the habits of the neighborhood never change, and it just reverts to itself eventually."

"So, we give up, Theodore. We just don't do anything?"

"No, we do what we can, and we move on. I mean, if people want to make it, they can and will. And if they don't, well that's a YP not a MP."

"No, Theodore, that is both our problem. My job is to convince them that there is a greater good that lives inside of all of us, and your job is to show them that someone cares. You have been given a gift and you have an obligation to share that gift. Not hoard it to make a list that only means something to the four hundred people on it. You do know that most of the world has no clue about this list and don't even read the magazine it's published in. Just like most people don't understand what it's like to have so much money, that you don't have a worry in the world. I mean, until now. You see, Theodore, these folks are richer than you may think."

"I don't understand, Abraham. You are confusing me. First, you tell me because I am rich, I can do so much good for the world. Then you tell me that being rich is not good for the world. Which is it?"

"Both, if you are a true capitalist, then you understand what your responsibility is as a capitalist. If you are just a greedy rich guy trying to be the greediest rich guy in the world, then you are not a capitalist anymore. You're just a guy with a lot of money and nothing to show for it. And one day when that most matters, your money won't be able to do a thing for you." And then it hit Theodore.

"Like when Amy died."

"Exactly, Theodore. With all your money, all you could do once you found out about your little girl was grieve. You could not bring her back to life, you could not call in a favor, all you could do is grieve. And for once in your life, you were the poorest man on earth. Because you had nothing of value that you could trade, buy, borrow, or steal to bring her back. And when you traded your car for my truck, I thought you understood that. But for the first time in my very long time on this planet, I had been fooled into believing you were starting to change. When I met you at the convenience store, it was not by accident. It was not coincidence, but providence. But your heart has been so hardened over all these years, that you can't see what you are doing to yourself. You are living with a lot of baggage and it's time to let go."

"What baggage, what are you talking about?

"I am talking about the death of your mother, the death of the pimp, now the death of your daughter. The sons you never talk to. The best friend that you never forgave for sleeping with a woman that you weren't even in love with. And then you shut yourself off from the world and made Shelley your go between. So, there you have it, the richest man in the world lives in complete isolation when the rest of the world needs him for more than a place on a list that they know nothing about."

"Abraham, how do you know so much about me?"

"Theodore, it's my job to know about you. I am your guardian angel. You see, you think you did all this all by yourself. And you feel like you are carrying so many people, I mean you do have indirect responsibility for over one hundred thousand employees. And that is appreciated. More than you may know. But here we are at a crossroads in your life, where you get to make new choices. And given what you have been through in the past few weeks, everyone would understand. But if you are not ready, then it's time for you to get on the road."

"My guardian angel, what are you talking about? I don't believe in angels, or…."

"God, I know, Theodore, I know you don't believe. But let me ask you one question and if you can answer it, you are free to go. And if you can't, then you must go back to Greensburgh and give it one more day. Deal?"

"No deal, but what is your question?"

"Theodore, how did you accumulate all the wealth you have now?"

"What?"

"How did you, all by yourself accumulate all your wealth?"

"I am not sure how to answer that."

"And do you know why that is?"

Rich Men Have No Friends

"No, tell me."

Abraham would not answer the question, and Theodore did not know the answer. A simple question could not be answered by Theodore. He was so caught up in his wealth that he had long forgotten that if not for the environment he grew up in, no matter how dysfunctional it was, he would not have had the drive and grit to do well in school. Had it not been for Pierre, he might not have been so driven to succeed in helping his once best friend. And if not for his mother, he would not have learned how to be street smart which had helped him survive a rough childhood. And if not for his daughter, he would not have learned to love again. And if he had not met Shelley, he might not have ever trusted someone again. In other words, a village had been behind him, and an angel named Abraham had been watching over him the entire time. But in his world, you don't remember how you got there or who helped you. You just believe that you did it all by yourself. And that was the reason Theodore could not be reasoned with.

"I tell you what, Abraham. I will go back to Greensburgh. On one condition, you tell me the answer to the question the next time I see you. Deal."

"That's not how this works, Theodore. I am not a negotiator. I don't do deals. I am what you would call in your world, a handler. I take care of things on behalf of...., well, it's neither here nor there. You would not understand anyway."

"Well, can I at least have the truck back? The folks there seemed to like me better when I was in the truck, and not the Bentley. "

Miraculously, the flat tire was no longer flat. And Abraham had a big smile on his face. Maybe, just maybe, Theodore had been listening after all.

"Theodore."

"Yes, Abraham."

"When you get back to Greensburgh, listen to the people. I mean really listen. And Theodore."

"Yes, Abraham."

"Drive safe, and there's someone waiting on you in the truck."

Phineas McNabb

Theodore walked over to the truck, and to his surprise there was Mr. Wimples. "What the he…." He turned around and to his surprise the Bentley and Abraham were gone. He never heard the car start, and not a sound, not a cloud of dust, nothing. Who was this guy? Theodore still did not believe.

Rich Men Have No Friends

39

As Theodore was making his way back to Greensburgh to give the town another chance, Shelley was back in Houston trying to figure out how to move forward. She had always been his trusted assistant, carrying out his orders and for that reason, she always felt she did not have any blood on her hands. What she did not understand was that just because you did not get out of the getaway car, that does not mean that you are not an accomplice to the crime.

In her case, being an accomplice was part of the larger plan to change a man whose heart was hardening to the point of no return. In other words, if he did not change his ways, then the entire world and its ultimate demise or strength to carry on was resting on his shoulders. She had been put in her position for a reason and Abraham had allowed it to happen.

Several years back, when her coffee shop was on the brink of collapse, a man pulled up in front and he was driving a 1978 Black Ford pickup truck. It was the final week before her closing, and she and her staff were in a funk. After all, they had been successful until the coffee shop across the street opened.

On this cool day in November, the sky was gray and there was a light but consistent rain coming down out of the sky. The streets were busy, but no one was coming into the shop. Most if not all her customers had started to frequent the other shop. The lower prices and extended hours had long passed her ability to keep afloat. This day, she sent all the staff home with pay. She felt they could move on with life if she assisted them with as much time as possible to look for other employment. As she was wiping down the counters and pondering what happened to her shop, tears started to flow down her cheeks. "Why me, Lord? I did the right thing. I left the money and the titles behind. My staff was my family. We did good by people. So why us. It does not make sense to me. Please help me understand."

Shelley had her back turned to the door and while she was talking to herself, a voice came into her ear from nowhere. "I need you to help me with something." She was startled by the voice given she had just been talking to herself and asking The Lord for guidance and understanding. She looked up at the roof of the shop and said, "What was that? What did you say?" And the voice said this time "Ms., can you assist me?" And then she felt a finger touch her shoulder. She leaped around and there was Abraham in his overalls, plaid shirt, boots and baseball hat.

"Oh, it's a customer, for a moment there I thought it was…"

"Who did you think it was, Shelley?"

"Hey, how do you know my name, sir?"

"It's on your name tag, Shelley. You, okay? I mean, I can come back."

"No sir, I can help you. Been a long day and I can't wait for it to end unfortunately."

"I'm sorry to hear that. Can I have a cup of decaf, black, no sugar, no cream please?"

"Sure, I can get that right up for you. Are you from around here? I don't recognize you."

"I'm not from anywhere in particular but this is my territory. I am like a salesman, but you don't buy what I am offering. I give it away. I meet people, get to know them, and if they like what I tell them, I give them something. Plain and simple."

"Hey, that sounds kinda shady, I think I need you to leave my establishment. I did not get your name by the way." Shelley was the child of military parents, and they had taught her that book sense without common sense was nonsense and book smarts without street smarts will get you killed.

"My name is Abraham, and there is nothing shady about me, Shelley. You know you are a long way from home. What brought you here from North Carolina? Fayetteville is a nice little town; my peer works that area."

"Okay, now this is getting weird. Who exactly are you, Abraham? And what do you really want?"

"Time, Shelley, just a few minutes of your time. The world needs more people like you, and I am here to tell you not to give up. I know your shop is closing in a few days, but I don't want you to give up."

"Why do you think I am giving up?"

"Well, your staff is looking for jobs but what have you been doing with your time? I mean have you started a job search for yourself."

"Abraham, I have not really thought about it. I put a lot of sweat and energy into this shop. This was my baby. You see I left the corporate grind to open this shop. And I am disappointed that it did not make it."

"So, why didn't you relocate to another area that had no competition directly in front of it? I mean, why did you stay and try to compete with the biggest player in the market?"

"Because I thought my loyal customers would stay loyal. The only guy who keeps coming in regularly is Mr. Hightower. He has been my most loyal customer all these years. I'm going to miss him. And I will miss my employees greatly. It just is not right, Abraham. How do you realize the American dream if someone is always coming along and trying to crush that dream? Not for me, but for the employees that I paid well, and gave them a decent living wage so that they too could live the American dream. It's just not right. I prayed on it but I guess my prayers fell on deaf ears."

"I would say just the opposite, Shelley. Your prayers were heard, but you are looking for a specific outcome and that is not how it works. The process is not for you to define but instead it is a process, nevertheless. But your prayers were heard."

"How do you know that, Abraham? I mean what are you, some guardian Angel from above."

"You could say that. Remember me saying that I give people something and it does not cost them anything?"

At this point, Shelley was confused but for some strange reason, Abraham had her full attention. He had made her stop and really pay attention to what he was saying. Although to this point, he had not said anything specific, he had in fact been very specific in his responses to her. And how did he know. She kept talking to him.

"Yes, I remember."

"Well, I am here to give you hope. I was driving by, noticed the sign saying you were closing in a few days, saw one employee inside and decided I wanted a cup of coffee. Now I could have gone across the street. I mean look at the place, all the bells and whistles, packed to the max, and everyone seems to be genuinely happy over there, right?"

"Well, yes, they do."

"But they don't have what this coffee shop has."

"And what's that, Abraham. What is that? I really want to know. Because counting you, I have had two customers today and that place has been moving since first thing this morning. What is it this shop has they don't have?"

"You, Shelley. They don't have you. Take a closer look at that shop and tell me what you see."

"I don't understand. People are going in and getting coffee and going their merry way. And the drive thru is packed with cars. So, what I see is a very successful business, Abraham."

"Right, but you don't see a coffee shop, Shelley. You see a business. Bring them in, take their order, and get them out. Make money. That's all that matters."

"How do you know that, Abraham?"

"I was just over there. Walked in, no one paid my any attention. I stood in line with people who were more consumed with themselves or just doing their job. No interaction, no Good Morning, just Can I Help You. That shop is full of people, but it lacks life, Shelley. It lacks life."

"And you are saying my shop has life. From where I stand, Abraham, I would say it is on its last legs."

"Shelley, you have taken the time to talk to me today, correct?"

"Yes, but...."

"No buts, you have taken the time to talk to me and get to know me. You have called me by my name the entire time we have been engaged in conversation. You mentioned another customer by name, a Mr. Hightower. That is because you are more than a barista, you are a people person and that's what made your shop highly successful."

"Then what happened, Abraham. Please enlighten me."

"Money hurt you, plain and simple."

"What do you mean money hurt me?"

"Those people across the street were so concerned about getting a better deal that they missed the whole point of your shop."

"Which is...."

"To serve the people, Shelley. You are a giver, Shelley. You were a top-notch consultant whose star was rising every year. You walked away from the salary, the perks, the stock options, and that life to open a coffee shop. A shop that benefited your employees and your customers in ways you may not fully understand. You were able to provide a service, and you were a faithful servant to the end. It's just that we live in a society that values money, a better bargain, and little to no interaction more than a good cup of coffee with a nice barista who happens to care about her employees and her customers. It was never about the money for you, was it?"

"Well yes, I mean no. I don't know what I mean."

"Shelley, how much were you making a year when you walked away from corporate America three years ago or so?"

"Well, that's personal but let's just say it was about one hundred fifty thousand dollars a year in salary alone."

"And what have you paid yourself since opening the shop?"

"I paid myself five thousand a month gross which amounts to about thirty-five hundred net. So about sixty thousand dollars a year. But what does that have to do with anything?"

"And why did you take the huge pay cut, Shelley? I mean that is a significant pay cut. Ninety thousand a year gone. And to open a coffee shop that you knew going in may or may not make it. But why did you really do it?"

"I wanted my life back. I was working seventy hours a week, traveling all the time. And on the weekends, I was too tired to enjoy the money. And I worked with people who I could no longer relate to. You see, my parents brought me up to appreciate the small things. And I was getting caught up. The nicest dresses, the nicest shoes, expensive purses. My car was costing me eight hundred dollars a month and I barely had time to drive it other than to work. It just was not fun anymore. And every client I visited only wanted to know how to cut costs. We never really engaged in how to make the product better, or service the client better, or find ways to be efficient to pay the employee more. It was always about the bottom line of the organization. I saw nothing wrong with that, it just wasn't me anymore."

"So, you left to open a coffee shop so that you could have your life back?"

"Yes, I think that sums it up correctly."

"And that is why you closed every day at four o'clock even though given your background you knew this may come back to haunt you one day. And you also knew that paying your employees a higher-than-normal wage plus a share of the profits annually might come back to haunt you as well."

"Yes, I knew that. But what's your point, Abraham?"

Phineas McNabb

"My point is you are confirming why in your past job the expectation was to affect the bottom line and nothing else. You were put out of the coffee business because you could not compete. Money drove the train, and that train is a powerful locomotive that left the tracks a long time ago. There is a fine line between capitalism and greed. I think we live in a society of unintended greed that we sell as capitalism. You, Shelley, were a capitalist, but you could not compete with the greedy shop across the street. Have you noticed that their prices are starting to go up again?"

"I did not until you just mentioned it. But I do remember someone stopping by and telling me that all the free stuff they were giving away and the lower prices were becoming a thing of the past."

"And you know why that is, Shelley. Come on, you're a smart person. Why is that?"

"Once they drive out the competition, then they can set whatever price they want, eliminate the perks, put on a façade of customer service that is not really about the customer, and push the profit straight to their bottom line. They priced me out the market and the real loser will ultimately be the consumer."

"And, Shelley, ultimately, they take the life out of the shop and the customer and reduce it to a business transaction. Your shop understood the business transaction is a direct result of fair pricing, paying employees a fair wage, and taking care of your customer. That's why you took the pay cut. You knew when you started that you did not need one hundred fifty thousand dollars a year to meet your needs. You needed it to meet your wants. But sixty thousand dollars allowed you to meet your needs and you paid your staff a fair wage to meet their needs as well. Make sense. The American Dream at its best."

"I do understand that, Abraham, but what's your point?"

"In this country, there is a new attitude that we have of everything must be cheap, give me the cheapest price possible. Well, that's a double-edged sword. You can get it cheap, but I can't pay my people that much, and then don't expect to receive a high level of customer service. It is a vicious cycle of dependencies that break down as soon as money becomes the sole driver."

Shelley was getting a lesson she had long since learned many years ago. Not in school, but from her parents. Treat others as you would want to be treated. And she done that. She paid herself a fair wage just as she did her staff. She treated her customers the way she wanted to be treated. And she wanted a profit, but not one that did not allow participation from her staff or one that would reduce the level of customer service or products she was serving. But that thought process ultimately put her out of business.

"Abraham, I appreciate you coming by today. You brought perspective that I never would have thought about. My shop was very successful, and I was doing the right thing. My business model worked, but when money became the only thing that mattered, well the model did not work anymore. And if money was going to be the only driver for me, well, then, I am okay going out of business. Sucks for my staff, though."

"Not really, Shelley. You showed them a different way to approach business. And if they take that to their next job, then that's one more person doing it the right way versus just going through the motions and getting through their day. You see, you are a salesman as well. And you offered your staff and your customers something money can't buy. And that is hope."

"Thanks, Abraham. Hey, why do you drive that old truck?"

"It gets me where I need to go, and it has no payment. It also reminds me of a time when material things were not as important. You should look at it. Runs really well."

"Let me look at that truck, Abraham. And Abraham?"

"Yes."

"I don't know who you are, but I have a feeling that you know who I am and for that I appreciate you stopping in today. You really gave me hope again. I think I will be just fine. Now, about this truck….."

Shelley would go outside with Abraham. She would laugh at the old radio in the truck, and the fact that the windows had to be rolled down by hand. This truck was old but had a certain appeal to it. She admired it and admired it. Finally, Abraham gave it to her. Right there on the spot, he gave it to her. And as she got in it to start it, something strange happened.

Shelley opened the door as it made a creaky sound. She looked for the keys and they were on the floor on the driver's side. She started the truck, it backfired twice and then it made a nice humming sound. She turned to give Abraham a thumbs up and he was nowhere to be found. When she went to pick up the keys, he had quietly strolled off into the crowd. Or had he?

She would go home, come back the next day and announce to her staff that the shop was closing for good and that she would pay them for the rest of the month. She also told them they had done the right thing, to hold their heads high, and take what they learned to their next venture.

Not soon thereafter, Theodore would call her, and offer a job. She was going back to the lion's den. If she learned anything from Abraham, and she learned plenty, she learned that money made the world go around so she might as well take advantage of that. Except, this time, she was clear with Theodore. She only worked Monday through Friday in the office, and not later than five in the evening. She did not mind being on call, but she would have work life balance and if that did not work for him, she was not his person. He relented and gave her what she asked for. And paid her a salary that was more than she made as a consultant. This new job would require a lot of her, and compromise everything she had done in her coffee shop. But there was a bigger picture. She needed to stay on mission.

Her reason for joining Theodore's staff had been predetermined by fate. And it was Theodore who caused it with a selfish act that would ultimately benefit Shelley more than it would benefit him.

Rich Men Have No Friends

40

It is Tuesday a little after noon. Theodore is in route back to Greensburgh. He told Abraham he would go back and stay one more day. One more day was all that would be needed to help him understand what it really meant to be the richest man in the world. The death of his daughter had affected him, but not enough to keep him from his goal. To become a trillionaire. And C.J. would be the cornerstone of making that happen. Maybe they could grab dinner tonight.

He spoke to Mr. Wimples, put on his seatbelt, and made the U-turn to head back to Greensburgh. He was about twelve miles out. He had not gone far when he surprisingly ran into Abraham, again. The truck looked the same although he was amazed that it had miraculously recovered from being broken down just this morning when he left town in his Bentley.

"Well, Mr. Wimples, we are headed back to this one stop light town for another day. And why, I don't know. But if it will help you adjust to not having Amy around anymore, I will do it for you." This was the first real sign that Theodore was not coping as well as he thought with the accident. He was projecting himself through a teddy bear. In other words, Mr. Wimples had become his good side while he still dealt with the dark side of his personality.

"So, what did you and Abraham talk about? I know, right. Who is he to tell me what to do with my money and about the greater good of man? He acts like he has a direct line to the man upstairs. I mean, assuming there is a man upstairs. Anyway, I did not fall for it. How about you?"

Mr. Wimples just stared at the dashboard, and as Theodore's faithful sidekick, he said nothing.

"I could not agree with you more. I mean the nerve of that guy."

As he was getting closer to Greensburgh, he saw a man walking down the side of the road. He was a white man, in his late forties, with a long beard and long hair. He had a black and brown German Sheppard on a leash. His pants were camouflage and tucked inside his boots. He had on a green shirt and a black hat that read US ARMY Veteran. He had a large backpack with what appeared to be a sleeping bag neatly rolled and sitting on top. His boots were jet black and had a shine that would cause you to see your reflection, like glass. On his backpack was a patch with an eagle's head on it and above it was the words Airborne. Theodore did not have a clue what that meant but he assumed the guy was trying to get somewhere. He checked his rearview mirror and slowed down beside the gentleman.

"Hey, where you headed today?"

"Greensburgh, Texas. I must be there by three today."

"I'm headed that way. Need a lift?"

"No, I am good. Thanks for asking, Sir."

"What's this Sir stuff. The name is Ted, Ted Hightower."

"Thanks, Ted, but I am good. I don't ride with strangers. Longstanding policy and not trying to break it today. Dynamite likes the fresh air." (Dynamite was his dog.)

"Are you sure about that? I really am headed that way with my friend here. He does not talk much though."

"Look, Sir, I don't want any trouble. Just need to be on my way and I suggest you do the same."

"I tell you what…."

At that point, the stranger reached into his belt buckle under his shirt and pulled a gun, a black Glock pistol and pointed at Theodore.

"Sir, I am going to tell you for the last time. Please move out. I am fine and my dog is fine. What we don't need is some serial killer riding around with a teddy bear in his front seat trying to lure me into his vehicle." Theodore by this time had slammed on the brakes, put the truck in park and raised both his hands away from the steering wheel.

"Look, I did not get your name……"

"Pete. Pete Dawkins, Sir."

"Well, look here, Pete. The man who gave me this truck said that I need to learn to give more and take less. All I am trying to give you is a ride into town. The teddy bear belonged to my daughter who passed away a couple of weeks ago. And as for being a serial killer, that is not who I am either. I'm just a guy on his way to Greensburgh trying to complete a mission that this man sent me on." Here is where it really got awkward for Theodore.

"Is this man's name Abraham, sir?"

"It is, but how do you know Abraham?" Theodore was really starting to get curious about Abraham.

Rich Men Have No Friends

"I met him several weeks ago in my hometown. I am from Luckspeak, Oklahoma, sir. I ran into him one night and he nearly saved my life. He was driving a truck just like this one."

"And he did not try to give it to you." Theodore smiled as he was being sarcastic. He still did not understand the meaning of these black trucks.

"Oh, no sir, he tried to give me his truck. But I had nothing to give him in return. And I don't like to owe people anything. He left it in front of my folks house for a couple of days and then one day it was gone again."

"I tell you what, we can ride together, and you can tell me all about your chance meeting with Abraham. I am still trying to figure the guy out. Has me totally baffled. Not sure why he keeps popping up. "

"He's an angel, sir. Your guardian angel. Did he not tell you that?"

"He did, but I don't believe in angels, well except for my daughter, Amy. She was my angel."

"Yes sir, well I guess I will take that ride after all. Come on Dynamite. Let's get in this nice fella's truck. I am tired anyway. It was a long trip trying to get here. Luckspeak is about five hundred miles from here."

"Get in, Pete. You can tell me the story on the way."

"Yes, sir."

"Ted, call me Ted."

"Okay, Ted."

Pete would get in the truck and dynamite would get in the rear cab area. They were on their way to Greensburgh. Ted was thinking to himself why people keep coming to this little town in Texas. What is drawing them all there? Is it some divine prophecy that all rich people move to Greensburgh? Apparently not because this homeless fellow with the shiny boots was headed there as well.

"Pete, what brings you to this part of the country anyway? Besides meeting Abraham. I mean what really pushed you to come all this way?"

"It was fate, sir. You see, the town I am from is slowly dying from the inside. All the jobs are gone, and all that is left is older folks like my parents and the people who can't leave. Many of them have turned to drugs, sir, I mean Ted. And it is killing my little hometown. The only town I have ever known. I spent twenty years in the military and

Phineas McNabb

when I returned home after retiring, it was not my hometown anymore." After twenty years in the military, calling someone sir or ma'am was a habit for Pete. It was the ultimate sign of respect, something that was becoming extinct in society.

"Why do you think that is?"

"The drugs, sir. The drugs are killing the town or rather finishing the job. Ever since the paper mill closed, the town has not been the same. That paper mill was everything to my hometown. Employed over two thousand people. Everyone in town worked at the papermill. Husbands and wives, eventually their kids, and their grandkids once they became adults. It was the main economic driver in town. If you did not go off to the military, or go off to college, then the paper mill was a good third option. And when that option went away, the young folks had nowhere to go but to the drugs and that life. Crime is way up in Luckspeak and it was not like that just ten years ago."

"When did the plant close?"

"Three years ago, sir. Now it is an old, abandoned building that is surrounded by a large chain link fence. The mayor tried to get some companies to look at Luckspeak, but you know how it is today. You can't get anyone to move to a small town in America anymore. One layoff, and you are stuck in a town with very limited options unless you live close to a big city like Houston, Atlanta, and those types of cities. Real shame too."

"Why do you say that, Pete?"

"Because those small towns and the people in them are the backbone of this country, Ted. There used to be a saying in one of those commercials that the thing that makes America is baseball, apple pie, and Chevrolet. When I left home, I knew my neighbors and we all looked out for each other. When I returned home from the military, it was like a totally different town. And frankly, it broke my heart, Ted."

Theodore was hearing a story that he could not relate to. He had grown up in a rough part of Houston, so for him hearing a guy be almost in mourning for his hometown was a foreign concept to him. And he had a penthouse that was fifty floors in the sky where all he could see was land, and buildings for miles. He had built himself a heaven on earth isolated from the world. And based on what Pete was talking about, that was why he had become the richest man in the world. So that he could get as far away from what sounded like a depressing life as possible. What he did not realize was he was now the cause of it, at least in the case of LakeSpeak and Greensburgh. He was not aware of that, but it would be revealed to him.

"Pete, what was the name of the company, the papermill company?"

"Siaptic Paper Company, one of the largest paper producers in the country at one time. The name of the company was Siaptic, Ted. Jobs paid well; they were paying fifteen dollars an hour to start when I left here twenty years ago to go into the military. The top pay was twenty-five dollars an hour for a shift supervisor, quality control expert or someone who had at least fifteen years on the job. And the union really took care of the people. I mean you could not ask for a better place to work. But then one day they told me the big bosses came in, told everyone the jobs were being sent overseas and the plant was being closed. Said something about efficiencies gained through automation and cheaper labor."

Theodore was very familiar with Siaptic. He was the person behind that closure. He had negotiated a deal to buy the company outright, and then sold the company to a company in South America who were already in the paper business.

Made two hundred million on that deal. He had never, ever spoken directly to someone who could tell him what the real domino effect of his actions was. He assumed that people were resilient like him and would simply bounce back.

But they did not have his money, his education, and more importantly his ability to live his life where home was wherever he paid cash and liked the amenities. For the folks of LuckSpeak, home was family reunions, Friday Night Football, the county fair, and front porches, iced tea and lemonade, and a local church that baptized everybody in town. There was no bounce back in a one employer town. When the plant left, the town lost its heart. And everyone knows that a body can't survive without its heart. Ted was indirectly responsible for the town's current plight. It was an unintended consequence.

They knew if you worked hard, and the plant was productive, the doors would stay open. It did not work like that anymore. If the work can be done for a cheaper rate elsewhere, then that is where the work went. And that created a lot of resentment in a town of mostly blue-collar workers who were second and third generation plant workers. Regardless of race, or background, the town was stronger because of the plants and that was what made this country great.

"Pete, you know that it was going to happen. It was just a matter of time. Those jobs would have been outsourced to keep prices down for the consumers here, that being you. If those jobs stayed here, then the cost of paper would have continued to rise to the point it would become unaffordable."

"Okay, Ted, now you sound like a politician trying to get my vote. That's hogwash and you know it."

"How is that hogwash?"

"Because if that were true, then why do we have so many billionaires and millionaires in this country. Don't' get me wrong, I am for the American Dream, and I want to see any man or woman realize their full potential. I spent twenty years in the military, and I get a nice pension, so I am not complaining but come on, a billion dollars in the bank. And I hear that the richest man in the world has over three hundred billion dollars, but he can't pay his people a fair wage and create jobs here in the United States."

"It's not that simple, Pete."

"Why not, why I bet to keep that plant open in LuckSpeak was probably no more than twenty or thirty million dollars tops. And that is a lot less than a billion dollars."

"Pete let's take that a little further. You said the people made fifteen dollars an hour if they had at least 15 years, right."

"Yes sir. And twenty-five dollars was top pay."

"So, let's just use your fifteen dollars and hour as a starting point. Just use that number which equates to about thirty-one thousand dollars a year, give or take, and that's not including benefits. And with over two thousand employees, that comes to roughly sixty million dollars a year in employee expenses alone. You said they had a union too, right."

"Yep, both my parents were in the union. The union got them a nice pension, sixty percent of their last three years' average pay. Together they get about sixty thousand dollars a year in pensions. "

"So that's another dynamic. How many people in town retired from the plant, Pete?"

Rich Men Have No Friends

"I don't know, of the ones still alive, there may two or three hundred collecting a pension."

"So that's another nine million or so dollars. All in with pensions and assuming the lowest rate of pay, that's about seventy-five million dollars a year."

"But is that sustainable, Pete. And if we assume everyone stays until they retire, then in the fifteenth year, everyone is making twenty-five dollars an hour, then we start knocking on one hundred million dollars. You see Pete, when the plant was first built some fifty or so years ago, the starting pay was probably in the single digits and the plant could make money. But it's hard to turn a profit when you have a one hundred million dollar spend. That's a billion every ten years just for employee expenses alone. That's tough for a company trying to make money in today's economy where competition is on every corner."

"You said a billion every ten years, right, Ted."

"I did."

"So, if the richest man in the world is worth one hundred billion dollars, he by himself could have kept the plant open another ten or twenty years and still have a lot of money left over, more than he will ever need. Or spent the money to create new opportunities for my townsfolk. Because the town is gone now. And what's left is a travesty, and it hurts me to see that. That's my home and I love it."

"It's not that simple, Pete. We live in a global economy now. And goods are manufactured where it makes the most sense financially to keep costs down. That's not a politician speaking but a guy who understands how the business world works." Ted did not want Pete to know who he really was. But he was giving Pete a quick lesson in economics.

"Look, Pete, it would have been ideal to keep that plant open, but the wages were just too high to sustain the plant and for the company to make a decent profit. I mean, I hear you, and no one wants a town to have the breath kicked out of it. And no one wants a drug problem as the alternative to hard working people who want to do a good job. I mean everyone is not cut out for college or the military and there should be a third option, I can't argue that. Anyway, we are coming into town now. Where are you headed."

"Greenspoint Village. My new home is waiting on me."

Phineas McNabb

"What new home?"

"Well, you see, Ted, there are people who still believe in the American dream and there is this pastor here in town, Pastor Johnson, they call him C.J and he has created a program for veterans like me. He is going to give me a home and a vehicle. All I must do is take a job in town for a fair wage and be a contributor to the community. What a concept, huh?" Pete was being sarcastic, and Ted heard him loud and clear. What was C.J. up to now?

"There it is up on the left. That's where I am going. 1622 Cascade Street. Should see it on the right as soon as you enter the neighborhood. "Theodore made the left turn and sure enough, it was the first house on the right.

He had seen this neighborhood when he was driving in with Mr. Wimples the day before. He pulled in the driveway and in the driveway was a black 1978 Ford Pickup truck and there was a red ribbon on the front door of the house. It was a yellow one story three-bedroom house, about one thousand twelve hundred square feet, with a nice front porch with three chairs just to the right of the front door. Above the number was a handmade sign that said Dawkins. And who should be standing on the front porch. It was C.J. and Sarah.

"Well, there's our new foreman. Pete, how you doing, man? How was your trip down?" C.J. ran up to Pete and gave him a big hug followed by Sarah. Dynamite had jumped out of the truck and had run to the backyard. Ted exited the truck as well. His curiosity was at an all-time high. What was the preacher up to now?

"I am good, Pastor. Mrs. Johnson, I presume?"

"It is, I have heard so much about you Pete. We are so glad you are here."

"Pete, everything is ready for you, and I know you are tired. Why don't you go in? Sarah can show you where everything is." Sarah and Pete went into the house with Dynamite in tow. Mr. Wimples was patiently waiting in the truck.

"Well, look who decided to come back and give us another chance. Ted, I thought you left but I see my friend persuaded you to stay. Welcome back."

"Look, C.J. I don't understand what is going on, but I must ask this. What's the deal with this Pete fellow? I mean he's not rich like the rest of you so what gives here?"

Rich Men Have No Friends

"You see, Ted, you immediately want to know what the money angle is. And in this case, there is a money angle but not what you think. Pete is a veteran."

"I know that, but what does that have to do with Greensburgh?"

"Pete is a veteran of three tours overseas to include Desert Storm. He got out of the service after he did his twenty years. He tried to go back home but it reminded him too much of the towns from the war zones he had left behind."

"I think that is a bit extreme, C.J. An old town that unfortunately lost its way when the paper mill closed is not like a war zone. I mean come on. This is America."

"Okay, Ted, let's break that down where we both can understand where Pete is coming from, okay. That's fair, isn't it." One thing Theodore would learn is not to argue with a pastor who also used to be an investment banker.

"First, all the jobs left. Then the plant became an eyesore to the town and eventually a rundown old, abandoned building. Now you have a town that is a shell of itself with no economic viability and a lot of economic casualties, in this case the people who are on government assistance and many who turn to drugs to try and get through the day. You see why to Pete that reminds him of things he saw overseas. He is not talking about war zones, but poor people with no way forward."

"Come on, Pastor. They have a choice. They can leave, I did. I was not born with a silver spoon in my mouth. I worked for everything I got. Hell, you had a better life than me. I am living proof that you can break the cycle."

"And you did, Ted. But then what did you do once you broke the cycle?"

"I don't follow."

"You have all this wealth, and so do I. I get it. But that wealth can't solve what pains you and I the most, the pain we will have for the rest of our lives. The loss of my parents and the loss of your daughter. I mean I know what you are going through, not as a dad, but as a son. I was so busy chasing money and the life, I forgot to go home one holiday. I mean, one holiday. And had I gone home as I always did, my parents might still be here today." Ted did not like what he was hearing, but he knew C.J. was right.

Phineas McNabb

"And my Amy might be here as well. I missed one birthday in five years. And now she's gone. And you're right. The money, the life, all that does not mean as much to me anymore. But what am I supposed to do? I mean seriously, if I don't keep busy, I will lose my mind."

"Ted, do you know what Pete is doing for us?"

"No, what?"

"He was part of an engineer battalion and they helped to rebuild towns in the countries that we fought in as part of the rebuilding efforts. He is good with heavy equipment and can drive anything from a forklift to a bulldozer. We offered him a job in return for a home and this nice black truck. You see, Ted, I can't give up. I understand math, and I know the uphill battle I am fighting. But if no one cares, and I just hoard all that money, then I am doing a disservice to Pete, to all I believe in and my parents."

"So, how do you do this then. Why start with the veterans first?"

"Ted, we had to start somewhere and in the case of Pete, he has known skills that will help to build this community. And he has contacts all over the country that he believes he can recruit to come here and help us with this. I can't save LuckSpeak, but I can revitalize Greensburgh. And who knows, if we are successful, we will move to another town, and maybe it is Luckspeak. So, we are building a community for veterans who want to grow Greensburgh and bring it back to what it once was."

"One problem, C.J. What happens when there are no more homes to build? Then what? I was trying to tell Pete this during the ride over. Unfortunately, a global economy and competition have created a situation where trying to revitalize towns that are no longer viable is a challenging venture. And frankly, not worth the investment. But I admire what you are doing. And if anyone can do it, it's you, the Rockstar of Wall Street."

"Ted, what are you going to do with all that money you have? I mean if I work for you on a consulting basis, and I just double your wealth, then you will be worth more than a lot of small countries. What's the point, I mean really tell me what is the point? Sarah has me convinced we are chasing the wrong things." At that point, Pete came out of the house and picked up C.J. and gave him a bear hug.

Rich Men Have No Friends

"Pastor, this is great. I really appreciate you. I feel like the richest man in the world today. I am on cloud nine." Ted spoke up as he was confused.

"Pete, how can you feel like you are the richest man in the world. I mean, I don't understand. How are you able to say that and how do you qualify it and quantify it?"

"Well, Ted, don't know what all that means you are trying to say but here is the bottom line as you call it, I believe. I have a home, my dog, and a second chance at life. And I moved to a community that wants me here, somewhere I can call home and help others to call it home. All my basic needs are met, and I get to give back. Because you know it's better to be a giver than a taker. I should know. I gave twenty years of my life so that folks can enjoy all the freedoms that come with living in this country. And as the book says, it is better to give than receive." C.J. looked at Ted and smiled directly at him as did Sarah.

"What book says that, Pete?"

"This one." Pete pulled out a small pocket bible that he had carried with him his entire career. And in the front of it was a small indenture the size of a dime. His bible had saved his once left when a bullet pierced his vest and stopped when it met his bible.

"There are people that say that I when I was in the military I fought for the economic interests of this country and that is a true statement that has been taken out of context. But that includes every single citizen who has the same dream I had as a kid. To be productive value add to society. And not someone who takes from the system, but someone who gives back. You see whether you are rich or poor, if all you do is take, then we will have no givers. And when we have no givers left, we have no country. Get it. Corruption is bred from greed, not capitalism. Capitalism is a good thing. When used in the right way. I mean, look at what is happening in Greensburgh. And so, for that reason, Ted, I feel like the richest man in the world today. Not based on my net worth. If I go by that I am worth a couple of hundred dollars and my next pension check. But I have my spiritual wealth, my physical wealth, my mental wealth, and now my financial wealth is improving, and all my needs are being met. Not my wants, but my needs. Get it."

Theodore smiled. "I get it, Pete. I get it." Sarah and C.J both smiled at Pete and Ted. For the first time in his life, Theodore understood what it really meant to be the richest man in the world. And it had nothing to do with money.

They would all leave Pete at his new house. It had been a long day. Theodore would go back to the Motel, check in, and have the special at the Diner later that night. He would then visit J.J at the bar and he and C.J. would talk in the morning. He was getting it finally but had not fully given up on his request for the two of them to be business partners. He was not totally convinced to give it all up yet. But tomorrow he would be. And if he could not be convinced tomorrow, then all this was a lost cause.

Rich Men Have No Friends

41

It is now Tuesday night. Theodore falls asleep with Mr. Wimples right beside him. Mr. Wimples has provided him with some stability through these past two days. The only time Theodore was a little irritated, as demonstrated by his running the red light, was when Mr. Wimples went missing. One question he had never asked was how Abraham ended up with Mr. Wimples. It mattered not, they were back together again, and all was good. As Theodore fell off into a deep sleep, he had the strangest dream. It was about Amy.

Theodore is walking along the beach. The sky is blue, the water is blue and there is a slight breeze coming in off the water. This appears to be an island for as far as he looks; he sees blue water and nothing else. About seventy yards inward is a lot of palm trees and a mountain off in the distance that extends into the clouds. He is barefooted, has on a white linen short sleeve shirt and white linen pants. There are birds flying over of all shapes and colors. It is a very beautiful day.

As he continues to walk along the beach, he does not know why he is here but there is a calm about him that he has never felt in his life. This is not like any beach he has ever visited, and this island is not like any place he has ever been to before. Where is he and why are there no other people here with him? He continues to walk for what seems like miles; in the distance he sees a little girl who appears to be about five years old in a white bathing suit. She is building sandcastles without a care in the world. Beside her is a teddy bear with swimming trunks on that looks vaguely familiar. As Theodore gets closer, he recognizes the little girl. It is Amy. It is Amy.

Theodore takes off running. Amy is alive. She's alive. As he gets closer to her, she never looks up. He keeps running and finally he is standing five feet from her. And he begins to cry and then his cries turn to laughter and then finally a big smile. And then she speaks.

"Hello, Daddy."

"Hello, Angel. How have you been doing, Angel?"

"I'm fine, Daddy. How have you been doing, Daddy?"

The entire time Amy is talking to Theodore she does not look up but continues to play in the sand. He has not moved any closer to her because he is in a state of shock and does not know what to do. So, they talk.

"Daddy?"

"Yes, sweetheart."

"Why did you stop loving me?"

"What do you mean, Amy? You are my Angel, the most important thing to ever happen to me in my life. I've missed you."

"Then why did you miss my party, Daddy. That man told me you were the richest man in the world the day I fell in the pool."

"What man, Angel?"

"That man who drives the black truck, daddy. He was at the house that day. And he told me you were the richest man in the world."

"I am the richest man in the world, honey. Honey, what was the man's name?"

"He did not say, Daddy. I just know when he pulled me out the water, he told me you would be all right." What Theodore did not realize was that Amy was talking about something he would not understand given his beliefs or non-beliefs in Angels and such. Amy was dead by the time they found her. But her young soul was innocent, and the Angel was there to take her to a place that would be her permanent home.

"Why did he tell you that, Amy? Amy?"

"Daddy, I was lying beside the pool, and I asked the man where you were. He told me that it was time for me to go home. And I asked him who he was daddy. I told him my home was high in the sky and you could see the whole world, daddy And I told him I sometimes lived there with you."

Amy was talking about the penthouse. Theodore did not know that she cherished the time they spent in the penthouse together with Mr. Wimples. She thought she lived in the sky and that is what she would tell her friends.

Ted began to cry. His little girl had been visited by her guardian angel, Abraham, as she was passing away. He was there to take her to her permanent home, one where she would spend the rest of her eternal life never to die again.

"That's right Amy, we had a home that was in the sky. And it does not feel like home anymore now that you are not there with me."

"Daddy?" Why did you miss my birthday party? You have never missed a birthday party."

"Daddy was away on business honey."

Rich Men Have No Friends

"You were away on business daddy. Was it to make money so you could stay the richest man in the world?"

"Well, yes, I mean no, it's complicated Amy. It's complicated." More tears began to come down his cheeks. Ted had no answer for his little girl. She had asked one of the most brilliant business minds of his time a very basic question and he had no answer. Book sense without common sense is nonsense.

"Daddy, I don't understand. You are the richest man in the world, right."

"I am, honey. I am."

"And do you know why you are the richest man in the world, daddy."

"Why, Amy."

"Because you had me, and mommy, and my two brothers. That's what makes you the richest man in the world daddy. That's what the man told me who told me he was taking me home. I've been looking for you daddy. It's good you are here but you must go now, daddy. I will see you soon."

"No, Amy, I want to stay here with you. I miss you."

"I miss you too, Daddy, but it is time for you to go." At that point, in the distance was a woman dressed in a long flowing white dress, and she was barefooted. He could barely make her out for the tears coming out of his eyes.

He was distraught. Here was his Amy and he could see her but not hug her. He could do nothing but gaze at his beautiful daughter one last time. The woman waved at Amy.

"I must go, Daddy. My MeMaw is waiting for me. I miss you daddy. Please tell mommy that it's not her fault." Amy stood up, ran off into the distance, grabbed the hand of the woman in the white dress and waved at Theodore. Theodore did not know it but his mother's efforts to save the girls on the street had revived her. She had pretty much stop dealing and using drugs and would spend most of her time trying to get girls off the streets. And for that she had been rewarded with having a granddaughter that she never knew. She had died many years before Amy was born. But they were now together.

"Amy, wait, I miss you. Wait, Angel, wait for Daddy." At that point he picked up the teddy bear that she had left behind and began to run towards them. And right when he was about to approach the palm

Phineas McNabb

trees, everything went black. Theodore woke up. It was four o'clock in the morning. He had been dreaming. He was in a cold sweat.

He looked beside him and there was Mr. Wimples. And when he looked closely at Mr. Wimples, he could see particles of White Sand on his face and on the shirt, he was wearing. What had just happened to Theodore? He needed to find Abraham and find out what he was doing with his daughter the day she died. It was too early to call anybody so he would lay there for the next four hours and then he would make a call. To Isabel, Amy's mom.

Rich Men Have No Friends

42

It was six o'clock in the morning in Malibu. The sky was blue, and the waves of the ocean were coming in. Isabel had a grassy area just beyond the pool where she did her morning yoga and exercise. The pool has been closed and has a cover over it. It has not been used since the accident.

Isabel was already up. The death of Amy was haunting her, and she was not handling it well. Like Theodore, she had dived back into her work best she could. She had a script, and the studio had told her to take her time and let them know when she would be ready to start filming. And as was her habit, she worked out every morning. She did thirty minutes of yoga to warm up and thirty minutes of exercises to get her mind and blood flowing. The last time she talked to Theodore, he blamed her for the accident, and she told him to leave.

A call from Theodore at this point would not be welcome and probably was not going to go well. But it was worth a try. And he had questions about the accident and Abraham.

The phone rang four times. Isabel stood up from her mat and looked at her phone. "Great, just what I need." But she answered anyway. "What, Theodore, what do you want?"

"Listen, Isabel. I need to ask some questions about the night of the accident. And I am sorry for calling you like this, but I need some answers. And I promise this is not about you nor do I blame you anymore. I just need answers. I am starting to lose it a little and I need closure. Please don't hang up."

"Theodore, you know everything. I mean you interrogated everyone to include me when you were here. What other questions could you have, I mean really. I need to move on, Theodore, which at this point is impossible. You calling me is not helping this situation at all."

"I understand, Isabel, but will you just give me five minutes. I promise I will be quick."

"Five minutes, Theodore."

"Do you remember seeing a man at the pool that night when you first found Amy? He would have had on a baseball hat, plaid shirt, overalls, you know the jeans with connections that go over your shoulder, and boots. Do you remember seeing anyone like that?"

"No, Theodore."

"Did anyone mention seeing a black truck at all?"

"No, Theodore. Do you think that Amy's death was not a drowning? What are you saying? You are scaring me right now."

"No, Isabel. So, no one saw a man or a black truck?"

"No, it never happened. Theodore, you okay/ I talked to Shelley and she said you were out indefinitely, and I also saw where you made her the new boss of HenPot Industries, your most coveted possession."

"That's not fair, Isabel."

And that's when the conversation went sideways.

"Not fair, Theodore. Our daughter is dead. Dead, Theodore! We will never see our precious Amy again. Was the business trip worth it?" I mean what happened, did you increase your net worth another million, hundred million, a billion? Amy was wrong about you, and I believed her."

"What does that mean. What do you mean she was wrong about me?"

"Amy said you were changing. She said you were nice to Shelley. She said you made Mr. Wimples your business partner, which I know sounds silly, but you give time to a stuffed animal. You did not even want her to have a dog when she asked. She said you were coming around. She said that you told her often that you loved me and that she was the best thing that ever happened to both you and me. She would tell me this every chance she got. She even said it to defend you when you could not make her birthday party. Without a tear, or a blink of the eye, she defended your actions and said that you loved her." Isabel began to tear up as did Theodore.

"Look, Isabel, if I had it to do over, I would do it differently. I wish I could have been there that night. It's not your fault. We are both her parents and for me to imply or say that it was your fault was selfish and I'm sorry for that, I really am."

"When will it be enough, Theodore? How many more millions do you need before you have made enough money? And when you make this money, then what? A new boat, a new house, more land, you planning to buy the moon, I mean what else is there? And then let me ask you this. Will it bring back our Amy and how does it change her legacy? You are the richest man in the world, and I am the most sought-after actress in the world. And right now, that fifty cents won't get us our Amy back. When does it end?"

Rich Men Have No Friends

"I don't know, Isabel. I don't know. But I really must go."

"And there it is, Theodore."

"What, what is it?"

"Every time the going gets tough, you get going. You run from everything. You never try to solve a problem, especially those that money can't solve. You have four ex-wives counting me, two sons you never speak to, and I know you provide for them, but you are never there for them. And now we have a dead daughter. All because you and I could not put our lives on hold and allow our daughter to be in the spotlight. Imagine what would have happened had we put our lives on hold and focused on Amy and your boys. Imagine if we had slowed life down, bought a house in the country and just focused on raising our Amy. Just imagine that, Theodore. We selfishly thought of ourselves. More Oscars, more money, but never thought about the thing that mattered most to us in this world, our Amy. And now she is dead."

"Isabel, listen...."

"No, you listen. I love you, Theodore. I know you never really loved me. I know all about putting money into my picture so you could meet me. And I knew the whole time you were married to me that you did not feel the way I did. But then Amy told me that you told her you loved me, and I was the best mom in the world. And that changed me. That night, I was watching Amy. She had been at my side the entire time. I looked away for a second, one lousy second, and now............." Isabel began to cry again.

Theodore was visibly shaken by the conversation at this point, but he was listening silently. He needed to hear this. After about thirty seconds, Isabel spoke again.

"Theodore, I am retiring from the movie industry. I am selling the house and moving to a quiet town. I have a friend and she told me there is a town there in Texas that is quiet and the people there live a rather simple life. Right now, what I need in my life is simplicity. I am tired of being around people who are not always genuine. I can't tell who my real friends are and where my fake friends begin. I have fifty million followers and I know for a fact that I don't have that much influence. One sixth of this country does not come to my movies or my box office numbers would be shattering all kinds of records. Don't get me wrong, I love being an actress but how can I go on and my daughter is dead. DEAD, THEODORE! OUR DAUGHTER IS DEAD! This house is too big for me. I mean why would a single woman need a six thousand square foot home. It's ridiculous. I know better. My parents did not raise me like this. I only agreed to buy this house because I thought we were going to be a family and have more children. Silly me. "

Little did Isabel know that Theodore was in that town Isabel was talking about. Greensburgh appeared to be a well-kept secret, but the word was getting out about this little town in Texas where life was simple, and your status and money meant nothing. No one cared. C.J. was trying to build something different and with the help of Abraham, he was building a town of people who had been transformed. They had all been shaken by an event that would change their perceptions about life, and what mattered the most in this world. A sense of belonging, a sense of community.

Where material things and money were irrelevant. In other words, they were meeting their needs, not their wants. And they were just fine with that.

Everyone wanted to go to this little simple town called Greensburgh and Theodore had been invited not once, but a second time. Sometime in life, you don't know a good thing when you see it. And Theodore could not see it because it was not for sale, and he could not take it. But it was being given to him.

"Theodore, I must go. I love you. I understand that you don't feel the same way. I have not filed the divorce papers yet. But I will get it done. I hope you understand. Bye, Theodore."

"Bye, Is..." She had already hung up. He was talking to no one.

Why had Abraham been with his daughter that night? He still had no explanation about who Abraham really was. He knew, but since he did not believe in Angels, well with exception of Amy, he refused to believe in Abraham. He had plenty of proof, but he was a non-believer. He had the truck that only a few people were privileged to drive. Abraham found Mr. Wimples for him. It appeared that Abraham was watching over Amy during her last few minutes on this earth. He had met Ruby, J.J. and Myrtle and heard their testimonials. He and C.J. had talked about a lifestyle that only the two of them could relate to. All the signs were there, but his heart was so hardened by

Rich Men Have No Friends

some bad advice from a stepdad many years ago and a pimp who killed his mother, that he was not able to change. And time was running out.

After he hung up the phone, he made himself some coffee, took a shower, put on his clothes, and headed out the door. He needed to see C.J. Myrtle's breakfast special would have to wait. Here was the richest man in the world and he needed answers. Answers money could not buy, nor could he google them. For the first time in a long time, Theodore was trying to solve a puzzle that required more than a textbook, or a calculator, or a team of twenty of the brightest minds money could buy.

Phineas McNabb

43

Shelley's alarm was going off. It was seven thirty Wednesday morning. Theodore has been gone now for three days. She had not heard from him except for the one text and a quick conversation that did not amount to much. He had given his Bentley away to a stranger and he was out there somewhere.

She slid out of bed, put on her bathrobe, and went to the bathroom to wash her face and brush her teeth. She was the chief executive officer of what was one of the most valuable companies in the world and she was charged with managing the money of the richest man in the world. Except for one thing. It did nothing for her. She had a sleepless night tossing and turning and she had concluded that she was not ready. She did not want the job.

Shelley had joined Theodore's company as his assistant ten years ago. When she originally came to work for him, she had never planned to stay this long. Her real goal was to learn as much as she could from him, save up some of that high salary he was paying her, and then she would go out on her own again. Except this time, if she could not beat them, she would join them. She would be an owner-operator for the very franchise that had put her out of business. But the checks kept coming and the bonuses kept coming. She had saved over almost one million dollars in cash. She had one million dollars in stock options in HenPot industries, her health insurance was paid for by the company and she was being paid more money than she could ever dream of.

But she was itching to get back out there and open her coffee shop again. Funny how that works. The money was like a drug and she was hooked. It was easy money. Although she was financially secure, she kept coming back. And for what?

Shelley got dressed, put on her favorite pair of jeans, her favorite sweatshirt, a pair of old socks and then she did nothing. She grabbed a book and began to read. She was not going to work today. She would call and leave a message for her assistant to clear her calendar. She was not coming in today and could not be disturbed, for any reason, by anybody. She closed the curtains in her place, cut on a small light and read herself back to sleep.

Rich Men Have No Friends

Amy's death was influencing everyone who knew her. And the effect was starting to take hold in ways that only C.J. would understand.

Phineas McNabb

44

Theodore showed up at C.J.'s house at eight in the morning. C.J. was barely back from his morning walk and had started breakfast when he heard a knock at his back door. He peaked through the curtain and there was Theodore. He turned over his pancakes and opened the door.

"Hey, C.J., I am sorry to come over so early but…."

"Ted, you are fine. Come on in. I am just cooking breakfast for the missus and me. A little pancakes, grits, turkey sausage, and some eggs. I have some coffee brewing on the stove. You should have breakfast with us this morning. Have a seat."

"You know what, C.J. I am barging on your quality time with Sarah. Why don't I come see you at the church later?"

"Nonsense have a seat, Ted. Remember, here in Greensburgh, you are not the richest man in the world but a man. A man who is trying to get answers to questions that money nor that staff of yours can buy. The answers you are looking for are gained through knowledge. A different kind of knowledge that you possess but don't know that you possess. The knowledge of life."

"I don't understand, C.J."

"It's not for you to understand. But it is to be understood."

"Okay, now I am confused. You mentioned breakfast." They both laughed. Theodore made the plates for Sarah, Theodore, and himself. The kitchen in their house was at the back of the house and looked out over a lake that ran through the back of town. It was a small comfortable kitchen. Island in the middle with white cabinets. There were three stools opposite the sink side of the island. The chairs had yellow flowered cushions. There was also a four-seater table that sat in the bay window. The bay window had plantation blinds as did the entire house. They were cracked slightly to allow sunlight in and a view of the lake. The table had a tablecloth that matched the cushions on the four chairs that matched the three stools. This kitchen was as comfortable and inviting as they come.

Theodore was not used to this type of home. A home that was full of life. The penthouse was nice when Amy was there but even then, he put his home next to his office. Never wanted to miss a deal. But it was obvious to him that this was the Johnson's home. And the church was up the street. The separation was necessary to give the proper balance to C.J. As Theodore was admiring the kitchen, Sarah came from the hallway and entered.

"Well, good morning, Mr. Hightower, how are you? C.J., you did not tell me we were having company for breakfast this morning. But we like good conversation so welcome, Mr. Hightower." Sarah made Theodore feel welcome in the Johnson home. He could not remember ever having a wife that made someone feel welcome in his home. But that was because his homes were just assets, things of value that normally appreciated. That was his main reason for buying them. He always bought his homes already assuming what the next buyer would pay for it.

For that reason, his homes did not have a personal touch. They were not Hightower family homes. They were HenPot/Hightower assets.

They began to have breakfast. C.J. put the butter and jelly on the table. He put some toast, biscuits, and bagels out. And there was a small fruit salad as well. Theodore was eating just like he did in those five-star places he frequented. The difference was this meal was warm and inviting in a different way.

"So, Sarah, how do you stay married to this guy for over twenty years.? I mean, I can't get it right for anything. I am in divorce number four. Can't find Mrs. Right. Or I am Mr. Wrong. Either way, me and marriage don't get along too well. What's the secret?" Theodore was trying to make small talk. He would save the talk with C.J. for later.

"The secret is patience, Ted. And realizing you are two different people who have two different ways of thinking and while that may seem like it would create conflict, it makes for a successful marriage in so many ways."

"I don't understand, Sarah. What do you mean that conflict creates a happy marriage? If that were true, I would still be with my first wife." They laughed.

"No, Theodore, I don't mean conflict as in arguing and fussing all the time. I mean having a balance. For example, if it were up to C.J., we would still be living in Houston in that big house we did not need and having four or five cars when we can only drive one at a time. We have always had enough money to buy whatever we wanted, but I never cared about that. Means nothing to me."

"Wait a minute, Sarah. Are you telling me that you don't like nice things?" Theodore was perplexed.

"Theodore, I did not marry C.J. for his money or because he was the Pastor of one of the most prominent churches in Houston. I married him because I genuinely loved him and wanted to spend the rest of my life with him. He could have been a maintenance man, worked in a call center or driven a cab. If he was a God-fearing man who was willing to do the right thing, he was the one."

"What do you mean do the right thing?"

"C.J. is a man. A man living in a world full of temptations, be it money, women, or any of the other things that can get a man in trouble on any given day. I expect him to make good decisions, own up to his faults, and try best he can to set the right example when it most counts."

"And that is?"

"When others are looking. You see, not only does he have responsibilities to me as his wife, but he also has responsibilities to his children, and to the congregation of his church, and to the people of this town who are backing him in his quest to bring it back to life. That's a lot of responsibility for one man. And there are times that responsibility becomes overwhelming and that is when he is most vulnerable to making a mistake. That's life, he's human."

"Wow, Sarah. What I hear you saying is it is not that he won't mess up because we all mess up. But it is the degree of the mess up, who affected it affect, and how does he handle it. And to the degree he can stay strong, and overcome it, and cause no harm to anyone but himself, then all is forgiven."

"Sort of. You almost have it right. Theodore is a grown man. He knows right from wrong. But he must make good decisions. Because the decisions he makes will always have a downstream effect on the people who trust and depend on him as well as the people who love him."

"And that is why you don't want him to do business with me. You don't see me as a good decision, do you?" Theodore was applying common sense.

"I see you as a man who is hurting, a man who lost his daughter. I can't imagine how you feel. But I know as a mother that when I heard about what happened to your Amy, my heart dropped. I shed a tear for you, and for my own children who I cherish more than anything in this world. So, as it relates to you, Theodore Hightower, I want to help you, but I can't. Because I can't bring your daughter back. But what I can do is tell you that you are a good man. I know in Houston, they see you as the richest man in the world, but I see you as a good man. And if you ask me, Mr. Hightower, I like the good man. And I have no problem with the rich man. If the rich man understands that it is better to be a good man with no riches than a rich man who is not good. I hope that I did not say too much or offend you in any way."

"No offense taken, Sarah. And thanks for your honesty. So, what I really hear you saying is you just tolerate C.J. and he's lucky to have you." They all laughed and finished their breakfast. C.J. grabbed his coat and he and Theodore made the short walk over to the church. They had business to discuss.

Phineas McNabb

45

Shelley has taken a short nap. The book never had a chance given how tired she was. Her phone rings. It is Jess.

"Shelley, everything okay? I just spoke to your assistant, and she said you are not coming into the office today. Said you had cancelled all your meetings."

"Yeah, about that, Jess. Look, I don't know if I can do this. I mean I don't have the energy or the drive to make Theodore money. I like working for him, the job is great, but I am not moved by how much money he has or accumulates going forward. And with Amy gone now, not sure there is a need for me anymore."

"Are you kidding me. The place would fall apart without you. Do you know that you are the only woman that he has lasted this long with Ted? You have been with him longer than any wife to date. You see, Shelley, you bring a sort of balance to his world. The fact that you don't care about money is why he sends you out to deliver his messages and the reason he uses you as a go between at the office there. He knows that when he puts a decision in your hands, it is not so you can self-promote or enrich yourself in any way. How many times have you asked him if you were getting a bonus this year?"

"Never, I have never asked him."

"Right, and you know the problem that most rich men have."

"No, what?"

"Employees who want more because they think they deserve a larger portion of the riches. Or friends that can't play a simple game of golf without trying to pitch you an idea or hit you up for money. Or businessmen that want you to put them in contact with someone or hire them. Or wives who are so caught up in your riches that they do more shopping and spending your money than they do spending quality time with you or the kids and making your house a home. So, you begin to trust no one. Then you come along, with not a care in the world. He came to your shop every day, and you never asked him anything other than did he want the usual? I am sure you knew who he was. Does that sound about right?"

"It does."

Rich Men Have No Friends

"And that is why he hired you. You are not a threat, and you won't get on his nerves. Let me guess, Pierre pitched a fit when he found out it was you that got the top job."

"Well, as a matter of fact he did but we are good now."

"And that's because Pierre does not get it. Guy carries you on his back, gives you a lifetime no cut contract, you are worth a billion dollars, and you still are not happy."

"Wait, Jess, what?"

"That's right, Pierre is a one percent holder of HenPot Industries and so his net worth is equated to Teds' on a percentage basis. And yet you and I do all the work. Not complaining as we are both well compensated for sure, but that is why Ted trusts you so much, get it?"

"I do get it. But I did not know he valued me like that."

"Look, Shelley, Ted is a shrewd businessman, believes that the only people who will survive are the takers and thinks the givers are soft and will eventually lose every time. So, as a taker, he takes whatever he wants because he is the richest man in the world. But he only takes that which will make him richer. A poor man never has to worry about Ted because in Ted's mine, he has nothing he wants."

"But is that the right way to be, Jess. A poor man has a lot to offer if given the opportunity and the right circumstances."

"You know that, and I know that. But a man like Ted. He sees no value in wasting his time on those types of people. He is not being mean, nor does he think less of them, they just can't add value to his bottom line. And for guys like Ted, all that matters is his bottom line."

"But then that makes the disenfranchised and the less fortunate the forgotten ones. If everyone of wealth or power just disregards a group of people because of their economic status, then it matters not to anyone what happens to them. And Jess, I know we are all better than that."

"Ted does what he can, Shelley, and as you know he has provided scholarships to kids, and he has his annual thing where he feeds a thousand families. And for a guy like Ted, he feels like he is making a fair contribution. And what's wild about this is he is right to some degree. Could he do more? Absolutely. The people who complain about rich people like Ted won't even let a family member stay with them whose down on their luck or donate five turkeys at Thanksgiving. But he is the bad guy? Frankly, we all could do better, we just choose not to. So, we blame the rich guy. He should solve all problems. The world does not work that way. We are all accountable, not just the rich guys."

And that was the thing that caused C.J. to leave the megachurch. He could not tell his congregation that he was the financial backer out of fear that if he dd, they would not contribute anything. And just as Jess was discussing it with Ted, they assumed that C.J. must be taking from the church given his lavish lifestyle, the big home, and all the cars. No good deed goes unpunished, or so they say.

"Wow, Jess, that was rather enlightening, and I had never thought about it that way. If we all gave and quit worrying about who isn't giving or how much they are giving, the world would be a better place. Who knew that such a simple concept might change the world as we know it?"

"So now, about that job and you not wanting it."

"I think I will stay a little longer. After all, can't keep Mr. Hightower on the straight and narrow if I am not here. Jess, I really enjoy working with you. And appreciate the conversation today. Guess I better get up and go to work."

"Great! Because if we had announced your resignation today, and his stock dropped which means he is not the richest man in the world anymore, he would have fired you."

"Jess, you can't fire someone after they resign."

"Shelley, you don't know Ted as well as I thought you did." They both laughed.

What Shelley had learned from Jess was invaluable information. She learned that the very rich lead isolated lives sometime by design but not because they think they are better than anyone. And she further learned that complaining about how much rich people give makes no sense when you are not doing your fair share. Hypocrites come from all walks of life. There is no qualification for pointing the finger at others.

Rich Men Have No Friends

46

Now that Shelley had decided to stay and was on the way back to the office, HenPot Industries was in fine hands. And Theodore could continue his business trip that had turned into quite the little adventure and was now turning into a sabbatical. His heart was softening, and unfortunately, it took the death of his daughter to make it happen.

It was now almost ten o'clock in the morning and C.J. and Theodore were back at the church in C.J.'s office. Ted had some questions, and he figured that C.J. was the only one that could answer them. Abraham, the dream, the pimp from so many years ago. He was slipping and afraid that he might go over the edge. His mental state was good as it related to business but as it related to Amy, he was a mess.

"C.J. how do you do it?"

"Do what, preach? Man, I love preaching. It runs in my family."

"No, how do you walk away from the money making so easy? I mean I understand you still dabble, and make a pretty good living doing it, but as much as I pushed you the other day, it is obvious to me that you really don't have it in your blood like you used to. It's like a hobby to you now. And it appears your happiness comes from this town, its people, and the things you are doing to make it better. How does someone walk away from French-Helliman and become a preacher for a small but prominent church, then become one of the leading preachers in the country for one of the largest churches in the country, and become a best-selling book writer, and just walk away?"

"It's complicated, Ted. And I don't know if you have the time to hear my story."

"Hey, if you were anyone else, I would not even care. But you and I are cut from the same cloth. Almost like brothers, if you will, so tell me why you walked away from the fame and fortune twice."

"Well, the first time, when I took over the church, my parents had just died, and I made a promise to my dad that I would come back and take his place when he retired. I just did not expect an early retirement, no disrespect intended to him or my mom. My father taught me early on that when you make a promise to someone, you must uphold it. So that one was a no-brainer. And I will admit at the time I thought I would do it in the interim and eventually I would move back to New

York, but it never happened and that was because of Sarah and the kids. You see, Ted, there were things going on around me that I could not control but they were reshaping my life and taking me on a different path. In my case, tragedy got me out the game and I never looked back."

"But just think of all the money you could have made. Hell, you might be the richest man in the world." Ted had a narrow focus, and that was money. It was the most important thing to him, so his conversations normally were about money, how to make it, how not to lose it, and what to spend it on.

"Ted, is that all you ever talk about, money? You do know there is more to life than money. I'm sorry, I did not mean that the way it sounded." C.J. was not trying to be insensitive to Amy and caught himself just in time.

"What I mean, Ted, is that I learned a valuable lesson from one of my church members in Houston when I had the megachurch. I was financing that church, and all its events and activities from my own funds, be it book sells or the investment company in Florida. I never took a salary, nor did I take any money from the church, ever. But I had a member to come visit me."

"Let me guess, begging for money. Rich church, with a well to do prominent preacher, and here they come begging. Gets on my nerves. Between taxes and charitable donations, you and I do more than our fair share."

"Says who, Ted."

"Says me and all the rich guys like me. You should understand. We pay more in taxes than one hundred people combined who make a decent living. And I bet you we give more than they do on a one for one dollar basis"

"There's just one problem with that theory, Ted. You assume you have done enough, that the average guy does not do anything. The average guy feels like the rich don't do enough but does do something in a lot of cases, but you are right some do nothing at all. And while everyone is worrying about what the other person is doing, a child goes hungry today, housing is not affordable in a lot of places, towns are dying a slow death economically and socially, and a family was just put on the street and are now homeless, and a young lady walks the street for twenty dollars because her pimp won't let her go back home. But anyway, about why I left the megachurch…"

"Sorry, that just really gets me worked up, C.J. I worked for everything I have. I was not always rich."

"I understand, but about the megachurch. I had a church member come to me who I did not really know. She had her three kids with her. All had been baptized at my church and I did not know any of them by name. I was rather embarrassed. You know kind of like companies that get so big that employees become numbers instead of people. And that was my problem, the members were becoming numbers, and I was just trying to grow the number, much like I grew an investment portfolio."

"Okay, what else, I mean that can't be the only thing."

"Then, Ted, she questioned how I was maintaining a big house, five cars, and wearing designer suits to church. What I did not understand is that the people I was serving, my congregation, had an average annual family salary of about fifty thousand dollars per year. So, when I showed up in my five-thousand-dollar suit, thirty-thousand-dollar watch, and pulled up in a two hundred-thousand-dollar car, it did not look good. It was the optics of it all. Just like when you gave Abraham your car. You did not know what to expect when you came to Greensburgh, so you wanted to fit in. To your surprise, a few of us here came from your world (the rich and famous) and never asked you who you were or how much money you have. Ken, Myrtle, J.J., Ruby nor I ever asked you what you did for a living, what title you carried or how much money you had."

"You know what, I never thought about that. You are right. No one ever mentioned money, status, or even where I went to school. Everyone here has just been genuinely nice to me."

"And because of that, Ted, you have been able to slowly let your guard down and not be such a shrewd guy. But getting back to the optics. The point that the member was making to me was it mattered not how my home, lifestyle, clothes, and cars were being paid for. As the leader of my people, the church that is, there was an expectation that I live a good life, but not one that would cause them to believe they were financing it at the expense of the church or those in need. Now translate that to your world."

"I don't understand."

Phineas McNabb

"Ted, everyday business decisions are made. Some are popular, some are not. Some have real impacts on towns like Greensburgh and Luckspeak, Oklahoma. And the people who make those decisions are not aware of the downstream affects because their intent is not to harm their fellow man, but they are trying to make money for their company, or in your case trying to make money for status reasons. And the logic is if I don't do it, someone else will. And I think everyone gets it now. But it does not remove the pain."

"What pain, Theodore?"

"The pain of a town dying that was once the heartbeat of that little community, that in some cases goes back fifty or a hundred years. You see, the people in Greensburgh all grew up here. And when the plant closed, it did not just layoff a bunch of people who could bounce back. It literally broke up families. Families that in some cases had worked in that plant over a couple of generations. A plant that funded the local library, the local high school that the whole city took pride in and traveled with the high school football team wherever they went. A town that grew into a small city that the locals would get dressed up and come to for their shopping downtown. The people who did not need a Houston because everything they needed was right here. Love, compassion for one another, and a sense of pride in their community."

"Okay, you are starting to sound like Pete. What does that have to do with me?"

"Everything and nothing, Ted. But let's get back to optics and perception. If I told you that you were the primary decision maker behind the plant closing in LuckSpeak and here in Greensburgh, what would you say."

"I would say I don't know what you are talking about. I would say that I am a businessman, and I can't be everywhere running an organization that has over twenty employees and indirectly at any point and time one hundred thousand employees and I can definitively say that I have never made a decision that would take the life out of a town in America. I love my country too much."

"And you really believe that don't you, Ted."

"I know it."

"Well, friend, don't stand up yet or you will fall back down in your chair."

"What do you mean, C.J.?"

Rich Men Have No Friends

"Ted, I know your model. Your team predicts the future by figuring out who has the most fat (employees that can be cut), and then you swoop in, buy the company, have your assistant and your lawyer push the executives to make decisions that will show some quote unquote efficiencies. Sound about right?"

"Well, yes, but it's all above board. I have not broken any laws."

"No, you can't be arrested for the downfall of a town or a community. Especially when you were not aware that the actions taken by those executives were not exactly what you were looking for. I mean, Ted you seem like a decent guy, not the guy we all read about. The Numb investor. You probably assumed they were trimming throughout the whole organization so that the impact was minimal."

"Well not exactly. I knew what they were doing but I did not realize in some cases that the plant was the only game in town. And when I learned that it was, I assumed that the people would bounce back or another company would move in, maybe even take over the plant. But now I see that never happened."

"Why would anyone do that Ted? It would require someone to sit down with a pen and paper, put together a plan, figure out how to negotiate with the local town to minimize the economic impact and in some cases not just target a large group of people and make it look like a well thought out plan."

"Now, C.J. you are smarter than that. Salaries keep escalating and it becomes difficult to compete and then the same worker who just so happens to be the consumer are not happy because the products they are buying cost too much. Again, I go back to having your cake and wanting to eat it too. Consumers want things cheap, but cheap comes with a price. And when that happens, goodbye Greensburgh, and goodbye Luckspeak. It's a vicious cycle with no happy ending for anyone involved. "

"You really believe that, Ted?"

"I know that. I lived it. My mom's boyfriend, the only one I ever learned anything from and whose lesson I go by to this day, taught me you can be a giver or a taker. He had given ten years to a plant. Started dating my mom who was not the easiest person to live with, and he would be late occasionally. What the plant did not know is that there were times they argued until the middle of the night or he had to go find her because she would get high, and so they laid him off. Did not care what his problems were at home, he was late, no longer of value and poof he was gone. He taught me one Christmas Eve that I had two choices, be the owner or be the employer. Be the taker or be the giver. I chose to be a taker. It was never about money or laying people off, it was about surviving, succeeding, and never being laid off. And to this day, I have never been laid off. Owners don't lay themselves off."

"And you go to bed telling yourself that every night."

"No, I actually go to bed every night being grateful that I was given a gift and I use it to the best of my ability."

"Who gave you that gift, Ted?"

"I'm not following you, C.J."

"If someone gave you a gift, who gave it to you?"

"Well, I did not mean it that way."

"You meant it exactly the way you said it and you are right you were given a gift."

"Okay, so what's your point?"

"My point is if a guy like you can figure out how to become the richest man in the world, then surely, he can figure out how to bring balance back to the country he loves. Surely, he can get along with other people who are rich as him and solve this problem. And the guy that heads up this group will probably end up with another title since you like titles."

"That was low, C.J."

"No, I am serious. You can be not only the richest guy in the world, but the guy who saved the world. I don't know if climate change is real, but I know the climate is changing. I don't know how serious homelessness is in the world, but I know we have homeless people. And I don't know how real the income inequality is given the amount of information that is fed to us some of which is exaggerated for effect and in some cases downright wrong, but all of those things are having an adverse effect on the people of this country so naturally the finger is pointed at you and I."

"What do you mean you and I?"

"Ted, the church used to be the backbone of the community. Let's not talk which religion but any religion. Faith used to be the backbone of the community. Many of the civil rights leaders came from the church. Some of the biggest evangelists in the country have advised and prayed with our Presidents. The church was once the place you sought salvation when you were going through a tough time or suffered the loss of a loved one. Now it has become a thing of the past for a high percentage of people. Not trying to convert you as I know how you feel about the subject."

"I don't know that I feel anything, C.J. I just find it hard to believe in something that allowed me to live in such a dysfunctional environment as a kid, having to suffer through boyfriend after boyfriend of my mom and right when you begin to like them, they go away. Having to deal with a mother I loved dearly but who could not stop doing the drugs. And then having to deal with her death at the hands of some low-level pimp. And now Amy. My drug of choice or my coping mechanism has been for me since I left college money. And I did not harm anyone, or at least I did not intentionally try to harm anyone given our discussion about Greensburgh and Luckspeak today."

"So, you are no different from your mom?" Ted jumped up out of his seat, balled up his fists and slammed them on the table.

"Hear me out, Ted. Hear me out."

"Okay, Pastor, but be careful. No one talks about my mom but me."

"Your mom sold drugs and used right? That's what you told me. Is that correct?"

"Yes."

"So, she was a taker as well. She took people's ability to think straight, may have ruined families, and may well have been responsible for people being on the street."

"Be careful, C.J." C.J. could see the red in Ted's face.

"And your drug of choice is money. You take away people's jobs although one might say unintentionally given the competitive market. You may have ruined families and may possibly be responsible for people being on the street. And the difference is you know better, but your mom was just trying to survive and feed you and your sister. That sound about right." Theodore calmed down and sat back down in his chair.

"That sums it up pretty much. I guess survival turned to greed, huh."

"You said it, I didn't. And my answer would be not that you are greedy. You don't know what to do. There is no easy answer. Remember I am the guy who was trying to do good for the church and left town. Not because I was chased out or forced to resign. But because I only wanted to do good for my members but all they were concerned about was the…"

"Money. I get it, C.J."

"Do you?"

"It's not about the money. It's about perception. It's all these doggone lists, and television shows about money, and bling bling, and songs about money. We have made money so important to us all that we lost sight of community, our fellow man, and most importantly having faith in each other and our ability to be resilient and take care of each other. We buy our kids hundred-dollar sneakers, two hundred-dollar phones, and luxury cars. Do you know my first car was a hooptie, as the kids call it? And I bought that with my own money once I started working when I went off to college."

"Who are you telling, Theodore? My parents had little money and made me walk until my senior year in college. My dad always told me he did just fine without one, and I would too. And you know what, he was right."

"At least you got the truth. My mom did not want me to know how much we struggled financially so she told me that I could not have a car as it might draw the attention of the police. Now how was a raggedy old car with manual windows and a am radio going to do that." They both laughed hysterically.

Theodore was so busy conversating with C.J. that he was not as consumed with his company, his money, his status as the richest man in the world, or the death of Amy. He was grieving, and his new family in Greensburgh was helping him get through it, one day at a time.

"So, C.J. about this Abraham fellow. Who is he?"

"Who did he tell you he was?"

"He claims to be my guardian angel. And I won't tell anyone else this, but I had a dream about him and in the dream, I saw my Amy and get to talk to her. And she told me about this man in the black pickup truck. Funny, huh!" C.J.'s face now had a very serious look to it.

Rich Men Have No Friends

"Not really, Ted. Look, I am not a fortune teller, and I don't read people's dreams for them. But I can tell you that it is not a coincidence that you had a dream about your daughter. I have dreams about my mother and father to this day. And I most often have dreams about my father when I am about to mess up or make a bad decision."

"Are you serious? Wait, don't answer that."

"As a heart attack, Ted. As a heart attack." They both laughed again.

"Hey, C.J., what does that mean, serious as a heart attack. I mean I think I know but what gives."

"Well, I learned it from Myrtle. You know how Myrtle likes to cook. Well, several years ago, she suffered a mild heart attack while at work. And she went on an on after she recovered how that really scared her when it happened and so when anyone asks her if she is serious, she says as a heart attack for emphasis."

"You know, I am glad I came to Greensburgh. My concern now is how do I deal with Amy. I mean I am trying to put up the good front, but it hurts, C.J., more than you will ever know. That little girl was changing me. And I messed up bad going on that trip, but it was a multi-million-dollar deal that really was going to do good things for a change. Instead of losing jobs, I was going to be creating jobs in a country that is going through some tough times. I mean the people there don't have food to eat. I have been working with some scientists and engineers to help the local people learn how to grow food in the most desolate of situations where the land is not necessarily compatible with growing your own food. It was Amy's idea. It was supposed to be her surprise when I returned to see her a few days after her birthday party."

"Amy's idea?"

"Yeah, she and Shelley, my assistant, were watching TV one night in the penthouse. Shelley was watching the news, and this documentary came on about this country and the plight of the people. So, I come back from my trip, and I ask Amy what she wants for her birthday."

"And she said?"

"She wanted me to save those people. She wanted me to find a way to give them food. And you know why she wanted me to do that?"

"Why, Ted?"

220

"Because her mother told her I was the richest man in the world. That little whipper snapper did not know a lot, but she knew that the richest man in the world could do anything."

"How did she know that, Ted?"

"Because my father-in-law, her grandfather, told her that I was like Solomon. And he told her the story of Solomon which I still don't know. But it left an impression on this little girl so she told me that I should save those people since I was like Solomon. Go figure." C.J. smiled from ear to ear.

"Sounds like your father-in-law is a pretty good guy."

"Can't stand him." They both laughed.

Rich Men Have No Friends

47

It is Wednesday, about noon. The sky is blue, the wind is calm, and it is a rather mild seventy-five degrees in Houston. Shelley is on her way to work after being at home for the balance of the morning. The pickup is running fine, she has the windows down and the radio is playing some beach music. She's patting the steering wheel to the beat of the music, and she has a big smile on her face. After talking to Jess, she feels much better about being the Chief Executive Officer for HenPot Industries. She is thinking through what steps she should take to ensure that she does no harm until Theodore is back in the picture.

As she enters the garage, her phone rings. It is Carol again. "Wonder what she wants" Shelley thinks to herself. She picks up as she is parking the truck. "Hey, Carol."

"Hey, how would you like to take a road trip with me?"

"To where?"

"Greensburgh, Texas. That's where Theodore is right now."

"I have never heard of Greensburgh, how far is it from Houston?"

"It's about a two-hour drive if the traffic is moving good. So, what do you say, Shelley, you want to go?"

"I don't know, Carol. I have a company to run and ......"

"Blah, blah, blah, you sound like Theodore. I'll be out front in ten minutes. It will be great. We can talk on the way."

"How did you find him, Carol?"

"I have friends in high places. You know the business world is not the only place you can network, Shelley."

"I know. I tell you what, is this a one-day trip or are we coming back today?"

"I don't know yet. You should probably plan on spending the night."

"Okay, I am going to stop by my place and pick up a few things and we can go."

"And Shelley, on second thought, I'll drive. I mean I like your pick up; I really do but I need my sunroof and satellite radio. Two hours is a long ride in that pickup. You okay with that."

"As long as you are driving, Carol, I am good. See you in twenty minutes."

Phineas McNabb

Shelley would call her assistant for the second time to tell her she would not be in today, and she would also call Jess and explain what she was doing so he would not worry. He would caution her against popping up on Theodore, but she explained who she was with. He would caution her even more once he heard Carol was going as well. His cautions would fall on deaf ears.

Carol would pull up front and pickup Shelley and they were on their way. Once they were on the highway, they had a long talk about this and that, but somehow circled back to Theodore.

"Shelley, what's it like working for Theodore or as you call him Mr. Hightower?"

"Well, he's very demanding, but he is fair. He does not ask me to do anything that he would not do himself. Well, except for the tough conversations. He's not good at visiting companies once he buys them because his purchases normally result in job cuts followed by layoffs. He has never been good at that piece."

"Then why does he do it? I mean he already has all the money he could ever need. I don't have one tenth the money he has, and I live a very good life. So, what gives?"

"At this point, I think he does it because it is all he knows. Mr. Hightower has been making money since he was in grad school at MIT. So, when he finally made it in this world, the way he made it was with money. I guess in his mind money is all he knows. How to make it, how to invest it, and how to spend it. And he only spends it on those things that will retain their value or in the best-case scenario increase in value. That's what gets him up every day. Well, that and Amy until the accident."

"What is it with this obsession with money nowadays. Don't get me wrong, I like money and I need money to get through the day, buy groceries, pay bills, help others and such. But why does every conversation have to be about money? I mean really!"

"You are right, Carol. I ran my own business, gave great customer service, but the bottom line became how much money I was charging versus my competitor. And my competitor drove prices down until I was out of business. There was no mutual competition based on who could provide the best service but instead who could give the best deal."

Rich Men Have No Friends

"And that right there is a problem within itself. Since no one tries to provide good service, it is either non-existent or costs an arm and a leg to get it. You know when I go to my congregation and ask them to donate to the church, it is like pulling hind teeth. And we really use the money to help the less fortunate all over the world. We have programs for those living in economic plight, the homeless, women trying to escape domestic abuse, young mothers who are struggling to raise their child or children but because I am a successful author, my members either think I am spending the money, or I should be giving more. And it's not about that."

"Carol, I blame this on us, me and you. This is a global problem that has been magnified by this country becoming a world of wants versus needs. If you want it, you can get it. I can finance it for you, you can borrow against your home, or if you are rich enough or have excellent credit, you can get it with no collateral and in some cases no money down. The problem with that is the bill comes due eventually. You and I are both capitalists and we are not even trying to be capitalists."

"I don't follow. I am not a capitalist; I am a pastor. Money does not define me."

"You sure about that. How many books have you sold thus far?"

"I don't know, five million or so to date."

"And did you keep the money?"

"Why of course, why would I not keep the money for my work?"

"Capitalist. You produced a good, the consumer bought it, and you received a monetary payment in return. And you priced that good to cover the expenses of making the product, and to distribute it and advertise it. And you did not charge just enough to cover those expenses, you made sure that you received a certain amount per item, or your agent did. Sound about right."

"Well, yeah but…"

"Capitalist. Carol, you are a capitalist. You are no different from Ted as it relates to making money."

"I am nothing like Ted. Laying people off is not something that I advocate at all. I mean I understand that businesses must do what is in the best interest of the organization, but the impact that has on people is horrible."

"What do you propose, Carol? I mean, you are a Pastor of one of the largest churches in America. You face the same problems in your environment."

"How so, Shelley?"

"You grew your church to the point now that you don't know all your members. There is no way you know all ten thousand or however many thousand you have. So, you delegate to other ministers or faith leaders in your organization to take care of those members, correct?"

"Yes."

"And when your secretary or whoever is keeping up with your membership tells you that you have lost five hundred members, who do you blame for that?"

"I don't follow, Shelley."

"You don't know who to blame because your organization is too big. You could have a faith leader who is in the wrong job, and not capable of leading or neglecting his department in this case members. And before you know it, membership is down but you don't know why. And then that reflects in your tithes which are down. And that puts the church at risk unless you use your own money from you book sales to prop it up, right?"

"Well, yes."

"And if you keep propping the church up, at some point you say to yourself you have a bad business model because you are losing money and you need money to keep the church going, right."

"Well, yes but I can replace the faith leaders if they are not doing their job and I do that on occasion."

"You lay them off, Carol. You relieve them of their duties because they are upsetting the business model and costing the church money, money it needs to survive and take care of those programs you manage to help the less fortunate?"

"But that is not like what Ted does."

"It's exactly what Mr. Hightower does. He studies a company, or rather the staff in Houston does. They look for those poor leaders, in this case, weak managers, who are driving off the customers, or members, and he replaces them. Then he looks at the amount of money coming into the organization and if it isn't profitable, he changes the business model. And that may mean layoffs, discontinuing a product or exiting a business altogether. Much like if you built a church in the middle of nowhere and nobody came. Would you keep that church open?"

"Absolutely, Shelley. The church is not a business. We are there to convert and help those seeking salvation. It's not about the money. Never was and never will be."

"Then why all the bells and whistles in the church today. Why all the lights, and cushioned seats, and churches that rival the nicest theaters or stadiums in town. Why all that? Don't answer. I will tell you. Because if you don't do it, they may not come. You, Pastor are a capitalist through and through. It's just that you did not intend to be when you started out. You really wanted to be like Paul, and Silas, and Timothy. But something changed along the way. You started to read your own headlines and before you knew it, you were no longer a preacher, and you were becoming a capitalist. A capitalist preacher. You can't help it because we live in a country that totally depends on…"

"Money. I get it Shelley. I don't know whether to be offended, upset, or enlightened. I think it is all the above at this point. Do you think my members feel the same way?"

"Think, I know they do. Just look at the number of people who question how much money you make, what type of car you drive, and where you live. I know because I read up on you. You should not be getting that kind of scrutiny as a Pastor. If you were Mr. Hightower, I would understand but you are a preacher, someone who is trying to help people and give them hope that today will be fine and there's better days coming. I have seen your sermons. You are very good at what you do. But for many people, the church has been reduced to just another business, not the backbone of the community. And unfortunately, much of that can be blamed on our obsession with things and money."

"Shelley, I could not agree with you more. When Theodore and I were growing up, our grandfather would drag us to church every Sunday. Theodore did not care for it too much and after the incident with my mom's boyfriend, well that hardened his heart for the rest of his life. But me, I kept going. And given the dysfunction in my home, it provided me with a place of comfort and understanding. It helped me to understand my environment and make the best of it. I forgave my mother for her hard life and its impact on Theodore and I. and I forgave Theodore for his quitting on something he did not understand and did not want to understand."

At this point, the dialogue was getting rather deep. Shelley was showing Carol that no matter where you were in life, to include being a leader in the church, money mattered. It was the catalyst that made the clock of life tick. And without it, the clock did not stop, but life would pass you by. Carol on the other hand saw it differently because she thought that in her role as a Pastor, she was above big business and money had nothing to do with who she was or what she did for a living.

"Let me ask you something, Carol? Why did you write the books initially?"

"To help people. I did not think I could get to enough people. I saw books as a vehicle to spread my message globally. I wanted to help those people who might not ever see a sermon or come to my church. Why?"

"Then why not price the books at cost for the customer. And take all profit for you off the table."

"Why would I do that?"

"Exactly, Carol. Why would you leave profit on the table, and you took the time to write these books expending your energy and valuable time to try and provide a service to those people you were trying to reach. You wanted a reward for your hard work. But is that what you are supposed to be doing, seeking a reward for your work through money or is the reward supposed to be reaching all those people which was your original intent?"

"I get it but explain how this relates to what you and Theodore do."

"Our reward is money, cut and dry. We know that and we know the downstream impacts of what we do. But it is not done without consideration for what is best for the consumer first, and then our shareholders, and finally our bottom line. In your case, you wrote books to reach a larger base of believers or consumers if you will, then you thought of your members and the needy who could benefit from your book profits, and finally you had to think of yourself. I mean, you did all the work."

"Well, that's right. I did do all the work."

"Did you do all the work? I mean who inspired you while you were inspiring everyone else?"

Rich Men Have No Friends

"I wrote those books all by myself. No one helped me. Wait, I get it. I was inspired and led by my beliefs and the ones I go to for guidance daily. I am just the messenger."

"Right, Carol. And Mr. Hightower is just the messenger of a different type no disrespect intended. He gets information given to him and he acts on it to try and make money for people and ultimately improve his bottom line. A lot of people have made money and become rich because of Mr. Hightower. He also has a charitable foundation and feeds over a thousand people during the holidays. And you probably did not know that the business trip he was on when Amy died was to try and help people in foreign country who are not able to get basic things like food. He was trying to solve a hunger problem in another country. That was his gift to Amy and that is why he was not there the night of the drowning."

"Are you serious?"

"Carol, the point I am trying to make to you is that you and your brother are different but trying to achieve the same things. You both are ridiculed and chastised for trying the best you can to do the right thing. The problem is we live in a society that has become so pessimistic that it is easier to find fault than to see the good in what people do. The church is not doing enough for the members, companies not paying enough salary. Preacher is living to opulent a lifestyle, richest man in the world not doing enough for those who are not rich. I mean it is a never-ending cycle of finger pointing that is getting this country and the people in it nowhere."

"What do you suggest, Shelley?"

"More action and less talk. Less transparency. I mean why does anyone need to know how much money you or your brother are worth? That is not inspirational to the average person trying to make it. It can be downright depressing. I don't want anyone to know how much I am worth. I just want to live my life normally, whether I have ten dollars in the bank or ten million. It should not matter to my neighbor, my friends, or a stranger I meet on the street. What should matter is how I treat people and how they treat me. That's the issue. Too much concern about money, net worth, who has the biggest car or house and not a simple how are you doing. Money can't solve everything and in the case of Mr. Hightower, it can't bring his Amy back. So, if we stop talking about money, and focus on what really matters, the world would be such a better place. I will defend Mr. Hightower not as a businessman but as a man. He worked hard, should not have to apologize for it, and how much money he has is really nobody's business."

"Wow, Shelley, you really don't hold back, do you."

"It's not that, Carol, but look at how much time we spent talking about money. I had to defend Mr. Hightower, then show you how you are participating in the same capitalistic system although I know that it is not your primary goal. And that got us nowhere. We should be talking about you and your brother, memories of the good times you had because I know it was not always like this. But money and religion divided the two of you, yet money and religion is what binds you."

"In what way, Shelley?"

"You are going to see your brother in two capacities. As his sister and as a Pastor who wants to be there for him. He on the other hand is trying to find closure on the death of his daughter and because of his lack of faith in anything but money, he does not know what to do. So, you are looking for the lost sheep, who this time just happens to be your brother. And he does not know it yet, but you are exactly what he is looking for."

"Shelley, you are a bright young lady. I see why Theodore hired you. And you are the only woman to have made it ten years with him. I need a Shelley. Have any sisters?" They both laughed.

This conversation that went on for quite a while started with money and ended with money. But what Carol finally understood is that money, if used for the right reasons is a good thing. And sometimes to do good things, there would be impacts that while perceived as negative, were necessary for the greater good. Shelley was working for Theodore for a reason.

His charitable foundation and the feeding of the thousand families had been her idea. Helping the people in the foreign country was Amy's idea. Both trying to do something for their fellow man. And both were capitalists. And there was nothing wrong with that.

Rich Men Have No Friends

48

It is almost two o'clock on Wednesday and Theodore has just awoken from a nap. After eating breakfast with C.J. and his wife, then meeting with C.J. at the church, he was tired and wanted to kick back for a little bit. He went back to the motel and went upstairs to relax. He closed the curtains, pulled his chair close to the bed and cut the TV on with the volume low enough to hear but not high enough to get engaged in what was on TV. He put Mr. Wimples in the other chair. He took off his shoes and put his feet up on the bed and took a long nap.

When he awoke from his nap, he opened the curtains and to his surprise the sun was gone. It was drizzling and the sky was getting a little dark. There was a storm brewing, and it was coming their way. Nevertheless, he needed to eat, he was hungry. He looked out the window and parked in front of the diner was a black truck. Could that be Abraham? No way. But maybe it was. He threw on his jacket and headed downstairs.

"Be back in a bit, Mr. Wimples. We should be leaving here late today or tomorrow morning. I've enjoyed my stay, but it is time to go home. What's that? Yeah, I miss her too."

As he was coming down the hall, Ruby was looking at a magazine and drinking a soda. "Hey, Ruby!"

"Hey, Ted."

"Bye, Ruby."

"Bye, Ted."

He ran across the street, water splashing under his feet until he got to the truck. Inside the truck was Abraham. Abraham cracked the window of the truck and spoke to him.

"Hey, Ted, how are you doing today?"

"I'm good but I have a question for you?"

"Okay, but don't you want to get out the rain?"

"No, I'm good, it's just water." Ted put on the hood from his jacket.

"Abraham, who exactly are you? I mean come on. Angels don't exist."

"Why do you call Amy your Angel, Ted?"

"Well, because she was innocent. She was not like the rest of this world. There was not a mean bone in her body. She would not hurt a fly. Amy was a good girl. She saw the good in people. She saw the good in me."

"And what you just described, Ted, is an Angel, but of a different kind."

"I don't understand, Abraham."

"You see, Ted, people are placed in your life at different times. Some are good, and some not so good. Some are good for you, and some need to be avoided. But they are all there to help shape you, mold you and in the case of Angels only, to be there for you when you are going through something or need some assistance with this thing you call life. You see, Ted, you don't do it by yourself. It takes more than you to get to where you are today. That's why the term self-made makes no sense at all."

"But I am self-made."

"You did it all by yourself."

"Sure did."

"Really?"

"Damn right."

"What was Pierre, you know the guy who your wife cheated on you with?"

"He was lost, and we related in a lot of ways, and I wanted to help the guy."

"What about your mom?"

"She had a hard life, it wasn't her fault, and I tried to do the best I could by her."

"What about Susan Flannery?"

"How do you know about Susan? She was down on her luck, mom tried to help her before that creep killed her, so I took care of it. She was a good girl who met up with the wrong people. But she is fine now because I helped her."

"What about Jess?"

"He was a good lawyer who had bad partners. I rescued him from them, and he lives a good life now."

"Wow, Ted. For a guy who people call Numb, you sound like a great guy. You are always looking out for someone else, like an angel."

Rich Men Have No Friends

"What?"

"I mean listen to you, and what about Shelley?"

"I mean I feel bad about how I hired her, but that shop would have folded anyway. I just expedited the process and she's worth more money now than she could ever dream of. I made it up to her ten times over."

"And you think you did that, all by yourself?"

"Why, yeah, I do."

"Anyway, let's get back to Amy. I was there that night. Saw the whole thing. It was a sad situation, but my job was to ensure she made it home and I did that."

"I don't understand, Abraham. What do you mean home?"

"Do you remember your dream?"

"I told the Pastor not to tell anyone about that."

"Louis did not tell me about that, Ted. I heard about it from Amy. You see Angels talk to each other. And she told me what you were trying to do and why you missed her birthday party. You are changing, Ted, but time is running out."

"What do you mean time is running out?"

"Ted, you believe or at least you did believe until recently that money could solve everything, right?"

"Well, yes. It just seems to make life so much easier. Money allows you to escape from the problems and challenges that the average person faces."

"You mean like growing up in a dysfunctional household where the parent barely has time for their children and the coping mechanism is something that provides a false high. And then you do it so long you lose sight of the things that really matter like love, compassion, and empathy for your fellow man."

"Hey, leave my mother and my childhood out of this."

"I was not talking about your mother, Ted. I am talking about you. I mean you have all this money but tell me what problem it has solved for you since Amy died. Has it helped you get over her memory, has it brought her back? Has it mended your relationship with Isabel? In the last three days, tell me where money was a factor in this little town called Greensburgh."

"Well, it has not been a factor at all. These nice folks have been so kind to me that they helped me not think about Amy as much. And hearing all their stories made me realize that I am not by myself. Everyone goes through something. And it does not matter how much money you have."

"Right, Ted. So, my job is to help you heal by providing whatever assistance and cover possible to ease your burden, in this case grieving for Amy. I am here to help you. Not to frighten you, or to get you to believe in me, but to help you. But know this, no one does anything by themselves. There is no such thing as being…"

"Self-made, I get it, Abraham. Abraham let's say for the sake of argument, that you are an Angel, and you were there for Amy. If that's true, then thank you. I really appreciate you being there for me. Now how do I go forward because I really miss my Angel?" A tear came down Theodore's cheek.

"Ted, it's the least I could do for you. But Ted, I don't deal in hypotheticals. You either believe or you don't, and you my friend are a believer, or you look silly standing in the middle of the rain talking to nobody. Because if I am not an Angel, then I am not here. Now you have a good day." They both laughed.

"You too, Abraham. You too." They both smiled. Ted slapped the side of the truck as a sign of affection and walked around the front. He had one more thing to say to Abraham. As he went to grab the door of the diner, he turned around and Abraham was gone. "Hey, Abrah……"

Myrtle had been standing in the door the entire time watching Ted talk to no one.

"Ted, who were you talking too. I mean, if you needed someone to pray with you, I would have come out there with you."

"What are you talking about, Myrtle."

"Well, you ran across the street, stopped, and started talking to yourself. Who were your talking to?"

"I was talking to a friend, Myrtle. A friend of Amy's."

"Okay, if you say so." Myrtle knew exactly what was happening, but it was not for her to intervene or comment on. She had been there herself and understood why Ted was in the middle of the street talking to himself.

"Now, what's this I hear about you standing me up this morning for that breakfast at C.J.s house. I mean, the nerve of you. I made the Ted special this morning. Newly added to the menu." She laughed and Ted smiled.

"Myrle, I will have whatever is easy for you. I have not eaten since this morning."

While Myrtle was in the back, C.J. came into the diner. "Hey, Ted, how was your nap?"

"How do you know I went to sleep?"

"Ted, you ate me out of house and home this morning. When you eat that much food, there is only one thing you can do. And that is taking a nap. Am I right?"

"You are right, C.J." They both smiled.

"Look, Ted, I need to tell you something. I am not going to be able to help you. After talking to Sarah, I have decided to remove myself from the company in Florida. I am turning it over to Thomas. Not closing it but removing myself from it. She's right, it's time to move on. Plus, I have too many projects as it is. I am full time pastor, trying to help rebuild this town and all our faith-based initiatives is more than I can handle. I had the computers removed in my office this morning. I am getting totally out of the game."

Myrtle brought Ted's plate out to him and a piece of pie and a cup of coffee for C.J. She then went back to the back to take care of some things.

"I get it, C.J. I mean you have a great wife, and this is a nice town full of nice people. I really envy you, man. I really do. If I could trade places with you, I would."

"Ted, you want to be a preacher. Wow!"

"Whoa, that is not what I mean! What I mean is you know exactly what you want to do, and I don't have a clue. Amy had given me a new purpose and that last project was fun. For once I was making money and doing good all at the same time. Then she dies, and the wind goes totally out of my sail."

"Ted, I don't know what to tell you. Until you let go of all the baggage you are carrying, you are not going to be able to go forward. And as for Amy, it's one day at a time, man. And it is not easy. I still think about my parents and on some days when I am alone, I still shed some tears and want like everything to hug them and tell them I love them one last time."

Phineas McNabb

"C.J., we are talking about my Angel, Amy. She was all that I had in this world other than the money. And she was starting to make me believe that there was more to life than money. Now that she is gone, how do I go forward? Because as you know, without Amy, all I have is my money and my title as the Richest Man in the World and right now I am not feeling rich at all. It hurts man, it hurts more than you can imagine." Theodore would grab his napkin and blow his nose. The tears were coming down much like the drizzle outside.

"Ted, I know someone who can help you understand what you are going through. But you need to have an open mind and hear her all the way out. Will you do that for me?"

"I guess, but you know my feeling about faith, Angels, and God."

"I do, but I just want you to hear her out. Will you do that for me?"

"I will."

"Myrtle, you ready to take that ride." Myrtle came from the back, and she pulled off her apron. She knew exactly what C.J. was talking about. Ted did not have a clue.

"I will pull the truck around now." Ted and C.J. finished their food. They were getting ready to take a ride to the plant, the abandoned plant that had been closed years ago. The plant had closed as a result of one of Theodore's deals.

Rich Men Have No Friends

49

Shelley and Carol had pulled off the highway by the Red Barn. They had taken the feeder and made the right. They were on the way to Greensburgh. The weather had taken a turn for the worst and the rain was coming down even harder. They were almost ten miles from Greensburgh when it happened.

A dog ran out in the middle of the street. Carol turned the wheel to avoid the dog. The car hydroplaned and they would veer off the road into a ditch. They got out of the car, and it was firmly stuck on its side. The right front wheel was bent. They were not going anywhere in that car.

"Well, that's just great. Shelley, this is the point where you will have to forgive me, but that old saying I'm about to lose my religion applies. Daggum dog." The dog, a German Shepard was across the street sitting under a tree happy to be alive and giving them the dog smile of he was happy to see them.

As they were assessing the seriousness of their situation, in the distance a black pickup truck was coming down the street. Inside the truck was a gentleman with a baseball hat on. He stopped to see if he could assist them. "Afternoon, ladies, can I give you a ride?"

"Abraham, is that you?" Carol and Shelley said it at the same time. Apparently, Carol knew him as well but the two of them had never discussed it. Why would they? People don't normally talk about their Angels. Might come across as weird.

"Shelley and Carol, well how have you both been doing?"

"Fine, Abraham, just fine. How about you?"

"Well, you both should know how I am doing trying to keep up with that Ted fellow. He's quite the guy. Nice guy, but quite the guy. He's the toughest assignment I have ever had."

"You too?" They both said it simultaneously again and then all three of them laughed.

"Here, take these jackets. I'll have Ken come get the car. He can get it fixed and have you back on the road tomorrow. But I believe you are both late, so we need to get moving." They took the jackets grabbed their packed bags and hopped in the truck with Abraham.

"You get home, Dynamite, and stay out of the road." It was Pete's dog. The car missed him and that was not a coincidence. And him being in the road was not a coincidence either. Fate was working on all cylinders. A storm was coming, and it was time. Theodore Hightower was in for another life-changing event. And Carol and Shelley needed to be there to help him as they had both done most of his life.

Rich Men Have No Friends

50

C.J., Myrtle, and Theodore all got into the front seat of her truck, and they drove two miles up the road to one of the old plant buildings that had been closed some years ago.

As they drove up to the plant, which was about fifty yards from the six-foot chain-link fence that surrounded the plant, there was tall grass where no one had obviously mowed in years. The parking lot looked like the driveway. Grass and weeds were growing through the surface. The Texas heat had not been kind to the place and looked like it was a lot older than it was. When they got close to the building, Myrtle stopped her truck. "That's close enough. Lord, be with me today." Ted looked at C.J. and then Myrtle. He was at a loss as to why they were there.

"Come on, Ted, I have something to show you."

"What is going on here, C.J.?"

"Ted, you told me you would hear her out, so hear her out."

"Okay, C.J. but I am not sure I like this." Myrtle and Ted started to walk towards the building. The rain was coming down harder, although they both had jackets with hoods.
An umbrella would do no good because the wind was picking up. There was a slight sound of thunder in the distance which meant there may be some lightning in the area. C.J. was keeping an eye out for both as he sat quietly in the truck.

"It's tough when you lose a child, Ted, you know. You tell yourself to get over it, but you never really shake yourself from the loss. And you play back in your head over and over if you had done something different, then it might not have happened."

"Myrtle, I don't know where this is going, but not sure this is going to help me."

"Keep walking with me and trust me, Ted. Trust me, like you did that assistant you have down in Houston and that beautiful child that you call your Angel. Just trust me." How did Myrtle know about his assistant? C.J. was also a very rich man with a lot of connections, that's how.

"So, as I was saying, Ted, the loss of a child can be tough on a parent. And even tougher on a single parent who is trying to make a living for herself and provide for a family of five on one income.

Phineas McNabb

That's right, I have five boys, all of them are the lights of my life. And I have always been proud of them. Raised them all by myself. I am not one of those women who look for someone to have pity on me. I am a prideful woman, and no work is beneath me when it comes to my kids. That's right. Loved them boys to death. One is a big shot lawyer in New Orleans, one is a policeman in Houston, one is in the military serving in Germany right now, and my youngest is in North Carolina studying to be a doctor. They all have made me so proud."

"Wow, you have a lot to be proud of, Myrtle."

"Not bad for a fry cook from Greensburgh, Texas, huh?"

"Myrtle, you missed one. Lawyer, policeman, doctor, soldier. But there is one missing."

"No, he's not missing Ted. James, my second to last child is not with us anymore."

"What do you mean? What happened?"

Just then they walked to a spot that was about ten feet from the building right below the highest point which was four stories high. Theodore was at a loss, but he would hear her out.

"The day the plant closed was extremely hard on everyone. You ever been to a family reunion, Ted. Probably not. But anyway, when you go to a family reunion in the south, people come from far and wide to eat, laugh, hug, reminisce and just catch up with each other. And this goes on for a couple of days, heck some people come in a week early to get the festivities going. Well, when the reunion winds down normally right after church on Sunday, everyone begins to pack up and go home. And if you are like me, a feeling of emptiness comes over you. Because the people you love so much that you wish you could be with every day all have to go back to their lives. So, for the whole week you were on this natural high and then your whole demeanor changes. You are no longer as happy as you were, and you may shed a few tears. And the reason you shed those tears, is because there is always a chance that is the last time you will ever see some of those folks again. Some stop coming, and some fold up their tent and go on to glory. They die, Ted."

"I understand but not sure how this relates to my Amy."

"Keep listening, Ted. You know for you to be the richest man in the world, you don't act so bright at times." Myrtle smiled at him. She was joking.

Rich Men Have No Friends

"So, anyway, the day the plant closed, everyone was sad. Some people did not know how they were going to make ends meet because they had been living check to check. Others had cashed out whatever money they had, and they were packed and ready to go. Some went to Houston, but others went as far as California, Atlanta and I heard that some went as far as New York City. And of those that relocated, most if not all have never come back. Now if they had relatives nearby, they might stop through for a quick minute. But these were people who had been in Greensburgh for years and years. So, the family reunion, which was permanent in this case, ended the day the plant closed."

"I'm sorry to hear that, Myrtle. Sounds like a group of good people."

"I fed all of them, they were good people. They were hard working, God fearing, honest, law-abiding people. They looked out for each other and would give the shirt off their back to help someone if they were down. No one had to worry about losing anything because someone else had their back."

"Myrtle, but you said they moved on and were able to continue with their lives."

"That's right, and they have homes in other places now and many of them are doing fine. But there's a difference. They are not home, Ted. They do not live in the town they call home, the community they call family, and they do not attend the church that their ancestors or in some their cases they helped to build. They are foreigners in their own country."

"I understand that, Myrtle, but we live in a global economy now. And everything is more connected than ever."

"How is that, Ted? Tell me how the people of Greensburgh who are scattered all over this country now are connected. And please don't tell me it's due to this high faluting technology. I think technology is wonderful, but nothing beats a face-to-face conversation with someone you have not seen in a long time." Theodore thought back to his dream about Amy and the last time that he saw her face to face.

"James and some of his friends decided to get a couple of kegs and do up on top of the plant. You know they wanted to hang out and just have one last good time at the plant. They could not be fired for drinking on the job because it was the last day. When the plant closed at five o'clock that evening, they went up on the roof. Must have been two hundred people up there. His fiancé, who worked in the same department as he did was up there as well. Well, they began to drink, and no one was paying attention to how much everyone was drinking, and things got a little out of hand. The rooftop had been off limits to employees because the overhang was only three feet high. All doors leading to the roof were normally locked."

"Not a good idea, Myrtle."

"Tell me about it. Well, anyway, James and some of his friends decided they were going to stand on the ledge and look out over the plants one last time. As he was trying to get up there, he got both feet up, but he lost his balance, and well…" Myrtle teared up in both eyes and Theodore did as well.

"Myrtle, I'm sorry to…."

"By the time the emergency folks got here, he was gone. They said he had a crushed skull and several broken bones. He was the only one who stayed home with me and the only one who worked in the plant just like me. He was proud of his brothers, but he wanted to be home. He said Greensburgh was his home."

"Myrtle, he died here."

"Right here, and I was at home when they called me. I remember it like it was yesterday. And Ted, I was mad for a long time about my James death, and I blamed myself, I blamed the plant for letting them up there, I blamed his friends, and I blamed the company who caused the closing. I grieved for a very long time."

"So, what made you stop grieving and go on with life, Myrtle?"

"That man sitting in that truck. And the man upstairs. When it first happened, I stopped going to church. I kept asking myself what God would let this happen to my boy. What God would let the plant close and just watch a city take a turn for the worse and become a shell of itself. All I kept thinking to myself is I have been believing in a myth. Because you see, when you get down, and things are not going right, you blame others, then you blame yourself, and then you don't know who to blame. And the reality is there is no one to blame. Not even James. It was an accident, and that's it. I had to learn to live with it and move on with my life."

C.J. exited the truck and the weather was getting a little rougher and the thunder was getting louder.

"But Myrtle, that's hard for me, Amy was my everything. She was my Angel from above."

"From where, Ted" Where from Above?"

"Come on Myrtle. You of all people should understand…"

"What I understand, Ted, is that the richest man in the world can't accept the fact that his daughter is gone and there is not a thing he can do about it now. And until you reconcile that within your heart, you will be the poorest man in the world for the rest of your life."

"Myrtle, you don't understand. At least you have your other boys. That must help."

"It does, but it does not replace my James. I loved my boys equally and unconditionally, but they each had a place in my heart. And what about you, you have two boys, and they lost a sister. Have you called them?"

"No."

"Amy had an aunt, have you called her?"

"Well no."

"So, as usual, the richest man in the world is only concerned about the richest man in the world and no one else. You are not grieving for Amy. You are grieving for Ted. You are angry because you can't fix this. And if this were anything else, your money would fix it. And that's the problem with worshiping money. It lets you down and then you have nowhere else to turn." Ted was mad now, at Myrtle, at himself, at anything and everything.

"So, what am I supposed to do, Myrtle? Act like it never happened, go on with life. Pretend she is no longer here. None of that will bring her back."

"No, it won't, Ted. And nothing will bring your mom back, either. The two most important women in your life, I mean the two women you loved more than anything is gone. And let me guess, you feel like you have blood on your hands in both cases. Correct."

"Well yes. If you want me to be blunt. Yes. WHY DID THAT MAN HAVE TO KILL MY MOTHER? SHE WAS ONLY TRYING TO HELP SUSAN. AND WHY WAS MY AMY TAKEN AWAY FROM ME SO SOON. WHAT HAVE I DONE TO DESERVE THIS? AND WHERE WAS YOUR GOD, C.J. WHEN ALL THIS HAPPENED? WHERE WAS HE?" Ted started to cry as his emotions were getting the best of him. He put his head into Myrtle's shoulder, and she held him tight.

At that point, the rain began to subside, and the thunder had all but stopped.

"Ted, it's going to be all right. But you are running out of time, friend. If you don't make some changes in your life, this is going to eat you alive from the inside out. And once that happens, you may not return. And there are too many people who love you and count on you every day to do the right thing. Stop worrying about being the richest man in the world and some old list in a magazine and go be the richest man in the world who made a difference. Be the man that everyone admires, except this time for your good deeds and not for your greed, no offense." Ted was sniffling but was able to utter some words.

"No, No, No, offense taken, Myrtle."

"Myrtle, I thought you said you did not like guys like me?"

"I don't like guys like Theodore Hightower. But this Ted guy, now he's alright with me. You know the guy who drives an old pickup and comes into town not flaunting his riches but just being an ordinary person like the rest of us. I love that guy and I call him a friend."

"Thanks, Myrtle."

"Now, I think those folks over there are waiting on you." Abraham, Carol, and Shelley had arrived at the plant. Apparently, Carol knew C.J. from his days as a preacher in Houston. She had reached out to him to find her brother only to find out he was in good hands the whole time. She and Shelley had exited the truck when Theodore and Myrtle first started talking. He had not heard them because of the weather.

Theodore looked at Shelley and Carol. He had not seen Carol since his mom's funeral and even there they were cordial but did not act like a brother and sister who had been through as much as they had in life. He ran towards them as they stood by the pickup truck, and they did not know what to expect. He hugged them both as hard as he could, and he cried an uncontrollable cry. No one said anything for a whole minute that seemed like an eternity. Carol spoke first.

"Hey, little brother."

"Hey, sis."

"Mr. Hightower."

"Shelley, and call me Ted, Shelley. Call me Ted." Theodore Hightower was gone just like Louis Johnson had left Houston a long time ago or so it seems. There were just Ted and C.J. and that was fine with them. They hugged again.

C.J. walked over to Myrtle and gave her a big hug. "Thanks, Myrtle, I know that wasn't easy."

"It gets easier each time, C.J. Not the death of my boy but being able to talk about it." C.J. had asked her to share that same testimonial with J.J. and Ruby when they first came to town. Her testimonial always had a way of making people she encountered realize that everyone has a story, none of us lead perfect lives. Not even the richest man in the world.

The sun was coming out and since they were all there and Myrtle had keys, Theodore asked for a tour of the plant if it was safe. She took him in, and Shelley, Carol, and C.J. tagged along. Ted began to realize that his decisions were not just business decisions after all.

He did not feel any guilt, but he did understand a little better what those decisions, even when made with the best of intentions, could do to a town and the people who lived in it. He had gotten a taste of small-town America, and he was in love. The sense of community, the friendliness of the people, the compassion for one another had made him a changed man.

"Hey, Pastor." He had walked off while Myrtle entertained Carol and Shelley. C.J. walked over to him as he gazed out the window, one that had not been boarded up or was shattered by kids jumping the fence to throw rocks.

"Yes, sir, Ted."

"I don't get it yet, but I am willing to give it a try. What time is service on Sunday?"

"Now Ted, don't force yourself to do something you are not ready to do yet. I appreciate the gesture."

"Listen, Rockstar, what time is the service on Sunday?"

"Eleven sharp. We have one service and one service only. It starts at eleven."

"I'll be there. See you Sunday."

"See you there, Ted."

"And Pastor."

"Yes."

"God bless you. I don't know what that means yet, but I am sure my Angel would want me to say that to you for taking care of her daddy."

C.J began to tear up as did Theodore and they grabbed each other by the hand, pulled in close and patted each other on the back.

"And thank you Ted, for teaching an old preacher that there is hope after all. There is hope that people like you and I with our influence, money, and power can use it for good things and when that happens, all things are possible."

"Amen, Pastor. Amen."

C.J. went back to check on the ladies. As Ted was looking out the window, off in the distance on the road was a 1978 Black Ford Truck. Except this time, it was a little different. It was clean and had a shine that reflected off the sun, and Abraham had on his Sunday best. White baseball hat, white shirt and well you know the rest. And gazing out the window in front of him was who else, Mr. Wimples. And the truck had a glow of light that was coming from inside where they were sitting.

Abraham waved at him and gave him a thumbs up. And he could have sworn that Mr. Wimples had a smile as well. He waved back at them. And this time he wanted proof that he was not dreaming or hallucinating. He called C.J. over.

"C.J., C.J, look! There he is!"

CJ ran over to see what Ted was making a fuss about.

"What, Ted, What's wrong."

"Look, look at......" Abraham and Mr. Wimples were gone. And he would probably never see them again. But never say never.

"Let me guess, you saw the Angel that you said does not exist."

"Well, yeah, I mean no. Heck, I don't know what I mean."

"Ted, it's all good man, let's get out of here.

Everyone left, they all went back to the diner and then the party carried over to J.J.'s place, The Bar. Sarah and Ken and Pete joined them along with some of the locals and they had a grand old time. Unfortunately, Ted, Shelley and Carol had to leave in the middle of the night. Jess called; the paparazzi were on their way. They did not know where to go yet but they heard that there was a sighting of the richest man in the world.

Rich Men Have No Friends

52

It is six months since Amy died. Theodore and Isabel reconciled and now live together on the outskirts of Houston east of the city in a modest but elegant home befitting a wealthy man, but a humble wealthy man. He has downsized his life in every way. All the cars and boats, and the fast lifestyle is behind him now. He has reconciled with his sons who came to visit him for a couple of weeks this past summer.

Theodore has reconciled Amy's death. He understands that his life and lifestyle had not killed Amy. It was a tragic accident that he was not responsible for. It did make him realize that there were more important things in life. He no longer cared about his net worth, as he understood that his true value was in how he lived his life as a man. And from this point on, he was going to do good things to make a change in the world.

He still has his company, but he has decided to make some changes there as well. Shelley is still the chief executive officer, and he has reinserted himself as the chairman. All his holdings have been sold off and he is now an investor, but no longer owns any companies. He is still the richest man in the world and that will change soon as well.

It is a Monday Morning, eight o'clock and the temperature outside is already eighty degrees. The sun is out, and Houston is as busy as ever. The conference room of HenPot industries is packed, standing room only. All twenty seats at the conference room table are occupied. And there are people sitting just to the rear of the people seated at the table. Shelley is sitting at one end of the table and Ted is sitting at the other end. He is having a meeting that will forever alter his business model going forward.

"Ladies and gentlemen, thank you all for coming today. In this room, we are represented by at least seventeen of the richest people in the world. And I have also invited three of my new friends from a small town I call my second home." (Myrtle, Ruby and J.J. were present in the room)

"You may recognize two of them, J.J. is a former six-time NBA champion and you all know Ruby, of the Warhill family. I appreciate you all taking my invitation as I am sure you heard others turned me down. And I am sure that some of your friends, who I think are still my friends in name only, tried to talk you out of coming today. But we have a problem, and we need to solve it for all our sake. The world is changing very quickly and, in some cases, not necessarily for the better. The people in this room have the financial resources, and the power and influence to do something about it. And let me be clear, I am not asking you to give up your wealth or is there an agenda to try and get you to do that at any point we work together over what I hope will be the rest of our lives. But we have a responsibility as we have been given a gift that has to keep on giving or it's just a gift that is going to be left unwrapped. To kick the meeting off, I have invited one of my closest advisors and dear friends, Pastor C.J., otherwise known as Louis Cletus Johnson. You all know him as the former Rockstar of Wall Street. No, that's not a legend, he really exists."

Theodore waved C.J. into the room and right on queue he came through the glass doors to the conference room.

"Ladies and gentlemen again welcome to all of you. I promise we won't waste your time today. I want to talk briefly about the packets we mailed to you over two months ago. I see many of you have brought them with you today. Our world is changing, and something must be done. I won't argue about climate change, but the climate is changing. We have a homelessness problem that needs to be addressed. People are going hungry in many parts of the world to include the United States. And the separation of the haves and have nots has reached a breaking point. If we don't begin to address these issues, even with baby steps, the future of your grandkids and your great grandkids as well as mine is at risk. Now please turn to page 4."

And so that's what happened to the richest man in the world. He used his ranking on a list, his wealth, and his power and influence to begin a dialogue to take real action to address the problems and challenges that plague this world today. If only it were that easy. Or is it? Only time will tell.

The End

Rich Men Have No Friends

Author's Note

Laughter does not cost anything. A hug does not cost anything. A conversation with a friend or a stranger does not cost anything. Doing a good deed for someone else does not cost anything. Memories of a good time spent with family do not cost anything. And simply helping a friend grieve the loss of a loved one does not cost anything. And why is that? Because money does not buy compassion, true love, or simply being there for your fellow man.

In a world that has so many real challenges that affect all mankind, money is not the solution but using it to do good things is. And when that happens, the world becomes a better place for all mankind. And the things that don't cost money become a priority for all.

www.ingramcontent.com/pod-product-compliance
Lightning Source LLC
Chambersburg PA
CBHW020636220526
45464CB00001B/169